PERSPECTIVES ON MINORITY GROUP MENTAL HEALTH

Edited by

Faye Untalan Munoz
Russell Endo

UNIVERSITY
PRESS OF
AMERICA

Library of Congress Catalog Card Number: 81-40848

TABLE OF CONTENTS

PREFACE   v

PART ONE: The Nature of the Problem   1

An Overview of Minority Group Mental Health Needs and Issues as
Presented to the President's Commission on Mental Health
    Delores L. Parron   3

Toward an Understanding of the Mental Health and Substance
Abuse Issues of Rural and Migrant Ethnic Minorities:
A Search for Common Experiences
    Robert A. Ryan and Joseph E. Trimble   23

PART TWO: The Context of Family Patterns   41

Black Family Lifestyles and the Mental Health of Black Americans
    Walter R. Allen and Sandra Stukes   43

Pacific/Asian American Families and Mental Health
    Barbara W.K. Yee and Sumiko T. Hennessy   53

The Mexican American Family and Interaction with Social Systems
    Marta Sotomayor   71

PART THREE: Service Delivery   83

A Theoretical Perspective for Delivery of Mental Health
Services to Minority Communities
    Barbara Bryant Solomon   85

The Need for Nontraditional Mental Health Programs in the Barrio
    Armando Morales   93

Trying to Make It Real: Issues and Concerns in the
Provision of Services for Minorities
    June Jackson Christmas   109

iii

PART FOUR: Manpower Development   133

   Federal Trends in Mental Health Manpower Programs
      William H. Denham   135

   **Minority Populations and Mental Health Manpower
   Development: Some Facts of Life**
      Madison Foster and Louis A. Ferman   143

   **The Politics of Mental Health Personnel and Its Impact
   on Minority Group Mental Health Services**
      Rodolfo B. Sanchez   157

PART FIVE: Research   169

   Ethnic Minority Research: Trends and Directions
      Stanley Sue   171

ABOUT THE CONTRIBUTORS   185

PREFACE

Interest in minority group mental health has increased in recent years. Evidence for this can be found, for example, in: a) the greater amount of research in this area especially on the effects of racism on mental health, the incidence of mental disorders among minority groups, and the ineffectiveness of existing service delivery approaches; b) the attention given to minority group problems and issues by the recent President's Commission on Mental Health; and c) the establishment of major Hispanic, Asian, Native American, and Black research and development centers by the National Institute of Mental Health. However, in spite of this increasing level of interest, mental health professionals are only beginning to develop a sensitivity to the significance of ethnic and racial differences. One small part of this problem is the relative lack of appropriate material for educational and training programs. This book is designed to fill a portion of that gap.

The twelve articles in this book are organized around five key areas: the nature of the problem, the context of family patterns, service delivery, manpower development, and research. The articles have been authored by recognized experts with extensive practical as well as research and/or academic experience. Eleven of the articles are being published here for the first time. Three of these were originally presented at the First National Conference on Minority Group Alcohol, Drug Abuse, and Mental Health Issues sponsored by the Alcohol, Drug Abuse, and Mental Health Administration; four were presented at conferences sponsored by the Western Interstate Commission for Higher Education or the American Public Health Association; and four articles were prepared specifically for this volume.

We would like to thank all of the authors for permission to publish their work. We are especially grateful to Walter Allen, Sandra Stukes, Delores Parron, Marta Sotomayor, Barbara Yee, and Sumiko Hennessy for writing papers specifically for this book. Thanks also go to the Bureau of Sociological Research, University of Colorado, and The Word Wizard of Boulder, Colorado for their help in the preparation of the final manuscript.

v

PART ONE

THE NATURE OF THE PROBLEM

This section provides an overview of major problems and issues related to minority group mental health. In the first article, Delores Parron presents a general discussion using materials prepared by the minority group Special Populations subpanels of the President's Commission on Mental Health. She reviews evidence showing that minority groups have serious mental health needs but are not receiving adequate or appropriate services. She examines barriers to service delivery and utilization and then discusses recommendations concerning the adoption of culturally relevant services; increased minority group participation in mental health planning, policy making, and service delivery; better training in minority group cultures for all practitioners; and more research into minority group mental health needs.

In the second article, Robert Ryan and Joseph Trimble describe the mental health and substance abuse problems of rural and migrant minorities. One important correlate of such problems is change (for example due to migration) although responses to change depend upon a variety of factors. There is a need to better understand minority group adaptation patterns and perceptions of mental health. The article concludes with suggestions for further research.

1

AN OVERVIEW OF MINORITY GROUP MENTAL HEALTH NEEDS AND ISSUES AS PRESENTED TO THE PRESIDENT'S COMMISSION ON MENTAL HEALTH

DELORES L. PARRON

The President's Commission on Mental Health was established by an Executive Order signed by President Carter on February 17, 1977 to review the mental health needs of the nation in order to make policy recommendations to the President. The charge of the one-year Commission was to identify how the mentally ill, emotionally disturbed, and mentally retarded were being served and who was being underserved. The Commission was to project how the President, the Congress, and the Federal Government could most effectively respond to mental health needs. The Commission was asked to recommend various methods for coordinating a unified public/private approach to mental health and people-helping services and to suggest what research support was needed to further the prevention and treatment of mental disabilities.

The twenty-member Commission, with First Lady Rosalynn Carter as honorary chairperson, was drawn from the fields of law, labor, social welfare, medicine, religion, education, public health, and consumer and patient's rights, and represented a broad spectrum of American life.

The Commission's work included public hearings in various sections of the country to determine the experiences of consumers, providers of services, state and local governments, and professional and civic groups with mental health needs and care. Thirty-two task panels comprised of volunteers from around the country collected information. Task panel studies included: delivery of mental health services; issues of cost and financing; research; prevention; legal/ethical issues; mental health personnel; public attitudes and understanding; community support systems; the mental health of families, children, and the elderly; access and barriers to care; and the mental health of special populations (minorities, the physically handicapped, and women).

The Task Panel on Special Populations

By definition, "special" denotes that which is distinguished by some unusual quality. When applied to minorities, women and the physically handicapped, this term takes on particular significance. Available statistics show that approximately 14 million persons in need of assistance for some kind of mental or emotional difficulty are not receiving services. The overwhelming majority of individuals in this category appear to be minorities, women, and the physically handicapped. For complex and varying reasons, the life chances of individuals in these special populations have been compromised in ways that have limited the realization of their full potential and deprived them of the opportunity to participate fully in American society and more specifically in the mental health system.

The special populations were designated by the Commission for particular attention because they represented a segment of American society which has been overrepresented in the statistics on mental disorders or, on the basis of numerous studies, were clearly underserved or inappropriately served by the mental health system in this country. The Task Panel on Special Populations was established by the Commission to ensure that the study of the mental health needs of the American population was truly reflective of America's diverse society. In choosing to collect data in this way, a bit of history was made. No other commission of this kind had ever actively sought input on minority groups through such a concerted effort.

Because the cultural background of each minority group is so distinct and diverse, the Commission elected to examine issues relating to the mental health of each group separately. Seven subpanels were therefore created. The subpanels focused on the concerns of the 51 percent of the population who are women, the three million Asian and Pacific Americans, 22 million Black Americans, 22 million Hispanic Americans, one million American Indians, 13 million Americans who are hearing-impaired and 500,000 persons who are profoundly deaf, and 40 million Americans with handicaps of various kinds.[1]

Each of the subpanels utilized the opportunity afforded them by the President's Commission on Mental Health to: 1) delineate the scope of mental disorders in their respective populations; 2) assess the state of mental health service delivery, research, and personnel needs; 3) designate necessary modifications of public policy governing the mental health delivery system, research, and personnel recruitment and training in order to make mental health services available, accessible, and acceptable; and 4) suggest strategies for research, treatment, and prevention of mental disorders. The subpanels made 181 specific recommendations to the Commission emphasizing the necessity of a comprehensive, integrated response to the needs of special populations by the mental health system. These recommendations were presented with detailed supporting documentation. The subpanel reports were included in the appendices which accompanied the Commission's report to the President.[2] What follows below is a concise

---

[1]One hundred sixteen individuals contributed their time and energy to the work of the Task Panel on Special Populations.

[2]The President's Commission on Mental Health. "Report on the Task Panel on Special Populations: Minorities, Women, Physically Handicapped." **Task Panel Reports Submitted to the President's Commission on Mental Health** Vol. III Appendix. Washington, D.C.: U.S. Government Printing Office, 1978.

summary of the highlights of four of the minority group reports. This summary does not attempt to be exhaustive. Instead, it focuses on several of the major mental health issues identified by these subpanels in defining the scope of mental disorders and the problems encountered in addressing these needs. The public policy response stimulated by the Commission's report will also be discussed.

An assessment of minority group mental health needs requires that attention be given to: 1) the nature and scope of mental and behavioral disorders; 2) barriers to the delivery of appropriate services (i.e., availability and accessibility of services); and 3) resources to provide personnel to staff services, to support research on the etiology, course, and prevention of mental disorders, and to design and implement mental health programs to serve minority groups.

The Nature and Scope of the Problems[3]

The Special Populations subpanels found that making a comprehensive statement about the nature and scope of mental disorders among minorities and estimating how many persons were in need of mental health interventions was a complex undertaking. This effort was complicated by the fact that a precise definition of mental health tends to be elusive. It was generally agreed, however, that mental health encompasses an order of concerns significantly broader than those represented by categorical mental illness.

Serious mental and behavioral disorders may arise from a broad range of biological, psychological, and sociocultural factors. Thus, the causes of mental disorders are often multiple and a resulting illness can represent complex interactions among these factors. It was assumed that the mental health of minority individuals could not be assessed in a vacuum. Rather, their mental health was viewed within the context of the total American cultural and societal system as well as within the perspectives of particular racial or ethnic minority groups.

In providing information to the Commission on the prevalence of mental disorders, the need for further epidemiological studies was very much apparent. Most studies have been based on existing systems of case findings and classifications of mental disorders. A most disturbing conclusion drawn from the examination of this data was its inadequacy for determining the burden of illness among minority populations. The nature, propor-

---

[3]It must be noted that comparable data are not currently available for each of the four major minority groups. In each case, the best data available relating to the health/mental health status of each group are reported here as they were reported by the Task Subpanels of the President's Commission on Mental Health. The data compiled by the minority subpanels represent the most cogent and accurate data available to date.

tion, and extent of mental health problems among minorities has not been accurately assessed. Available data are usually on the utilizers of services or from the census. However census data have been notoriously inaccurate when it comes to counting minorities, and utilization data are inconsistent in the manner in which they categorize minorities. Both sources of data often ignore persons who may need services but are not receiving help.

Implementation of Public Law 94-311, requiring that health statistics be broken down by race, ethnicity, and sex, has been hampered by poorly defined procedures. For example, Hispanics are generally not considered a separate racial group; they may be placed within either the white or the minority category when questions concerning race are asked. In the 1970 Census, about 93 percent of the Hispanics identified themselves as being of the white race. Inclusion of Hispanics in the white category tends to increase the mortality and morbidity rates for whites. Therefore, less of a difference is found between the mortality and morbidity rates of whites as compared to Blacks when Hispanics are considered part of the white group (Health Resources Administration, 1977: 4). A major problem with this kind of reporting has been the inappropriate assessment of the service needs of persons of Hispanic background. Another result of this kind of reporting has been an inadequate data base of understanding and addressing crucial issues in mental health. Periodic reexamination of the nature and scope of mental health problems represents a necessary contribution to the ongoing process of effective planning for the needs of minority groups. Instruments designed to provide a statistical-normative distribution of psychiatric symptomatology in the general population have only rarely been used and those that are available have problems when applied to minorty populations. Little attention has been given to developing criteria and instruments to identify potential "needers" of service (i.e., those whose symptoms may be part of a larger syndrome which includes the inability to perform in normally expected social roles).

Data provided by the Health Resources Administration, U.S. Public Health Service (1977), summarize the following important facts about the mental health of racial minorities and Hispanics:

1. Racial minorities use most mental health facilites at greater rates than whites. They make the greatest use of: 1) inpatient as compared to outpatient facilities, and 2) publicly funded as compared to private facilities.

2. The admission rate to state and county mental health hospitals for racial minorities is twice that of whites. However, whites have a 15 percent higher rate than Hispanics.

3. The rate of inpatient admission to state and county mental hospitals for racial minorities diagnosed as schizophrenic is over two and one-half times the rates for Hispanics and whites. For alcohol disorders, the admission rate for racial minorities is three and one-half times the rates for Hispanics and one and one-half times the rate for whites. For drug disorders, Hispanics and racial minorities have about three times the admission rate of whites.

ASIAN AND PACIFIC AMERICANS

Data on the incidence and prevalence of mental disorders among Asian and Pacific Americans have only recently begun to be gathered and analyzed. Currently these data are insufficient. Asian and Pacific Americans are one of the most complex, diverse, and misunderstood minority groups in the United States. Asian and Pacific Americans include Chinese, Japanese, Koreans, Filipinos, East Indians, Pakistanis, Thais, Hawaiians, Guamanians, Samoans, persons from the United States Trust Territories in the Pacific, Cambodians, Vietnamese, and other Indochinese "refugees." It is estimated that by 1980, the number of Asian and Pacific Americans in the United States will exceed three million. This represents a two-fold increase since 1970, largely due to the rapid increase in new Asian and Pacific American immigrants.

"At risk" groups within the Asian and Pacific American population include: 1) Indochinese "refugees"; 2) Asian wives of American servicemen; 3) recent immigrants, especially the elderly and children; 4) persons in areas undergoing rapid cultural change (for example, parts of Hawaii, Samoa, Micronesia, Guam, and other Trust Territories); and 5) individuals with multiple problems (for example, physical and developmental disabilities concurrent with specific mental health care needs). Asian and Pacific Americans are victims of the same social, economic, and political inequities that have victimized other minorities. Below subsistence-level incomes, high rates of unemployment, inadequate health care, and alienation and powerlessness are difficulties that also confront Asian/Pacific populations. These problems taken singly and, more often, together produce stress and increase vulnerability to mental disorders.

Studies show that Asian and Pacific Americans tend to be brought to the attention of mental health services only at the point of acute breakdown or crisis. In a study conducted in Seattle, Sue (1977) found Asians to have a far higher proportion of individuals diagnosed as having "psychosis" than other groups. Of Asian and Pacific American patients, 22.4 percent were diagnosed as "psychotic" compared to 12.7 percent of white patients, 17.6 percent of Native American patients, 13.8 percent of Black patients and 14.5 percent of Chicano patients. In comparing a sample of Chinese patients with a randomly selected control group, Brown and his colleagues (1973) found that the Chinese were less likely to utilize existing mental health services; those who did tended to be more disturbed than their white counterparts.

In a comparative study of 17 community mental health centers in Seattle, Sue and McKinney (1975) observed that over a three year period Asians, though accounting for 2.4 percent of the total population, represented only 0.7 percent of the patient population. A review of the San Francisco Community Health Services (1977) revealed that over a seven month period (July 1976 - January 1977), only two percent of the patients served in community mental health services were Chinese. This statistic may seem insignificant until one notes that the Chinese account for close to ten percent of the population in that city.

BLACK AMERICANS

Stressful factors such as racism and discrimination, rising expectations but limited opportunities, life in the inner city, and cultural conflict create special risks for Black Americans. These factors appear to erode their capacity for adequate social functioning and increase the probability of psychological stress and physical and mental illnesses.

Blacks comprise 11 percent of the U.S. population or about 20 million persons. Census data indicate that the Black population continues to be more highly concentrated in the central cities of metropolitan areas. The downward swing in the U.S. economy since 1974 and the attendant rise in unemployment have hit Blacks the hardest. Since 1975, nearly 14 percent of Blacks, compared to 8 percent of whites, have been unemployed. It has been well established that unemployment creates stressful situations for laid-off workers and their families. Stress has long been recognized as a major contributor to a variety of physical and emotional disorders (Brenner, 1979). The Census Bureau also reports that 31 percent of Black Americans, as compared to nine percent of white persons, live in poverty. The overall income position of Black families relative to white families has declined since 1970.

These factors point to the social milieu, not individual Blacks, as the target for change and are germane to the goals of mental health programs in Black communities. The Special Populations subpanel on Black Americans (1978) noted: "Of the twin evils of our time, racism and poverty, racism ranks first and poverty second as etiologies of the difficulties Black Americans face. Neither of these maladies is endemic to the Black community. Both are generated, operated, and perpetuated by the white community and the institutions it dominates."

The nature and scope of mental disorders among Black Americans is illustrated by the following data:

1. Many Black adults are under the care of a variety of institutions, and some of these adults have children. In 1970, the rates of institutionalized persons per 100,000 population were 1412.7 for Blacks, but only 1004.3 for whites (Cannon and Locke, 1977).

2. Black males consistently show the highest rates of mental disorder. In state hospital data, Black males from ages 18-34 show an extremely high rate compared to other age and racial groups (Miller and Miller, 1973).

3. Data suggest that commitments of disordered persons for treatment occur somewhat sooner for Blacks than whites. Black admissions to mental institutions are less likely to be voluntary and Blacks are less likely to be committed by a spouse or offspring (Gary, 1977).

4. Blacks are more likely to be in mental institutions than whites and are twice as likely to suffer fatal consequences from psychoses and neuroses (Levitan et al., 1975).

5. It has been reported that the treatment Blacks receive in mental health agencies is different from that received by whites (Gary, 1977). The following differences have been observed: 1) diagnoses are less accurate for Blacks (Gross et al., 1969; Cooper, 1973); 2) the disposition of Black cases is more nonspecific (Lowinger and Dobie, 1966); 3) Blacks are more likely to be seen for diagnosis (Jackson et al., 1974); and 4) Blacks are less likely to be selected for insight therapy than whites (Rosenthal and Frank, 1970).

6. Blacks are more than eight times as likely to become instititutional-ized for drug addiction than whites; death from alcoholism is three times more common among Blacks than whites (Staples, 1976).

HISPANIC AMERICANS

Hispanic Americans constitute a significant and rapidly growing segment of the American people. Hispanic Americans are a heterogeneous popula-tion which includes individuals of Mexican, Puerto Rican, Cuban, and South or Central American descent. The 1970 Census counted 9.6 million persons of Spanish origin in the United States. The 1975 Populations Report raised the number to 11.2 million, which can be considered a conservative base figure. Other estimates which take into account the census undercount, increase from births, and legal as well as undocumented immigration indi-cate that probably more than 23 million Hispanics live in the United States today. Although projections diverge widely on the basis of baselines and growth rates, it is expected that by the year 2000 the number of Hispanic Americans will be between 26.5 and 55.3 million. By moderate estimates, they will become the largest minority group in the U.S. within the next 25 years (Macias, 1977).

Hispanic Americans are largely urban dwellers; 84 percent of them reside in metropolitan areas, particularly in the central cities. One out of every two families of Hispanic origin lives in the central city of a metro-politan area, as compared to one of four families in the general popula-tion. The Spanish language continues to be a most significant aspect of the Hispanic cultural heritage. Over 80 percent of Hispanic Americans report Spanish as their native language, while 20 percent report having difficulty with English.

There is little valid and reliable national data about the mental health status of Hispanic Americans. This lack of an adequate data base has resulted from the failure to identify Hispanics as a distinct group in the compilation of epidemiological data and other health statistics. There are, however, other indicators which compel us to conclude that Hispanic Amer-icans are a population "at risk" concerning mental illness.

The plight of Hispanic Americans has been extensively documented (Padilla and Ruiz, 1973; Padilla et al., 1975). They have been found to suffer the impact of economic, social, and political inequities to a much greater extent than the general population. Low income, unemployment, underemployment, undereducation, poor housing, prejudice and discrimina-tion, and cultural and linguistic barriers have been compounded by the low quality and quantity of mental health services available to Hispanics. This situation has perpetuated the stress to which Hispanic Americans are subjected and which often results in the increased prevalence of substance abuse, alcoholism, and juvenile delinquency. Personal suffering and the waste of human resources are more difficult to evaluate but are nevertheless equally important consequences of the social condition of Hispanics in the United States.

Although the social and economic conditions noted above render Hispanic Americans vulnerable to psychological and emotional stress, they underutilize available mental health services. Utilization rates vary for different groups and in different geographic locations. These rates rarely exceed 50 percent--that is, Hispanic representation among recipients of services is one half (or less) of their representation in the general population (Brandon, 1975; Solis, 1977; Bachrach, 1975).

AMERICAN INDIANS

The mental health of American Indians and Alaska Natives cannot be viewed within the context of the traditional mental health system. Any discussion or definition of mental health as it relates to Indian peoples must take place within the context of Indian peoples' history and the strengths associated with their culture. Indianness and being an Indian, identification with a tribal entity, identification with a particular place, and harmony with the earth constitute integral parts of the definition of health among Indian peoples.

The American Indian Policy Review Commission (1977) in its 1977 report to Congress notes:

> No recitation of cold statistics can adequatly portray the human misery and suffering experienced by the majority of Indian and Alaska Native peoples on reservations and in numerous villages in Alaska. However, when the impact of these statistics is measured against the unfulfilled hopes and aspirations of scores of Indians which have been cut short by unnecessary illness and deaths, and against the alarmingly high number of Indian families which have been devastated by social disintegration caused by mental illness and alcoholism, then the conditions become real and meaningful.

In viewing the life situation of the American Indian one must examine social, economic, and political realities. Years of colonization and neglect have left the Indian with inadequate resources.

The economic situation for the American Indian has always been bleak. The average family income for Indians on reservations is below the poverty level. Unemployment is extremely high, from 60-70 percent on some reservations to 20 percent on "more prosperous" reservations. The average paycheck is not cashed on the reservation and the dollar turns over only once at the reservation level. Unemployment among American Indians has

been noted as a highly significant factor in the etiology of mental health problems, family disruption, and alcoholism.

The effects of colonization and racism have taken their toll on Indian communities. The lack of opportunity to plan for themselves and control their own decision-making has eaten away at the self-reliance and stability of the Indian people.

The most severe and widespread health problem among American Indians is alcoholism and its consequences: cirrhosis and its complications, neuropsychiatric disorders, and nutritional deficiencies. The majority of accidents among Indians, especially fatal ones, are associated with alcohol as are nearly all homicides, assaults, suicides, and suicide attempts. The loss of personal freedom and productivity, the breakup of families, and the hardship and humiliation involved are considerable although not easily measured (Hoffman and Noem, 1975).

A 1973 General Accounting Office survey of six health care units serving American Indians reported that an estimated 60 percent of the caseload was directly or indirecly related to alcohol. During 1972, 1,097 patients made 2,637 visits for episodic and habitual drinking, alcohol addiction, intoxication, and delirium tremens. In 1973, 75-80 percent of American Indian suicides were alcohol-related, two or three times the national rate. The National Center for Health Statistics reported that in 1972, suicide was one of the three fastest growing causes of death among American Indians (Fredric, 1975).

Drug abuse is becoming a significant problem for American Indians. In the first three months of 1974 alone, the number of drug abuse cases reported by American Indian mental health programs jumped by almost 50 percent. This increase has continued. Alcoholism and alcohol abuse, however, are the major mental health problems that directly and indirectly affect the entire American Indian community (Downey, 1976).

Barriers to Service Delivery and Utilization

As noted ealier, statistics (as inadequate as they are) show that there are approximately 14 million persons in need of mental health services who are not receiving services. The overwhelming proportion of individuals in this category are members of special populations. The issues related to this underservice or inappropriate service are related to serious deficits in: 1) the availability of service (too few choices in terms of where services can be obtained); 2) accessibility of services, particularly in terms of cost; 3) acceptability of existing services in terms of the attention these services give to the unique needs, values, and belief systems of those who seek them; and 4) accountability of services to the groups they seek to serve.

ASIAN AND PACIFIC AMERICANS

Historically, the utilization of existing mental health services by the Asian community, in comparison with other minority groups, has been very low. It would appear that low utilization rates may be attributed to certain cultural values and practices which are characteristic of most Asian groups. Murase (1977) notes that among Asian groups the concept of "face" (i.e., presenting one's best side at all possible cost) may be in conflict with the "confessional" character of the therapeutic situation. Other issues focus around the concept and practice of self-determination. Enumerating alternatives or options is part of Western therapeutic intervention. This technique may be bewildering to the Asian patient, not because of difficulty in matching options with problems, but because the Asian patient may feel disobedient and disloyal by not selecting the option valued by the therapist. In Asian cultures, it is acceptable for one to assume a very dependent role in times of crisis and for significant people in the patient's life to offer much support; consequently, it may be appropriate to indulge the patient at a time when he or she is experiencing extreme humiliation and loss of self-esteem.

Studies show that when visible, culturally relevant programs for Asians are provided, there is a significant increase in the number of Asians seeking those services. For example, in Seattle the number of Asians utilizing an Asian American counseling and referral service in one year was approximately equal to the total number of Asians utilizing 18 other community mental health centers over a three year period (Sue and McKinney, 1975). True (1975) reported that an Asian community-based mental health program in Oakland saw 131 Chinese Americans in its first year of operation in contrast to three Chinese out of a total of 500 persons utilizing a central outpatient facility. She also found that the diagnostic categories of Asian patients treated at the Asian community-based facility were comparable to those of other county health facilities. This suggests that an indigenous, community-based facility with bilingual staff will serve not only a much larger population of people in need but also people at varying stages of need and not just those in states of acute breakdown (Murase, 1977). Hatanaka et al. (1975) reported data for an Asian community-based program in Los Angeles which suggest that the presence of comprehensive, accessible, and ethnically appropriate services increased the rate of utilization by Asians by approximately 200 percent over a three year period.

BLACK AMERICANS

Many studies have provided data on how conditions in the ghetto contribute to stress, whether in an urban location such as Chicago or in a rural one such as Mound Bayou, Mississippi. Stress has been found to be highly correlated with the health and mental health of Black Americans. Research has shown that admissions to mental hospitals rise in times of unemployment and decrease during economic upturns. With the rate of unemployment among Blacks continuing to move steadily upward, the implications for all segments of the Black community are demoralizing.

Besides the unemployed, "at risk" populations among American Blacks include children who suffer the consequences of poor prenatal care, poor nutrition and health care, and illiteracy; youth who are alienated and find solace in illicit drugs and alcohol; elderly who often have little education, income, and medical care, with this vulnerability often heightened by the risk of assault and robbery; and women who suffer the double jeopardy of sexism and racism.

In spite of abundant evidence that persons who are not functioning to capacity are economic liabilities, pressures to improve the health and mental health of Black people have not received significant attention from decision-makers. A growing body of research indicates that the reason Blacks do not avail themselves of physical and mental health services is not because of a lack of desire for such services so much as the attitude of health care givers (Byron, 1975). Other factors which mitigate against Blacks using health/mental health services include: 1) lack of awareness of the availability of such services; 2) reliance on traditional media to inform Blacks of the existence of such services; 3) inadequate transportation to and from health/mental health delivery agencies; 4) scheduled hours that are more convenient for health/mental health delivery personnel than for the potential Black consumers (Byron, 1975).

The lack of funding to address the specific fiscal complexities of programs in minority neighborhoods, and the special needs for consultation and education, outreach programs, and research necessary to develop innovative treatment approaches make it difficult to establish community mental health centers that can survive and meet the needs of Blacks.

A major barrier to the access and utilization of the mental health delivery system by the Black community appears to be the identity of the mental health practitioner. Blacks are poorly represented in the mental health disciplines. The supply of qualified professionals and paraprofessionals continues to lag behind the increasing demand for services. It is essential to increase the representation of Blacks (and other minorities) in the mental health professions for an important reason relating to the issue of trust. Blacks have experienced abuse by non-Black mental health and health practitioners. They are reluctant to use health/mental health facilities for they accurately perceive that they may be mistreated. Efforts to ameliorate this situation by recruiting, training, and employing Blacks in the mental health disciplines at all levels of responsibility and expertise have proven less than successful. Some new approaches to solving personnel issues are imperative. Until such time as the cadre of Black mental health personnel is sufficiently large and can accommodate the needs of Black Americans, it will be necessary to prepare nonBlack mental health professionals and paraprofessionals to understand the nuances in problems that confront Black consumers of mental health services.

HISPANIC AMERICANS

A number of hypotheses have been advanced to explain the underutilization of mental health services by Hispanic Americans. The major factors appear to be structural in nature and pertain to the availability, accessibility, and acceptability of services in terms of their relevance to the socio-cultural characteristics of Hispanic Americans. When Hispanics do receive services, these are usually of inferior quality. Often, diagnosis is based on assessment procedures developed for the Anglo population which have no demonstrated validity or applicability for Hispanics. Additionally, Hispanics are more likely to receive somatic and psychopharmacological treatment and less likely to receive individual or group psychotherapy. When psychotherapy is provided, it is often based on culturally irrelevant treatment modalities. Under these conditions, it is not surprising that Hispanics tend to terminate treatment prematurely (Padilla et al., 1975; Yamamoto et al., 1968).

Another problem related to the quality of services is that Hispanics are more often served by paraprofessionals than professionals. While the former are an important part of mental health care, they obviously do not have the training to provide the quality of service which the professional mental health worker can provide (Casas and Lopez, 1977).

Beyond a doubt, this nation has very few programs aimed at serving the specific needs of Spanish-speaking peoples. Hispanics are not receiving adequate mental health care and underutilize existing services, although a high incidence of mental health problems is known to occur among this population. Hispanics need more mental health services because as a group they are only partially acculturated and marginally integrated economically; as a consequence they are subject to a number of "high stress indicators." These indicators, known to be correlated with personality disintegration and the subsequent need for treatment intervention, include: 1) poor communication skills in English; 2) the poverty cycle--limited education, lower income, depressed social status, deteriorated housing, and minimal political influence; 3) the survival of traits from a rural agrarian culture which are relatively ineffectual in an urban technical society; 4) the seasonal migration of some workers; and 5) the stressful problem of acculturation to a society which appears prejudicial, hostile, and rejecting. Consequently, the entire pattern of service delivery to Hispanics must be reviewed in the light of the principles of biculturality and the right to treatment in accordance to one's own cultural perspective (Padilla et al., 1975).

AMERICAN INDIANS

Service delivery systems for American Indians are fragmented and this represents a severe problem for Indian communities. There is little or no coordination at either the local or Federal levels.

The urban Indian, for example, has been placed in a very difficult situation. Even though the Snyder Act authorizes services for all Indians no matter where they reside, a lack of funding has caused the Indian Health Service (IHS) to restrict services to Indians who reside on reservations. Thus, services to urban Indians are severely limited.

State and county relationships with Indian tribes and communities have not been good. Services are refused to Indian people in the erroneous belief that all Indians are eligible for Federal programs. Because of jurisdictional disputes between some states and Indian tribal governments, services such as foster care placement, nursing home care, juvenile care, food stamps, and other county-based programs have been denied.

State governments receive funds from the Department of Health and Human Services based on the size of their state populations (which include Indians), but those funds are not equitably shared with Indian tribes. Tribes also complain that they are included in various state plans without their knowledge. Comprehensive community mental health centers sometimes plan nonexistent services for tribal communities.

Health care is part of the trust relationship between the Federal government and the Indian people, even though this relationship is often cited as a "mysterious one." The IHS has had many problems and has come under increasingly severe criticism. Appropriations from Congress have not kept up with the level of needs. Recruitment of staff is difficult and retention is even more difficult. Facilities and equipment are sustandard. The American Indian Policy Review Commission commented in 1977 that it was "kind to say that Indian health is substandard." Many IHS persons attribute their problems to Congress and the lack of adequate funding.

One problem frequently mentioned by the IHS administration is poor staff morale at the local level. Tribal persons are asked to work as a means to raise morale and thus to better recruit and retain IHS personnel. Tribes in rural areas of North and South Dakota, Montana, and other remote areas also share the same problems as any rural area in recruiting physicans.

The current relationship between the IHS and the Indian people is best characterized as one between a colonizer and the colonized. The struggle for power, the increasing resentment of the Indian people, and the frustrations of the service providers are typical of this relationship. IHS personnel—in their frustrations--often fall into the trap of "blaming the victim."

The literature on American Indians reveals a state of confusion concerning the kinds of mental health treatment that would be necessary and appropriate. Mental health related problems such as alcohol abuse, drug overdose, suicide attempts, depression, obesity, and sexual acting-out have seemed overwhelming to many who provide services to American Indians. A cycle of dependency and rejection has been established at times. Patients have complained of long waits, insensitive caretakers, and lack of proper treatment; and the care givers have complained of long hours, ungrateful patients, and a hostile community. Some psychiatric consultants to the Indian Health Service have found it more appropriate to provide attention and support to care providers than to the Indian clients.

There is currently a sharp difference in philosophy between mental health care providers in the IHS and the recipients of services. Indians at the local level (both urban and reservation) want to design, plan, and manage their own services. They insist that only this kind of approach will be helpful and successful. Indian Health Service providers still operate within the framework of increased funding for services directly from the IHS.

Removing Barriers to Utilization

It was evident from the information gathered by the Special Populations subpanels that the mental health system has a long way to go in providing services for minorities as well as women and the physically handicapped. Writing new legislation to make services available and pumping money into monolithic, generic service programs will not be solutions unless: 1) the services are skillfully tailored to be culturally relevant to the populations they are to serve; 2) these populations are partners in the planning and development of services; and 3) these populations are involved, in reasonable numbers, in the delivery of services at all levels from administration to line staff.

Entitlement to services through mechanisms such as Medicaid/Medicare or national health service does not mean that minority groups will automatically use these services. Again, what is necessary are appropriate, culturally relevant, and high quality services. In addition, issues related to factors which are suspected to be barriers to utilization (e.g., stigma, lack of consumer awareness) may continue to be relevant unless efforts are made in the areas of outreach and education about mental health.

The question may be raised that providing an improved and equitable mental health system means providing an expensive system. But, from a very similar perspective, it is also expensive in social and economic terms to have large numbers of persons whose personal and social functioning is significantly impaired by mental disorders, many of which could be mitigated, if not fully remitted, by adequate mental health treatment.

Racism cannot be overlooked as a major barrier to the utilization of mental health services by minorities. Eradicating this barrier will perhaps be the most difficult task to accomplish; however, strenuous effort toward that goal is critical.

The response of the President's Commission on Mental Health to the data submitted by the Special Populations subpanels was to recommend an increased emphasis on mental health service delivery, research, and training aimed at providing for the mental health needs of minority persons.

Among the Commission's recommendations to move the nation closer toward the goal of making quality care at reasonable cost available to all Americans were: 1) a new Federal grant program for community mental health services to create services where none currently exist, to supplement existing services that are inadequate, and to increase ways that communities can develop a comprehensive network of services; 2) a new national priority to end the neglect of the chronically mentally ill by providing Federal incentives--$50 million a year for five years--to further phase down large state mental hospitals, upgrade care in the remaining smaller hospitals, and develop needed community-based services; 3) inclusion of appropriate coverage for mental health care in any plans for national health insurance and improved mental health coverage in Medicare and Medicaid; 4) a concerted national effort to prevent mental disabilities chiefly through increased availability of maternal and infant care and early childhood development assistance; and 5) increased Federal investments in research on the causes and treatment of mental illness, mental retardation, drug abuse, and alcoholism. The Commission urged "a strategy developed and implemented by partners--the private sector with the public sector, the Federal government with state and local governments, those working in mental health with those working in general health and related human services."

For the proposed new Federal grant program, the Commission recommended that priority be given to communities that are unserved and underserved; to services for children, adolescents, and the elderly; to specialized services for minority group populations; and to services for people with chronic mental illness. The Commission recommended a funding level of $75 million in the first year and $100 million for each of the following two years. These new dollars would be in addition to funds required to support the nation's existing community mental health centers.

The Commission also recommended: 1) increased links between existing community supports (families, schools, churches, self-help groups) and formal mental health services; 2) new directions for the Federal support of training to promote a better distribution of mental health personnel throughout the country and more personnel trained to meet the special needs of minorities, children, adolescents, and the elderly; 3) stronger protection for the basic rights of the mentally disabled and establishment of advocacy systems for the mentally ill; 4) adoption by each state of a "bill of rights" for the mentally disabled; and 5) specific steps to improve public understanding and acceptance of the mentally ill and mental illness.

The analyses, findings, and recommendations of the Commission have formed a blueprint for the Mental Health Systems Act as well as related initiatives in such areas as training, financing, services for the chronically mentally ill, research, and other issues pertinent to the delivery of mental health services. Some new Federal policies have significant implications for minority group populations.

THE MENTAL HEALTH SYSTEMS ACT

The President's Commission recommended a new service system which would give special attention to the unserved and underserved including the elderly, minorities, children, and the chronically mentally ill. While working towards comprehensive services there must be flexibility to allow areas with unique needs and limited resources to first initiate mental health programs for the most underserved.

Each title and section of the Mental Health Systems Act is a direct response to a Commission recommendation. Title IV of the Systems Act, especially, provides for assistance to communities that wish to initiate services which are designed to meet the unique needs of special populations. Priority would be given to areas with limited mental health services.

Heretofore, organizations which wanted to initiate mental health services targeted on a specific population that was unserved or underserved could not receive funding without being committed to the development of the required services of a community mental health center or without trying to affiliate with such a center. The initiation grant mechanism of the Systems Act now provides these organizations with a source of funding.

FINANCING MENTAL HEALTH SERVICES

The Commission defined the following principles for coverage of mental illness under any national health insurance program:

1. Reasonable array of services to be covered
2. Cost-sharing on the same basis as for other illnesses
3. Freedom of choice for consumers

Regarding Medicare, the Commission recommended:

1. Provider status for community mental health centers
2. Encouragement of partial hospitalization utilization
3. Increases in outpatient reimbursement to $750
4. Reduction of beneficiary co-insurance to 20 percent
5. Extension of coverage for inpatient care

Regarding Medicaid, the Commission called for eliminating discrimination against the mentally ill and increasing incentives for deinstitutionalization. It also recommended the development of a new system for paying nonmedical costs related to caring for the chronically mentally ill--either through social security insurance or a new Federal income support system.

The Department of Health and Human Services has proposed Medicare amendments raising the outpatient reimbursment to $750 and lowering co-insurance to 20 percent. In addition, the Department has developed a demonstration program under Medicare dealing with the feasibility of: 1) granting provider status to ambulatory care facilities such as community mental health centers; and 2) increasing the coverage of partial hospitalization by allowing two days of partial hospitalization to be reimbursed at the rate of one inpatient day.

As part of the process of developing a national plan for the chronically wmentally ill, a review of Federal income maintenance and health/mental health financing mechanisms to eliminate barriers to appropriate care is under way.

MENTAL HEALTH PERSONNEL

The President's Commission recommended increasing the number of minority mental health personnel and promoting better linkages between health and mental health by developing the mental health skills and knowledge of primary care physicians. The Commission also recommended increasing the number of mental health professionals trained to work with the special populations of children, adolescents, and the elderly.

The National Institute of Mental Health (NIMH) has made an increase in

the number of minority mental health professionals a major priority. Funds
have been designated for grants to minority and other institutions for the
training of mental health professionals and paraprofessionals.

NIMH training program activities for 1980 include:

1. Minority Access to Research Careers Program, similar to a program
   at the National Institutes of Health
2. Extramural Associates Program to increase the participation of
   minority group managers under the Intergovernment Personnel Act
3. A state-of-the-art conference on research and clinical training curricula for minority group students
4. Fellowships for upgrading the skills of minority group faculty

NIMH has also launched a new initiative to develop the mental health
skills of primary care physicians. Most people in need of mental health
services receive help from a primary care physician who lacks adequate
mental health training. Increasing the mental health skills of primary care
physicians will increase the level of mental health services for minority
groups.

RESEARCH

The President's Commission stated that the nation's research capacity in
the areas of alcohol, drug abuse, and mental health must be restored and
increased, and that there is a need to expand epidemiological and service
delivery research. In 1979, the budget for mental health research was
increased by $13 million. The President's budget for 1980 increased the
NIMH research budget by $27 million. Increased funding is being directed
towards:

1. Improvement of mental health delivery systems serving minorities,
   including diagnostic and treatment methods and demonstrations of
   effective service models.
2. Identification of the factors which promote or contribute to the
   survival and maintenance of minority group mental health.
3. Development of effective intervention methodologies designed to
   eliminate racist structures and behaviors within varied settings.
4. Six research and development centers (two for Blacks, two for Hispanics, one for American Indians and Alaska natives, and one for
   Asian Americans) which will increase the number of minority group
   researchers and expand the base of knowledge about the special
   problems of minority groups.

BASIC RIGHTS

The President's Commission recommended that an advocacy system be
established for the representation of the mentally disabled and that a bill
of rights for the mentally disabled be developed. The Department of
Health and Human Services has proposed a demonstration program on the
most effective way of insuring the protection and advocacy of rights as
well as an assessment and evaluation of current state and local internal and
external advocacy programs.

Toward the Future: A Concluding Note

As we move through the 1980s, one can only hope that the ground gained in the interest of high-quality, accessible, appropriate, and affordable mental health care for minority populations will not be lost in the competition for limited resources and the distressing regression of attitudes towards minority groups. If minority mental health advocates are to realize in the 1980s the new directions that emerged from the world of the Special Populations subpanels, alliances and coalitions among various groups must be formed. Operating from a position of significant political power, it will be critical that attention also be given to those sociocultural components that contribute to the diminished status of minority group persons and their overrepresentation among the mentally ill. Since prevention is an essential component of a unified and rational mental health system, measures to improve the quality of life of minorities are a necessary corollary.

References

American Indian Policy Review Commission. **Final Report.** Submitted to Congress, May 17, 1977.

Bachrach, L. **Utilization of State and County Mental Hospitals by Spanish Americans in 1972.** Rockville, MD: National Institute of Mental Health, 1975.

Brandon, R. "Differential Use of Mental Health Services: Social Pathology or Class Victimization?" in M. Guttentag and E. Struening (eds.), **Handbook of Evaluation Research.** Beverly Hills: Sage, 1975.

Brenner, M. "Personal Stability and Economic Security," **Social Policy** 8 (May/June 1979), 2-4.

Brown, T. et al. "Mental Illness and the Role of Mental Health Facilities in Chinatown," in S. Sue and N. Wagner (eds.), **Asian Americans: Psychological Perspectives.** Palo Alto: Science and Behavior Books, 1973.

Byron, F. "Development of Quantitative Indices of Institutional Change with Regard to Racial Minorities and Women in NIMH Extramural Programs." Unpublished report prepared for the Center for Minority Group Mental Health Programs. National Institute of Mental Health, 1975.

Cannon, M. and Locke, B. "Being Black is Detrimental to One's Mental Health: Myth or Reality," **Phylon** 38 (1977), 408-428.

Casas, J. and Lopez, S. **Summary Report: Working Conference on the Political and Economic Status of Hispanic Community Mental Health Centers.** Los Angeles: Spanish Speaking Mental Health Research Center, 1977.

Cooper, S. "A Look at the Effect of Racism on Clinical Work," **Social Casework** 54 (1973), 76-84.

Downey, G. "The Exclusion of American Indians from the U.S. Health Care System: An American Travesty," **Modern Health Care** 5 (1976), 22-31.

Fredric, C. **Suicide, Homicide and Alcoholism Among American Indians: Guidelines for Help.** Washington, DC: U.S. Government Printing Office, 1975.

Gary, L. "A Preliminary Statement on Mental Health Problems in Black Communities." Paper prepared for the Subpanel on Black Americans, President's Commission on Mental Health, 1977.

Gross, H. et al. "The Effect of Race and Sex on the Variation of Diagnosis and Disposition in a Psychiatric Emergency Room," **Journal of Nervous and Mental Disease** 148 (1969), 638-642.

Hatanaka, H. et al. "The Utilization of Mental Health Services in the Los Angeles Area," in W. Ishikawa and N. Archer (eds.), **Service Delivery in Pan Asian Communities.** San Diego: Pacific/Asian Coalition, 1975.

Health Resources Administration. **Health of the Disadvantaged.** Washington, DC: U.S. Government Printing Office, 1977.

Hoffman, H., and Hoem, A. "Adjustment of Chippewa Indian Alcoholics to a Predominantly White Treatment Program," **Psychological Reports** 37 (1975).

Jackson, A., et al. "Race as a Variable Affecting the Treatment Involvement of Children," **Journal of the American Academy of Child Psychiatry** 13 (1974).

Levitan, S., et al. **Still a Dream: The Changing Status of Blacks Since 1960.** Cambridge: Harvard University Press, 1975.

Lowinger, P., and Dobie, W. "Attitudes and Emotions of the Psychiatrist in the Initial Interview," **American Journal of Psychotherapy** 20 (1966), 17-34.

Macias, R. "U.S. Hispanics in 2000 A.D.--Projecting the Number," **Agenda** 7 (1977), 16-20.

Miller, J. and Miller, K. "Mental Health," in K. Miller and R. Dreger (eds.), **Comparative Studies of Blacks and Whites in the United States.** New York: Seminar Press, 1973.

Murase, K. "Asian Mental Health From the Community Perspective." Paper presented at a conference on "Three Perspectives of Asian American Mental Health--The Individual, the Family, the Community," 1977.

Padilla, A., and Ruiz, R. **Latino Mental Health: A Review of the Literature.** Washington, DC: U.S. Government Printing Office, 1973.

Padilla, A., et al. "Community Mental Health Services for the Spanish Speaking/Surnamed Population," **American Psychologist** 30 (1975), 892-905.

"Report of the Special Populations Subpanel on the Mental Health of Black Americans," in **Task Panel Reports Submitted to the President's Commission on Mental Health,** Vol. III Appendix. Washington, DC: U.S. Government Printing Office, 1978.

Rosenthal, D. and Frank, J. "Fate of Psychiatric Clinic Outpatients Assigned to Psychotherapy," **Journal of Nervous and Mental Diseases** 127 (1958), 337-347.

Solis, A. "Utilization of Community Mental Health Services by the Spanish Surnamed Populations in California Counties with Five Percent or More Spanish Surnamed Population, 1976-1977." Paper presented at the Working Conference on the Political and Economic Status of Hispanic Community Mental Health Centers, 1977.

Staples, R. **Introduction to Black Sociology.** New York: McGraw Hill, 1976.

Sue, S. "Community Mental Health Services to Minority Groups: Some Optimism, Some Pessimism," **American Psychologist** 32 (1977), 616-625.

Sue, S., and McKinney, H. "Asian Americans in the Community Mental Health Care System," **American Journal of Orthopsychiatry** 45 (1975), 111-118.

True, R. "Mental Health Services in a Chinese American Community," in W. Ishikawa and N. Archer (eds.), **Service Delivery in Pan Asian Communities.** San Diego: Pacific/Asian Coalition, 1975.

Yamamoto, J., et al. "Cultural Problems in Psychiatric Therapy," **Archives of General Psychiatry,** 19 (1968), 45-49.

TOWARD AN UNDERSTANDING OF THE MENTAL HEALTH AND SUBSTANCE ABUSE ISSUES OF RURAL AND MIGRANT ETHNIC MINORITIES: A SEARCH FOR COMMON EXPERIENCES

ROBERT A. RYAN
JOSEPH E. TRIMBLE

Overview

Addressing the special needs and problems of rural and migrant ethnic minorities is a complex and demanding task. The breadth of the subject by itself is extensive. When the areas of alcohol, drug abuse, and mental health are added, the task becomes more complex. Moreover, America's salient ethnic minority groups are complex social systems. No single treatise has effectively identified the broad range of psychosocial characteristics particular to any one group. Some groups, like the American Indian, have received enormous attention from social scientists; yet, despite this attention, large knowledge gaps persist. Nonetheless, data does exist that identifies common ethnic minority experiences, particularly the kind generated by racism. In addition, small bits of knowledge are available which point to particular needs and problems that encompass mental health and substance abuse issues.

Many American Indians, Asian Americans, Blacks, and Hispanics argue that each respective group is unique (Trimble, 1977; Williams, 1976; Yee, 1975; Okura, 1975; Sue and Chin, 1976). Moreover, many ethnic minority scholars and lay-people alike emphasize the range of differences inherent within each group. Sue (1977: 617) amplified this when he stated: "Even the concepts of Native Americans and Asian Americans encompass many different groups." Participants at a 1977 meeting on The Mental Health Needs of Hispanic-American Communities pointed out that: "Hispanics are not a homogeneous group . . . each differs in some respects and this variability must be recognized" (Hispanic Mental Health Professionals, 1977: 1). Among Native Americans, there are well over 200 separate tribes, each markedly different from the others. Add to this tribal diversity the scatterings of Indians and Alaska Natives in urban and rural communities across the country, each believing that their problems are unique, and one has a sense of the enormity of the complications. An understanding of the unique dimensions of each ethnic minority group is essential if science and the government are to be responsive and effective in delivering services and programs.

If America's ethnic minorities have one overwhelming commonality, it is their rootedness in the land and their shared understanding of the rural lifestyle. Indeed, American Indians, Blacks, and Hispanics historically share common rural beginnings. The first Asians imported to the United States were placed in rural railroad and mining work camps. Today, about 50 percent of each ethnic minority group still resides in rural communities, with the exception of Asian Americans.

Many urban ethnic minority families have direct ties with kin still living in rural areas. Also recent census information shows a reversal of the rural-to-urban migration trend among Blacks, Hispanics and Indians. Blacks from northern cities are beginning to resettle in areas of the South, seeking not only an improved economic lifestyle but a rural environment as well. This same type of thing is occurring among Indians and, on a smaller scale, among Hispanics. The swelling of rural environments by ethnic minorities can introduce unforeseen problems different from those experienced in major urban centers.

Internal migration, whether voluntary or involuntary, is not a new and different experience for ethnic minorities. Hispanics, to a large extent, make up the greatest percentage of migrant workers in this country. The migrant worker is accustomed to movement, to settlement and resettlement. Constant movement in an effort to sustain economic welfare has created a distinct and unique lifestyle for the migrant worker. Coping and adaptation strategies are tightly woven in a social fabric whose foundation is built on social and environmental change.

Just as the migrant ethnic minority anticipates and expects change, the rural ethnic minority prefers the slow-paced sedentary lifestyle. Change in the rural area, whether it be a village on Norton Sound in Alaska, a reservation in South Dakota, a border town in south Texas, or a small town in Arkansas, comes slowly and, when it does, painfully and reluctantly. Rural folk prefer the status quo and seem to permit only the kinds of change that will make the quality of life just a little better.

Thus, among present-day ethnic minorities, we have a strange set of circumstances. For rural folk, change is not particularly welcomed. The rural migrant worker expects and seemingly adapts effectively to change. Somewhere in between these two orientations exists the urban ethnic minority person who is returning to the rural lifestyle. Settlement and resettlement in rural areas can and will present a myriad of coping and adaptation difficulties for the urban-to-rural returnee and for permanent residents of the rural town or migrant camp. It is difficult to predict the nature and extent of these difficulties simply because social scientists, for the most part, have concentrated their research efforts on understanding the rural-to-urban phenomenon and urban lifestyles.

A partial understanding of the nature of these difficulties can be gained from assessing a collection of findings concerning the rural-to-urban problems of ethnic minorities and the coping patterns of rural and migrant communities. To make the task a little easier, emphasis will be placed on mental health and substance abuse, primarily because they are areas that have a strong relationship with coping and adaptation strategies. In discussing the mental health and substance abuse of rural and migrant ethnic minorities, we take the position that: 1) ethnic folk are not well prepared to tolerate stress when confronted with **abrupt social change;** 2) salient cultural characteristics and lifestyle experiences affect the degree of responsiveness to social support institutions; and 3) increasing contacts between rural and migrant communities with their urban counterparts are likely to create undesirable circumstances and could induce the need to devise alternative coping strategies to meet economic and psychosocial demands.

Ethnic Minority Perceptions of Mental Health

Social science and biomedical attempts to understand the mental health experiences of ethnic minorities are derived from conventional wisdom rooted in an "occidental psychiatric orientation"; research is molded around that orientation and cast into the time-worn tradition of the scientific method. The combination of these factors has largely contributed to the way mental health experiences are investigated and subsequently interpreted. Thus the contemporary understanding of mental health and substance abuse among rural and migrant minorities is biased; nature and folk interpretations are limited and rarely covered in the literature (cf. Padilla and Ruiz, 1973; Attneave and Kelso, 1977; Morishima, et al., 1978).

How rural folk perceive mental health experiences and addictive behavior is essential if science and government ever hope to provide solutions to "deviant behavior." The few studies that exist on this subject show that: 1) migrant Hispanics view mental illness as a "misfortune," one that "can be cured," and something for which "one should not be punished" (Derbyshire, 1970); treatment is often centered around the use of informal community helping networks (Fabrega and Metzger, 1968); 2) mental illness is a state of mind among the more traditional Sioux and is viewed as an achieved status within the native world view (Trimble and Medicine, 1976); and 3) for many rural Blacks hallucinations, delusions, and "psychotic-like" behavior reveal an individual's relationship with a greater spiritual force; an individual in a "psychotic" state of mind is seen as one who is in closer contact with religious entities than the average person (Fisher, 1977).

Traditional ethnic minority conceptions are deeply entrenched in history and customs. Madsen (1961) and Trimble and Medicine (1976) strongly urge modern-day practitioners to closely examine the traditional beliefs instead of ridiculing them as superstitious and unfounded in reality.

There is every reason to believe that rural and migrant minorities have little understanding of contemporary psychiatric nosologies and typologies (Karno and Edgerton, 1969). An uneven fit exists between "educated" investigations and interpretations and rural minority folklore. It seems reasonable to suggest that, as science and government continue to work from a model founded outside the environment in which the problem occurs, accrued knowledge will continue to be inappropriate for dealing with substantive issues embedded in rural folklore. Future efforts should tap into the folklore of this country's rural and migrant minorities and assume a reasonable compromise in the methods and interpretations used. In the meantime, we are faced with knowledge that caters to the needs of researchers, practitioners, and decision-makers to guide our level of understanding.

Current Mental Health Understandings

Price and Sikes (1974), in their extensive review of rural-urban migration research, agree that mental health data on the adaptation experiences of ethnic minorities is inconclusive. Although most people experience difficulty adapting and coping with a new environment, urban or rural, the level of stress is typically minimal and short-lived. Among migrant workers specifically, adjustments to new surroundings are dealt with through the use of long-standing, well-refined coping strategies; mental disorders that occur are typically minor and small in scale. Migrants expect change and prepare themselves psychologically to deal with new circumstances. However, it is usually the unexpected events that create adjustment problems which can be manifested in a number of ways.

Mental health studies of rural-urban migrants typically make use of mental health hospital admissions data to determine incidence levels. Lee (1957) compiled data among first admissions to New York hospitals and after controlling for race, age, and sex found that migrants had higher first admissions rates than nonmigrants for each diagnosed and classified form of psychosis, both overall and at specific levels. Using a similar methodological approach, Struening et al. (1970) found that Black and Puerto Rican migrants to New York City had higher rates of hospitalization for mental illness than permanent residents. In addition, Struening et al. (1970: 246) found that "the number of migrants and the number of relatively permanent residents of the same ethnic group played virtually identical roles in predicting the indicators of social, health and mental health problems." Again, using hospital admissions data, Locke and Duvall (1964) found that nonmigrant Ohio natives had lower first-admission rates than out-of-state migrants.

Mental illness among migrants is often attributed to the experiences created by social mobility and the degree to which they are accustomed to that phenomenon. If social mobility is a causative factor, it should be looked at more systematically. For example Kleiner and Parker (1965) found a higher incidence of mental illness among Philadelphia Blacks than rural southern Black migrants. In addition they found that migrants from other areas had lower rates than natives but higher rates than rural southern migrants. In a more comprehensive study of 2,000 first-admission Black patients to Pennsylvania psychiatric hospitals, Kleiner and Parker (1959) found an overrepresentation of Pennsylvania natives and northern migrants and an underrepresentation of southern migrants. Levels of goal-striving behavior and ethnic identity problems were found to be more prevalent among northern Blacks than southern migrants (Kleiner and Parker, 1970); these psychosocial characteristics are similar to those found among groups of the mentally ill. The higher rates of mental disorders characteristic of northern Blacks cannot be solely attributed to social mobility as the northern migrants were found to be more mobile than the southern migrants (Kleiner and Parker, 1970). Social and geographic mobility may be differentially related to psychiatric disturbance; however, sole attribution of higher rates to migrant groups alone is not totally accurate (Micklin and Leon, 1978).

COMMUNITY SUPPORT SYSTEMS

Factors such as educational attainment, sex status, and "immediate life experiences" may contribute more to the incidence of mental illness than social mobility. Fried et al. (1971) found that the single most important factor in adjustment among Black migrants to Boston was the loss of close ties to people left behind and, more generally, the home environment. Additional factors such as low educational levels, lack of job skills and, for women, social isolation, were found by Fried to contribute to the incidence of emotional disturbance among rural-to-urban migrants. Relatives, as well, can play a significant role in easing the adjustment of migrants as substantiated by Omari (1956) in a study of 200 Black migrants in Beloit, Wisconsin. Thus the presence of relatives and friends combined with the length of city residence can be very instrumental in offsetting mental disorders and psychological stress.

Even though support systems may ease adjustment and coping difficulties, stresses created by the migration itself may be the most likely precipitant of mental disorders (Murphy, 1965). Migrant youth, in particular, are very susceptible to peer group influences that have created stress between adolescents and their families (Moses, 1958) and have also led to status anxiety, alienation, and powerlessness due in part to the low status ascribed to migrant families (McQueen, 1959). American Indian and Hispanic youth who arrive in the cities with their families often experience identity and value difficulties in their relations with their nonethnic counterparts (Dinges et al., 1977; Ablon, 1965). To strengthen the need for ethnic identity, relocated American Indians will often exclude non-Indians from formal and informal relations (Ablon, 1964) and restrict youth from joining friendships outside the Indian cultural milieu (Barter and Barter, 1974).

The support provided by the presence of people from the same ethnic minority group also seems to be a salient factor in preventing certain forms of mental illness among migrants. Bagley (1968) examined "anomie" as a cause of delinquency and emotional problems among Black migrants. He noted that decreases in diagnosed mental illness are directly associated with increased time in the city and that relatives and friends can often play an important role in curbing one's sense of anomie. Presence of "one's own kind" can provide a cushion for the migrant by assisting in the informal socialization into the normative patterns of the urban neighborhood. Breed (1966), in studying the effects of migration on suicide, found "duration of residence" to be a key factor in adjustment to and accomodation of the urban lifestyle. While there is some evidence to support the significance of helpful influences provided by relatives and persons from the same ethnic background, more research is needed to identify the nature and character- istics of the informal community helping networks.

CULTURAL DIFFERENCES

The settlement experiences of rural-to-urban migrants contain conflicts and stresses that stem from the cultural background of the individual and family. The presence of kin and "a colony of one's own kind" are helpful indeed; however, the migrant eventually has to deal with those outside the "cultural circle of awareness." Karno and Edgerton (1969) and Torrey (1969) emphasize that California Hispanics are subjected to a variety of stress indicators which are closely related to mental disturbances and self- destructive behavior. Malzburg (1956, 1965) found that migrant Puerto Rican males have a higher standardized rate of first admissions than non- Puerto Ricans in New York and suggests that high rates are due, for the most part, to cultural and social characteristics. In support of this, Srole et al. (1962: 293) maintain that a "complex of exogenous sociocultural forces and pressure converging with endogenous selection processes may create turbulent effects" for migrant Puerto Ricans.

Language is also a major barrier to adjustment and adaptation to the urban environment. Countless numbers of Hispanics, American Indians, and Asian Americans have experienced alienation, rejection, and despair from an inability to effectively communicate with potential employees and service agency personnel. Jewel (1952) relates the terrifying experiences of a Navajo male who was erroneously diagnosed as a psychotic because no resident in a Denver mental hsopital could comprehend the Navajo lan- guage; the unusual syntax of Navajo made it appear that this person was speaking in a garbled language indicative of psychotic behavior. Wester- meyer (1978) similarly recounts the tragic experiences of Vietnamese relocated to urban areas without any English language training whatsoever; many Vietnamese arrived in communities where no one understood their language.

The impact of cultural differences between migrants and urban natives cannot be underscored enough. Fabrega (1970) confirmed the hypothesis that Mexican American mental patients exhibit greater disorganizaton, regression, and grossly psychotic behavior because of the general lateness of their hospitalization by their families. It seems that "unacculturated" Mexican Americans have underlying cultural perspectives towards mental illness itself that affect the way they respond to the need for treatment; rural Hispanic families take a humanistic approach to helping the individual that largely departs from approaches used in urban areas (Fabrega and Metzger, 1968). Wignal and Koppin (1967: 146) capture the significance of the impact of language and culture on migration and mental health. They maintain that "cultural differences may account for the significantly higher admission rate of Mexican American males . . . here the rate may serve as a measure of the amount of stress produced by acculturation." As a rem- edy, Anders (1977) argues that one should strive for a clear understanding of a migrant's values, linguistic and cultural background.

Perhaps the single most important contributing factor to lifestyle adjustment to migration is racism. While relatives and the community can provide support for the migrant, little if anything can prevent the individual from experiencing job discrimination and the racist attitudes and behavior of the dominant American culture. As if struggling with the new environment is not enough, the ethnic minority migrant can be subjected to an impairment of self-image, to denial and deception that could lead to increased feelings of inadequacy, withdrawal, and self-deprecation (Marmor, 1977). Despite the presence of hard and fast civil rights regulations and affirmative action programs, migrant minorities continue to complain about discrimination and racist practices. Frustrations produced by racist practices tend to increase stress (a major causative factor in psychological disturbances), social deviancy, and mental illness (Kramer et al., 1973).

FORCED MIGRATION

Thus far the discussion has emphasized the experiences, accounts, and admissions rates of rural-to-urban ethnic minority migrants. Implicit in this discussion is the assumption that the rationale behind relocation and urban settlement is purely voluntary on the migrant's part. However, there are large communities of rural folk who have no choice in the decision to move; they are forced wittingly or unwittingly to leave their traditional homes to reside in new and unfamiliar environments. Forced movements of ethnic minority groups may involve isolated family units or the mass movement of an entire community. During the move, families and significant segments of the group may be separated, in some cases never to reunite (Trimble, 1977).

Some groups are forced to relocate through economic need or decisions imposed by actions of local, state, or federal governments. Numerous rural families have been forced to make room for the construction of superhighways, hydroelectric dams, nuclear reactors, and fuel-related processing plants (Chapin, 1954). This uprooting of ethnic minority families occurs largely against their will and has created stress due to acculturation and resettlement (Trimble, 1978).

Forced migration is still occurring in rural segments of the country. Currently, for example, the United States is negotiating with the Navajo and Hopi tribes in Arizona to resolve long disputed land claims. One result of this land entitlement issue will be the relocation of some 700 Navajo families. The Navajo may adjust, as they have done for centuries; however, there is a strong likelihood that the families will experience emotional duress as a consequence of the experience (Dinges, 1977).

Forced migration has always been an issue in the history of America's ethnic minorities. Migrants, whether they be from Africa, Mexico, Asia, or some remote corner of this country, have always experienced difficulties including (but not limited to) the disruption of families and kinship ties, loss of employment and frequent drastic shifts in occupational career lines, settlement in strange communities, and the likelihood of stress and psychiatric duress. Forced migration issues are of extreme importance in understanding the causes and consequences of future population movements. In contrast to voluntary migration, forced movement is more insidious and potentially destructive for the group and individual (cf. Trimble, 1977).

SUMMARY

The incidence of mental illness among rural and migrant minorities presents a confusing picture. Most of the studies emphasize the nature of mental illness among most rural ethnic minorities. Many of the studies show higher rates of disturbance among migrants; others show higher rates for nonmigrants. The rationale behind the onset of disturbance is equally unclear. Social and geographic mobility are offered as explanations. However, migration may not necessarily be the sole cause of emotional problems (Kantor, 1969). Instead, environmental changes resulting from migration may create situations to which the migrant may or may not be able to adjust without mental health consequences. Nonetheless it is generally argued that stresses connected with migration and settlement are salient contributing factors in the etiology of emotional difficulties.

If findings on the etiology of migrant mental illness are mixed, so too are the procedures used to investigate the problem. Sanua (1970) argues that the use of hospital statistics to measure relationships between mental illness and migration lead to "guess" generalizations. Furthermore, he maintains that research could be more fruitful if both migrant characteristics and the circumstances under which the move occurred are fully considered.

Thus the adjustments of migrant ethnic minorities are complicated phenomena and difficult to put into perspective. Add to this the dearth of information on rural mental health in general, and the situation becomes more complex. In summary, the lack of understanding surrounding the rationale for movement and the absence of objective criteria leads to the conclusion "that there is no consistent pattern of failure of migrants to adjust" (Price and Sikes, 1974: 27).

Substance Abuse: Towards Some Understanding

People often turn to alcohol and addictive drugs as a response to emotional problems to "take the edge off of reality." Rural and migrant ethnic minorities, like their urban counterparts, are experiencing increased abuses of addictive substances. Beigel et al. (1974), in an extensive study of alcohol and drug use, found that American Indians rated alcoholism as the most serious health problem; Blacks and Mexican Americans rated it as the second most serious problem, ahead of heart disease and cancer.

Many attribute the high incidence of alcohol and drug abuse to the same conditions that create mental illness for rural migrants (cf. Padilla and Ruiz, 1974). Ferracuti (1967) adds to this long list of factors by asserting that drug addiction in particular is more common in areas that undergo rapid social change. Values are challenged and those who follow traditional folk customs are often forced to make a choice. The presence of **agringados** in south Texas has created value conflicts with long-time residents and has produced a high percentage of problem drinkers (Madsen, 1964). Drug and alcohol use, viewed as an escape mechanism, can continue unchecked so long as practitioners fail to recognize the cultural subtleties inherent in rural folklore.

Abuse of "hard drugs" is not nearly the problem on Indian reservations that it is in urban ghettos (Attneave and Beiser, 1974). Instead of cocaine, opium, and heroin, Indian youth have turned to sniffing glue, gasoline, paint, and spray cans with propellant gases. "In nearly every community," Attneave and Beiser (1974: 88) maintain, "there are adults in their 20s who have serious brain damage and other complications arising from this condition."

Drug abuse among rural American Indians is small in contrast to the alarming rates of alcohol abuse. Alcohol abuse rates in excess of 60 percent are not uncommon in many rural Indian communities (cf. Brod, 1974; Street et al., 1976). Whittaker (1966) attributes the high incidence to the: 1) high degree of interpsychic stresses caused by insecure life on the reservation; disintegration of the tribal culture; and suppression of aggressive tendencies and loathesome feelings towards whites and the government; 2) lack of a suitable substitute for relieving mental stresses; and 3) utilitarian cultural views regarding alcohol consumption that typically receive approval from most community members.

Alcoholism is also a major problem for many American Indians who relocate to the urban environment (Ryan and Ryan, 1978). Ablon (1965) found that alcoholism on the reservation is a factor in deciding to relocate to cities; however, it is the families with drinking problems who are least likely to adjust to urban life. A change in environment and lifestyle probably gives the Indian problem drinker a greater excuse to continue drinking. As such, inability to adjust to an urban lifestyle is a major causal factor of Indian alcoholism in urban settings (Price, 1968).

The adjustment difficulties of urban American Indians stem from a number of factors including: 1) poor acculturation, 2) social and economic deprivation, 3) lack of marketable job skills, and 4) anomie (Burns et al., 1974). A large part of the resulting psychological stress, anxiety and frustration is vented through heavy alcohol abuse; alcoholism, however, is a symptom, not a cause. "The dearth of mental health data is greater for American Indians, as so little is known about Indians living in cities . . . urban migration is a very traumatic experience for Indians and . . . urban living is extremely stressful as it heightens the cultural conflict " (Chadwick and Stauss, 1974: 2).

Rural-to-urban adjustment problems are also manifested in alcohol abuse among Hispanics and Blacks. Madsen (1964) and Jessor et al. (1968) emphasize the stress-inducing circumstances surrounding Mexican American abuse of alcohol in urban settings. Jessor et al. (1968) isolated salient personality and sociocultural circumstances that give rise to deviant behavior and alcohol abuse among Indians and Hispanics. Deviancy is learned, goal-oriented and adaptive, demonstrating that alcoholism can become an internalized pattern of behavior, however self-destructive, that enables an Indian or Hispanic to cope with stressful conditions.

While drug abuse is not a major problem among migrant Indians, the same cannot be said for Blacks and Mexican Americans. In some communities, heroin, for example, is more accessible to Mexican Americans than Blacks (Redlinger and Michel, 1970). Differential accessibility to drugs can be a major factor in narcotics abuse rates among migrant ethnic minorities. The presence of friends and members of the same ethnic group can enhance the likelihood of access to drugs, particularly if the drug pipeline is controlled by "one's own kind." Redlinger and Michel (1970) point out that Mexican Americans in south Texas do not trust Blacks and, as a result, limit the supplies of drugs from Mexico to themselves.

If there is a paucity of information of substance abuse among rural and migrant Blacks, Hispanics, and American Indians, then there is even less information available on Asian Americans. What information that is available suffers from severe limitations and certain erroneous conclusions. Although five articles have been published on the topic (LaBarre, 1946; Barnett, 1955; Wang, 1968; Chu, 1972; and Singer, 1972) only Barnett and Wang offer useful information. These articles concentrate on Chinese drinking behavior and characterize it as: 1) heavy but restrictive in the display of violence and aggressive behavior while intoxicated; 2) a matter of course with little or no ambivalence towards it; 3) a group phenomenon where one rarely drinks to excess in solitude; 4) a behavior that is taught to Asian youth; and 5) sanctioned but only at moderate levels.

SUMMARY

As one would expect, substance abuse incidences and experiences among rural and migrant ethnic minorities resemble those concerning mental health. Abuse of alcohol and narcotics is a symptom as is mental illness. Abuse of addictive substances is brought on as a result of an inability to effectively cope with adjustments to the urban lifestyle or to changes occurring in the rural or reservation environment. Available information is somewhat restrictive in scope largely because the bulk of alcohol and drug research is conducted on urban residents. However slim the information, it still would be safe to conclude that substance abuse is a response to a variety of identifiable stress-producing agents. The extent to which social mobility and environmental change affect substance abuse levels is open to question.

General Summary and Recommendations

Salient mental health and substance abuse findings concerning rural and migrant ethnic minorities have been presented. The articles discussed capture major themes in the research literature. Where appropriate, emphasis has been placed on identifying knowledge gaps.

Current understandings of ethnic minorities are derived from contemporary psychiatric and scientific orientations. Findings generated by these approaches cater to the needs of academicians, professionals, practitioners, and decision-makers but miss the mark when reflected against ethnic folklore; very few studies have attempted to examine mental health and substance abuse from the native worldview.

Understanding, prediction, and control are the major goals of science. From the review conducted in this paper, it would indeed seem plausible to suggest that science has not come too far. For the most part, mental health and substance abuse are still largely at the understanding stage. There is not enough data to accurately predict how we will cope with change due to migration. General categories of knowledge exist; however, they are insufficient for predicting behavior with absolute certainty.

There is another side to the issue. Research on rural and migrant ethnic minorities is presumptuous; many investigators assume that rural and migrant folk have little understanding of their needs and problems. Moreover, many assume that migrant folk do not have the knowledge and skills to prevent problems. Oddly enough, cultural groups have evolved prevention and treatment strategies for practically every known condition. Future understandings can gain immensely if efforts are focused on identifying indigenous mechanisms used to control and prevent emotional problems and abuses of narcotics and alcohol.

In conclusion, the presence of knowledge gaps requires specific attention. Some of the important areas in which work is needed are listed below.

1. The physical and mental health of migrants compared to urban nonmigrants with appropriate controls for situational characteristics, migrant experiences, age, susceptibility to emotional disturbances, occupational backgrounds, etc.

2. The psychosocial characteristics of the effectively coping person who has managed to accomodate and adjust to new environments.

3. Comparisons of urban-born children of rural-to-urban migrants with urban-born children of urban nonmigrants and urban-to-urban migrants.

4. Identification of salient coping mechanisms that foster transcultural competence in adapting to varieties of mental health conditions.

5. Knowledge of the characteristics and motivations of returnees to rural areas compared with initial migrants, nonreturnees, and rural nonmigrants.

6. Knowledge related to the implementation of training programs aimed at utilizing the talents of local residents for establishing prevention and control strategies.

34   Minority Group Mental Health

7. Knowledge related to accelerated efforts at eliminating racial bar-
    riers that block attempts to successfully cope with new and changing
    environments.

8. Development of research paradigms that more accurately reflect
    cultural perspectives and lifestyles.

9. Longitudinal or cross-lagged cohort studies to monitor mobility exper-
    iences and psychiatric disturbances which would allow for within and
    between group comparisons.

10. Knowledge related to the identification and implementation of pre-
    vention strategies that utilize known effective contemporary proce-
    dures in tandem with traditional cultural practices.

References

Ablon, J. "American Indian Relocation: Problems of Dependency and
    Management in the City," **Phylon** 26 (1965), 362-371.

_____. "Relocated American Indians in the San Francisco Bay Area: Social
    Interaction and Indian Identity," **Human Organization** 23 (1964),
    296-304

Anders, A. et al. "Why Did We Not Establish a Separate Complete Program
    for Spanish-Speaking Patients," in E. Padilla and A. Padilla (eds.),
    Transcultural Psychiatry: An Hispanic Perspective. Los Angeles:
    Spanish Speaking Mental Health Research Center, 1977.

Attneave, C.L. and Kelso, D.R. **American Indian Annotated Bibliography of
    Mental Health.** Seattle: University of Washington, 1977.

Bagley, C. "Migration, Race, and Mental Health: A Review of Some Re-
    cent Research," **Race** 9 (1968), 343-356.

Barnett, M.L. "Alcoholism Among the Cantonese of New York City: An
    Anthropological Study," in O. Diethelm (ed.), **Etiology of Chronic
    Alcoholism.** Springfield, IL: Thomas, 1955.

Barter, E.R. and Barter, J.T. "Urban Indians and Mental Health Problems,"
    Psychiatric Annals 4 (1974), 37-43.

Beigel, A., et al. "Planning for the Development of Comprehensive Com-
    munity Alcoholism Services: Assessing Community Awareness and
    Attitudes," **American Journal of Psychiatry** 55 (1974), 1116-1121.

Beiser, M., and Attneave, C.L. **Mental Health Services for American
    Indians: Neither Feast nor Famine.** Portland, OR: White Cloud Cen-
    ter, 1978.

Breed, W. "Suicide, Migration and Race: A Study of Cases in New Orleans," Journal of Social Issues 22 (1966), 30-43.

Brod, T.M. "Alcoholism as a Mental Health Problem of Native Americans: A Review of the Literature," Archives of General Psychiatry 32 (1975), 1385-1391.

Burns, M., Daily, J.M., and Moskowitz, H. Drinking Practices and Problems of Urban American Indians in Los Angeles. Santa Monica: Planning Analysis and Research Institute, 1974.

Chadwick, B.A., and Stauss, J.H. "Assimilation of American Indians into Urban Society: The Seattle Case," Human Organization 34 (1975), 359-369.

Chapin, F.S. In the Shadow of a Defense Plant: A Study of Urbanization in Rural South Carolina. Chapel Hill: University of North Carolina, Institute for Research in Social Change, 1954.

Chu, G. "Drinking Patterns and Attitudes of Rooming-House Chinese in San Francisco," Quarterly Journal Studies of Alcohol 6 (1972), 58-68.

Derbyshire, R.L. "Adaptation of Adolescent Mexican Americans to United States Society," in E.B. Brody (ed.), Behavior in New Environments: Adaptation of Migrant Populations. Beverly Hills: Sage, 1970.

Dinges, N. "Mental Health Implications of the Hopi-Navajo Land Dispute." Paper presented at the American Psychological Association Annual Meeting, 1977.

Dinges, N., Trimble, J., and Hollenbeck, A. Socialization of American Indian Adolescents: A Review of the Literature. Seattle: Battelle Human Affairs Research Centers, 1976.

Fabrega, H. "Mexican Americans in Texas: Some Social Psychiatric Features," in E.B. Brody (ed.), Behavior in New Environments: Adaptation of Migrant Populations. Beverly Hills: Sage, 1970.

Fabrega, H., and Metzger, D. "Psychiatric Illness in a Small Latino Community," Psychiatry 31 (1968), 339-351.

Ferracuti, F. "Juvenile Delinquency and Social Change in Puerto Rico," Criminalia 33 (1967), 569-573.

Fisher, H.G. Personal communication, 1977.

Fried, M., et al. A Study of the Demographic and Social Determinants of Functional Achievement in a Negro Population. Final report submitted to the Office of Economic Opportunity, OEO Contract # B 89-4279. Chestnut Hill, MA: Boston College, Institute of Human Sciences, 1971.

Hispanic Mental Health Professionals. **Conclusions and Recommendations of the Meeting on Mental Health Needs of Hispanic-American Communities in the U.S.A.** New Haven, CT: Yale University, 1977.

Jessor, R., et al. **Society, Personality, and Deviant Behavior: A Study of Tri-ethnic Community.** New York: Holt, Rinehart & Winston, 1968.

Jewell, D.P. "A Case of a 'Psychotic' Navajo Indian Male," **Human Organization** 11 (1952), 32-36.

Kantor, M.B. **Mobility and Mental Health.** Springfield: Thomas, 1965.

_____. "The Enigma of Ethnicity in a Psychiatric Clinic," **Archives of General Psychiatry** 14 (1966), 516-520.

Karno, M., and Edgerton, R.B. "Perception of Mental Illness in a Mexican-American Community," **Archives of General Psychiatry** 20 (1969), 233-238.

Kleiner, R.J., and Parker, S. "Goal Striving and Psychosomatic Symptoms in a Migrant and Non-Migrant Population," in M.B. Kantor (ed.), **Mobility and Mental Health.** Springfield: Thomas, 1965.

Kleiner, R.J., and Parker, S. "Social-Psychosocial Aspects of Migration and Mental Disorder in a Negro Population," in E.G. Brody (ed.), **Behavior in New Environments: Adaptation of Migrant Populations.** Beverly Hills: Sage, 1970.

Kramer, B.M. "Racism and Mental Health as a Field of Thought and Action," in C. Willie et al. (eds.), **Racism and Mental Health.** Pittsburgh: University of Pittsburgh, 1973.

LaBarre, W. "Chinese Food and Drink," in R. McCarthy (ed.), **Drinking and Intoxication.** Glencoe: Free Press, 1946.

Lee, E.S. "Migration and Mental Disease: New York State, 1949-1951," in C.V. Kiser (ed.), **Selected Studies of Migration Since World War II.** New York: Milbank Memorial Fund, 1957.

Locke, B.Z., and Duvall, H.J. "Migration and Mental Illness," **Eugenics Quarterly** 11 (1964), 216-221.

Madsen, W. **Society and Health in the Lower Rio Grande Valley.** Austin: Hogg Foundation for Mental Health, 1961.

_____. "The Alcoholic Agringado," **American Anthropologist** 66 (1964), 355-361.

Malzberg, B. "Mental Disease Among the Puerto Ricans in New York City, 1949-1951," **Journal of Nervous and Mental Disease** 123 (1956), 262-269.

_____. **Mental Disease Among the Puerto Rican Population of New York State, 1960-1961.** Albany: Research Foundation for Mental Hygiene, Inc., 1965.

Marmor, J. "The Psychodynamics of Prejudice," in E. Padilla and A. Padilla (eds.), **Transcultural Psychiatry: An Hispanic Perspective.** Los Angeles: Spanish Speaking Mental Health Research Center, 1977.

McQueen, A.J. **A Study of Anomie Among Lower Class Negro Migrants.** Unpublished doctoral dissertation, University of Michigan, 1959.

Micklin, M., and Leon, C.A. "Life Change and Psychiatric Disturbance in a South American City: The Effects of Geographic and Social Mobility," **Journal of Health and Social Behavior** 19(1978), 92-107.

Morishima, J., Sue, S., Teng, N., Zane, N., and Cram, J. **Handbook of Asian American Mental Health Research, Vol. 1: An Annotated Bibliography.** Washington, DC: U.S. Government Printing Office, 1979.

Moses, E.R. **Migrant Negro Youth: A Study of Culture Conflict and Patterns of Accomodation.** Unpublished doctoral dissertation, University of Pennsylvania, 1948.

Murphy, H.B. "Migration and the Major Mental Disorders: A Reappraisal," in M.B. Kantor (ed.), **Mobility and Mental Health.** Springfield: Thomas, 1965.

Okura, K.P. "Asian American Programs in the National Institute of Mental Health." Paper presented at the American Psychological Association Annual Meeting, 1975.

Omari, T.P. "Factors Associated with Urban Adjustment of Rural Southern Migrants," **Social Forces** 35 (1956), 47-52.

Padilla, A., and Ruiz, R.A. **Latino Mental Health: A Review of Literature.** Rockville: National Institute of Mental Health, 1973.

Price, J.A. "The Migration and Adaptations of American Indians to Los Angeles," **Human Organization** 27 (1968), 168-175.

Redlinger, L.J., and Michel, J.B. "Ecological Variations in Heroin Abuse," **Sociological Quarterly** 11 (1970), 219-229.

Research Task Force of the National Institute of Mental Health. **Research in the Service of Mental Health.** Rockville, MD: Alcohol, Drug Abuse and Mental Health Administration, 1975.

Ryan, L.M., and Ryan, R.A. "Alcoholism--Usage Among American Indian People: An Overview." Unpublished paper, 1978.

Sanua, V.D. "Immigration, Migration and Mental Illness: A Review of the Literature with Special Emphasis on Schizophrenia," in E.G. Brody (ed.), **Behavior in New Environments: Adaptation of Migrant Populations.** Beverly Hills: Sage, 1970.

Singer,K. "Drinking Patterns and Alcoholism Among the Chinese," **British Journal of Addiction** 67 (1972), 3-14.

Srole, L., et al. **Mental Health in the Metropolis.** New York: McGraw-Hill, 1962.

Street, P.B., Wood, R.C., and Chowenhill, R.C. **Alcohol Use Among Native Americans: A Selected Annotated Bibliography.** Berkeley: Social Research Group, School of Public Health, University of California, 1976.

Struening, E.L., Rabkin, J.G. and Peck, H.R. "Migration and Ethnic Membership in Relation to Social Problems," in E.G. Brody (ed.), **Behavior in New Environments: Adaptation of Migrant Populations.** Beverly Hills: Sage, 1970.

Sue, S. "Community Mental Health Services to Minority Groups: Some Optimism, Some Pessimism," **American Psychologist** 32 (1977), 616-624.

Torrey, E.F. "The Case for the Indigenous Therapist," **Archives of General Psychiatry** 20 (1960), 365-373.

Trimble, J.E. "Issues of Forced Relocation and Migration of Cultural Groups," in D. Hoopes, P. Pedersen, and G. Renwich (eds.), **Issues in Cross-Cultural Education Training and Development, Vol. III.** Georgetown: Society for Cross-Cultural Education, Training and Research, 1977.

Trimble, J.E., and Medicine, B. "Theoretical Models and Levels of Interpretation in Mental Health," in J. Westermeyer (ed.), **Anthropology and Mental Health.** The Hague: Mouton, 1976.

Wang, R.P. "A Study of Alcoholism in Chinatown," **International Journal of Social Psychiatry** 14 (1968), 260-267.

Westermeyer, J. Personal communication, 1978.

Whittaker, J.O. "The Problem of Alcoholism Among American Reservation Indians," **Alcoholism** 2 (1966), 141-146.

Wignall, C.M., and Koppin, L.L. "Mexican-American Usage of State Mental Hospital Facilities," **Community Mental Health Journal** 3 (1967), 137-148.

Williams, J.R. A Comparison of the Self-Concepts of Alcoholic and Non-alcoholic Males of Indian and NonIndian Ancestry in Terms of Scores on the Tennessee Self-Concept Scale. Unpublished doctoral dissertation, University of South Dakota, 1976.

Yee, A.H. "Identity Crises for Asian Americans: A Personal View," The Scooper: An Asian American Publication (December 1975).

PART TWO

THE CONTEXT OF FAMILY PATTERNS

Many of the adaptations of minority groups to social, economic, and political conditions in this country are reflected in their patterns of family life. This section is concerned with the implications of such patterns for mental health practices.

In the first article, Walter Allen and Sandra Stukes describe the status of mental health services for Blacks, the importance of Black families for the maintenance of mental health, and six classes of common coping mechanisms. The authors also point out some policy consequences of their discussion.

Barbara Yee and Sumiko Hennessy begin the next article by reviewing the mental health status and history of Pacific/Asian groups. Common family characteristics relevant for mental health practices are then examined. Finally a series of technical suggestions and broad policy recommendations are presented.

In the third article, Marta Sotomayor provides a reinterpretation of the Chicano family structure which highlights the role of extended kinship networks and the influence of outside social systems. She stresses the need to recognize positive aspects of family life such as the extended family pattern and the sense of mutual obligation which permeates relationships. Sotomayor argues for interventions which carefully distinguish between sociocultural elements that need to be preserved and those to be changed.

BLACK FAMILY LIFESTYLES AND THE MENTAL HEALTH OF BLACK AMERICANS

WALTER R. ALLEN
SANDRA STUKES

Introduction

The assessment of the mental health status of Black Americans as well as the formulation of appropriate mental health delivery systems continues to be frustrated by a variety of factors. This paper examines relationships between Black family lifestyles and the mental health status of Black Americans. We begin with a brief overview of mental health services to Black Americans. In this context, current issues surrounding the social and economic characteristics of Blacks as these relate to mental health status are given special attention. We next consider Black family structures and functioning in relation to their influence on Black mental health status. We conclude with a discussion of the social policy implications of our findings for mental health service delivery systems in Black communities.

The mental well-being of twenty-five million Black Americans cannot be candidly addressed without acknowledging the impacts of racism and discrimination on Black communities. The President's Commission on Mental Health, Special Populations Subpanel: Mental Health of Black Americans, states that for Black Americans:

> It is largely the environment created by institutional racism, rather than intrapsychic deficiencies in Black Americans as a group, that is responsible for the overrepresentation of Blacks among the mentally disabled (Task Panel Reports, 1978: 823).

While there is currently no general agreement over the definitions of mental health or mental illnesses as they relate to Black Americans, certain factors tend to be central in most assessments of Black mental well-being. These include a stress on:

1. The interdependence between individual Blacks and the larger sociocultural environment as respresented by formal and informal associations, the community, and societal institutions (i.e., schools, churches, hospitals, etc.).

2. The importance of Black families, and the values, lifestyles, and behaviors which they maintain.

3. The historical development of health services for Black communities and the legacies of past practices which currently influence the delivery of health services to Black Americans.

4. The social and economic statuses of Black Americans (as historically created) and how these relate to the overall health status of this group.

5. The biological, psychological, and cultural factors which influence the mental health of Black Americans.

Mental Health Services and Black America:
Background Considerations

Historically, Black Americans have been discriminated against in the organization, development, and delivery of mental health care services. Such discrimination has occurred at both the individual and institutional levels. Black Americans tended to be excluded or placed in separate but unequal facilities once they were determined to be mentally ill. Not only were Blacks excluded from treatment in many facilities but their numbers were also limited among those admitted to the ranks of mental health-related professions. Mental health hopsitals, community mental health centers, and the mental health professions were, and continue to be, largely administered and controlled by whites (Johnson, 1978). As a result, the interests and needs of Black communities relative to mental health services have yet to be adequately addressed. Among the many factors accounting for the lack of consensus between mental health services as currently organized and Black Americans, the following stand out: 1) the underrepresentation of Black professionals in mental health fields; 2) significant observed differences in the treatment and diagnosis of mental illness; and 3) the continuing economic disadvantages of race in this society.

The most recent published data on Black representation in the mental health disciplines indicate that there are small proportions of Blacks in psychiatry, psychology, social work, and psychiatric nursing. Fewer than two percent of the individuals in the above disciplines are Blacks (with the exception of social work professionals, where the proportion is 7.6 percent) (Cannon and Locke, 1977). Clearly, more Black Americans must be admitted into the mental health-related professions in order to improve mental service delivery, accessibility, and evaluation processes in Black communities. While some progress has been made in this respect, current rates of black enrollment in training programs and professional certification remain woefully inadequate.

Black mental health service preferences are revealed by recent research; in numerous instances, these preferences differ from those common to the larger society. A 1977 study of Black adults in Baltimore showed that nearly the same proportion would choose to consult ministers (10 percent) as would choose to consult psychiatrists (14 percent) in times of mental distress, while only five percent would consider consulting staff members at community mental health centers (Gary, 1978: 38). Similar preferences for informal over formal mental health services were revealed in McAdoo's (1977) study of middle-income Black families. While strongly desirous of counseling and supportive services to aid in stress management, Black parents tended to underutilize existing agencies. The perceived insensitivity of these agencies motivated this sample to opt, instead, for reliance on informal community mechanisms (e.g., ministers, family, friends, etc.) for assistance in the management of life stresses and the maintenance of positive mental health.

Despite clear preferences among Blacks for alternative arrangements, current mental health services rely heavily on institutionalization in the treatment of Black mental health problems. Thus, recent mental health service data reveal the following trends:

1. Black rates of institutionalization have increased since 1950. Where decreases have been observed, the relative deinstitutionalization for Blacks has been less than for whites (Sharpley, 1977).

2. Black males consistently show the highest rates of mental disorder and institutionalization according to state hospital data. Black males aged 18-34 show significantly higher rates than any other race-age group in this society (Task Panel Reports, 1978: 845).

3. Black admissions to mental institutions are less commonly voluntary than is true for whites. Moreover the decision to commit Blacks to mental institutions is more routinely made by agents other than spouses or offspring (Task Panel Reports, 1978: 831).

Indisputable in these trends is a pattern of mental health services to Blacks that are inconsistent with their preferences for community-based treatment of mental illness.

In this time of economic recession, spiraling inflation, and inflated unemployment rates, the purchasing power of Black Americans has drastically declined (Hill, 1979). Given that ours is a society where mental health and well-being are goods to be bartered and sold in the marketplace, the implications for mental health services to Black Americans are clear. The extreme economic disadvantages of Black Americans have historically frustrated their efforts to obtain satisfactory mental health care. Limited financial resources inhibited their ability to purchase the few suitable services that were available while at the same time providing little economic incentive to mental health professionals to develop specialized services for the market which Blacks represented. To some extent the huge infusion of government monies into minority mental health care during the last twenty years has helped to mute the impacts of the Black economic position on mental health services for Blacks. Nevertheless, these economic effects are apparent and will become increasingly so assuming that the twin societal trends of diminishing Black (relative) economic status and government cutbacks in social programs continue through the 1980s.

Sparse numbers of Black mental health professionals, inappropriate mental health care system responses, and Black economic deprivation, then, provide the backdrop for observed relationships between mental health services and Black America. For the most part, Black mental health care needs have been inadequately addressed by the various mental health care institutions and professions. Out of this a dilemma arises. How have Black Americans managed to maintain a modicum of positive mental health? What structures or arrangements fill the voids resulting from the poor fit between Black community mental health needs and available mental health services? Since reliance on family and kin networks for assistance in the fulfillment of needs is a strong characteristic of Black life, we thought it wise to look to Black family systems for an answer. Specifically, we are concerned with the contributions made by Black families to the maintenance of positive mental health among their members.

Family Systems and Mental Health in Black Communities

Of all the vital functions performed by family systems in our society, perhaps the single most important is that of protectorate. Families serve as buffering mechanisms between their members and the larger society. Acting as advocates, stabilizers, and defenders for their members who are at times confronted by societal forces that are simply overwhelming, families make real and tangible contributions to the maintenance of personal mental health. Some family researchers go so far as to suggest that institutional division of labor has evolved in our society to a point where families now exist largely for purposes of emotional gratification. According to these researchers, many functions traditionally assigned to families have since been assumed by other institutions in the society (e.g., care of aged and infirmed members, education, religious training, etc.). While other societal institutions are involved, we are convinced of the primacy attributed families (or their less formal—though no less real—substitutes) in the maintenance of stable personalities. For this reason an understanding of family variations in "coping" styles, skills, and patterns is essential for a complete grasp of alternative models for preventative and corrective action in the area of mental health.

In our opinion, Black families represent prototypes of effective family systems in their performance of these mental health maintenance functions. In spite of historic deprivation, discrimination, and their concomitants in this society, Black families have continued to produce creative, productive, and stable individuals. They have successfully nurtured and maintained their members through centuries of societal indifference, if not outright hostility, toward their welfare. Paradoxically, Black families have received few accolades for their admirable work in this sphere. Negativisms and oversights in research approaches continue to retard recognition of the skill and dedication with which Black families marshall limited resources to maintain positive mental health in Black communities.

The lifestyles of Black families are heterogeneous, varying in kinshp structure, geographic location, values, and social class status. However, certain predominant patterns persist. The simple nuclear or two-parent neolocal household is the prevalent structure found among Black people (McAdoo, 1977; Stukes, 1979). Findings indicate that the second and third most frequently found household types among Blacks are sole-adult units and one-parent households respectively (Stukes, 1979). Additionally, Black families evidence higher proportions of extended households than whites, indicating a greater tendency to incorporate additional relatives and non-relatives into the family unit.

Predictably, the structure and type of households where individuals live are related to their mental well-being and help-seeking behaviors. Stukes (1979) found that Black respondents living in nuclear and extended households were more likely to talk to others about concerns, while lower percentages of those in sole-adult and one-parent households discussed their problems with other people. All Black respondents, irrespective of household type or structure, were more likely to seek help from relatives or friends than from mental health professionals. Thus the importance we attribute to Black families in the maintenance of positive mental health among Black Americans would seem to be a correct emphasis.

Efforts to improve mental health services to Black Americans must include consideration of the various family networks of which they are a part as well as their particular patterns of help-seeking behavior. The records of mental health agencies in Black communities to date indicate that such factors are often not sufficiently considered when designing mental health support and service delivery programs. To insure that effective, sensitive mental health services are available to Black Americans, the distinctive features of their family life must be given appropriate attention. Among the many issues to be addressed by mental health policy makers and practitioners in this respect are matters surrounding the established coping mechanisms of Black families.

Black Families: Coping Mechanisms

Limited research experience most certainly contributes to our lack of information on Black family coping styles and skills. However, several important classes of Black family coping behavior potentially relevant to mental health can be identified.

1. **Role Flexibility.** Due to historic necessity, Black families have found it necessary to display amazing flexibility in family role definition, responsibility, and performance. Children commonly assist with the care and socialization of younger siblings; children and wives share economic maintenance responsibilities with the husband-father; sex role expectations are less stereotypic and alternative family arrangements are more prevalent than is the case among families in the wider society (Lewis, 1975; Nobles, 1974; Hill, 1971; Scanzoni, 1971).

2. **Close-Knit Kinship Systems.** Black families as a rule tend to be well integrated into larger kin-friend networks. Researchers have shown that such relationships represent invaluable ways of supplementing material, emotional and social resources. Coping is enhanced because the family finds itself with a larger pool of resources upon which to draw (Stack, 1974; Hill, 1971; Aschenbrenner, 1975; McAdoo, 1977).

3. **Culture-Specific Norms.** Black communities are characterized in a majority of cases by bicultural norms. Individuals draw on "mainstream" and "subcultural" values--as the situation dictates--for prescriptions of appropriate behaviors. Again, the ability to cope is strengthened since subcultural values "stretch" conventional norms to fit the imperatives of the situation (Rodman, 1969; Ladner, 1971; Nobles, 1974).

4. **Parallel Institutions.** Institutions in the Black community that parallel those in the white community also contribute substantially to personal adjustment. Individuals denied access to organizations, institutions, and positions of status in the wider society find satisfying alternatives in their Black community-based counterparts (e.g., Black businesses, fraternal orders, leadership roles in Black institutions, Black child adoption institutions, etc.). In addition, certain Black institutions--most notably the church--have traditionally represented sources of individual support and comfort in the struggle for adjustment to life's rigors (Hill, 1971; Blackwell, 1975).

5. **Race and Personal Identity/Pride.** Membership in and identification with the race has also been shown to yield positive benefits for Black Americans. A stronger sense of purpose, greater security in self, easier acceptance of frustration, and better developed self-identities are but a few of the commonly cited outgrowths of such racial pride and identification (Noble, 1974; Gurin and Epps, 1975; McCarthy and Yancy, 1971).

6. **Pooling Economic Resources.** Black Americans have been required to maintain dual wage-earner households, exchange services, develop extended households, and exploit alternative income producing sources in order to survive economically. Statistics have shown that even with such innovations, Black families on a whole are less well off economically than white families (Allen, 1979; Hill, 1980; Stack, 1974).

The identified coping mechanisms common to Black families are among those having obvious relevance for the maintenance of positive mental health. We suspect that with extensive research many more will be discovered. Certainly attention should be paid to identifying such structures. Afterwards, mental health delivery systems could be organized so as to complement these already existing mental health maintenance structures. To the extent that mental health services are successfully interfaced with Black family coping mechanisms, the overall mental health status of Black communities can be expected to greatly improve. In order to achieve such ends, social policy in the area of Black families and mental health will need to become more systematic.

Social Policy: Black Families and Mental Health

Historically, governmental social policies vis-a-vis Black families have had beneficial as well as detrimental consequences.   In numerous instances government agencies, policies, and representatives have been found to be working at cross-purposes with one another.   Thus the achievements of one program were undercut by another program, some services were duplicated while other needs went unserved, and families were fragmented into different service populations (e.g., children, aged, handicapped, etc.) rather than being addressed as the comprehensive systems that they represent.   In short, our cultural stress on nonintervention by government in family affairs has encouraged the creation of policies by default.

Consistent perspectives are definitely reflected in government policies toward families.   Unfortunately, since these perspectives are not clearly articulated but rather implicit, the best interests of Black families are not necessarily served.   Under these implicit government family perspectives, adequate economic resources, middle class goals, traditional family arrangements, and the white experience are assumed to be normative.   Since Black families violate these assumptions to varying degrees, they are penalized by government policies and practices that either reject outright, or fail to consider, important issues in their special circumstances.   Needless to say, current government family policies do not serve the interests of any family group completely; even those interests characteristic of white middle class families are not fully served or addressed.   The difference is that these families generally have more resources, relative to Black families, on which to draw in order to either buffer their members from negative government social policies or to focus on the task of making desired changes in such policies.   Continued limitations in economic, political, and social resources leave Black families more dependent on government intervention while at the same time lessening their influence over decisions which determine the nature of these interventions.

A major challenge for mental health services during the 1980s will revolve around how to upgrade these services to Black Americans while accomodating the exigencies of reduced expenditures.   In the past, periods of economic scarcity have resulted in the severest penalties for those with the least political clout.   Family interests have thus been subordinated to those of private industry, women have lost their jobs to men, and Blacks have lost economic ground to their white counterparts.   A change is long overdue for this "last hired, first fired" philosophy, particularly as it pertains to the availability of quality mental health services.

Mental health researchers and practitioners concerned with the mental health/well-being of Blacks, minorities, and the poor can contribute towards radical change in our society by challenging the unspoken assumption that only when there is excess is there enough for social service expenditures to aid these populations.   Certainly cutbacks in oil subsidies, capital gains tax breaks, and interest write-offs on private homes are to be preferred to cutbacks in the already minimal food, clothing, and energy allotments of those on fixed incomes. Reversing the perverse logic of the past, we need to argue for cutbacks which concentrate the financial burdens on those best able to bear them--the upper-middle and upper classes. Given the clout of these groups in the influence-peddling and lobbying arenas, the achievement of such changes will likely prove problematic. Nevertheless, professionals and laypeople with interests in mental well-being should go on record as arguing for such humanistically-oriented changes in government social policies vis-a-vis Black families specifically and all non-mainstream families generally.

Finally, we call for a broadening of government sensitivity to the needs and conditions of Black family life in this country. While the President's economic advisors feel they can tolerate a nationwide unemployment rate of eight percent, Detroit inner-city Black families cannot tolerate the over-thirty percent unemployment rate this "national average" translates into for them. Nor can they long tolerate the groundswell of social problems and mental anguish certain to accompany such crisis levels of economic deprivation. It is all a matter of perspective--and for too long the perspectives of Black families have been glossed over or ignored in the formulation of government social policy.

Conclusions and Implications

In closing it should also be noted that while we endeavor to accentuate the positive strengths of Black families as these relate to mental health, one should not lose sight of social reality. A large proportion of Black families presently find themselves in extremely precarious positions. In fact, the economic stability of most Black families is worse now, relative to whites, than ever before during the past 25 years. Current census statistics on Black-white occupational classification and annual incomes attest to this fact. Since Black families (as is true of all families in industrial societies) are heavily reliant on societal institutions for the creation of environments conducive to their positive development, we must recognize the limits of mere coping. A sincere commitment by the public and private sectors to the improvement of the economic status of the Black community is a necessary condition to the fostering of positive mental health in Black families. Black individuals receive significant emotional support in the loving, caring environments of their families. What they and their families need most now are additional structural supports in the form of jobs, adequate incomes, quality housing, and equality of opportunity. Until such structural supports are widely available, maintenance of positive mental health in Black communities will continue to be problematic, for as we intuitively know, emotional support--no matter how plentiful--goes only so far in our society.

While Black families are the specific focus of this discussion, many of the points made are pertinent to other non-mainstream families (e.g., poor, other minority, rural, and aged families, etc.). Government mental health delivery systems integrated with indigenous mental health maintenance networks would seem most likely to achieve maximal coverage of non-mainstream community mental health needs. By the same token, further research into the specialized mental well-being statuses and needs of non-mainstream communities seems warranted. Central to all of this is the need for a conscious commitment by government at all levels to the improvement of the mental health and well-being of previously neglected segments of our population, those people judged as somehow falling outside the mainstream and consequently penalized.

References

Allen, W. "Class, Culture and Family Organization: The Effects of Class and Race on Family Structure in Urban America," **Journal of Comparative Family Studies** 10 (Autumn 1979), 33-44.

_____. "The Search for Applicable Theories of Black Family Life," **Journal of Marriage and the Family** 40 (February 1978), 117-129.

Aschenbrenner, J. **Lifelines: Black Families in Chicago.** New York: Holt, Rinehart and Winston, 1975.

Beck, D.F. **Marriage and the Family Under Challenge: An Outline of Issues, Trends and Alternatives,** 2nd Edition. New York: Family Service Association of America, 1976.

Blackwell, J. **The Black Community: Diversity and Unity.** New York: Dodd, Mead and Company, 1975.

Brenner, M.H. "Personality Stability and Economic Security," **Social Policy** 8 (May-June 1977), 2-4.

Cannon, M.S., and Locke, B.Z. "Being Black is Detrimental to One's Mental Health: Myth or Reality?" **Phylon** 38 (December 1977), 408-428.

Gary, L.E. **Support Systems in Black Communities: Implications for Mental Health Services for Children and Youth.** Occasional Paper, Vol. 3, No. 4. Washington, DC: Institute for Urban Affairs and Research, Howard University, 1978.

Gurin, P., and Epps, E. **Black Consciousness, Identity and Achievement.** New York: Wiley, 1975.

Hill, R. **The Strengths of Black Families.** New York: Emerson Hall, 1971.

Hill, R. (ed.). **The Widening Economic Gap.** Washington, DC: The National Urban League, 1979.

Hill, R. "Black Families in the 70's," in James Williams (ed.), **The State of Black America, 1980.** Washington, DC: The National Urban League, 1980.

Johnson, A.E. "The Organization of Mental Health Services Delivery," in Lawrence Gary (ed.), **Mental Health: A Challenge to the Black Community.** Philadelphia: Dorrance and Company, 1978.

Ladner, J. **Tomorrow's Tomorrow.** Garden City, NY: Doubleday and Company, 1971.

Lewis, D. "The Black Family: Socialization and Sex Roles," **Phylon** 36 (Fall 1975), 221-237.

McAdoo, H.P. **The Impact of Extended Family Variables Upon the Upward Mobility of Black Families: Final Report.** Columbia, MD: Columbia Research Systems, Inc., 1977.

McCarthy, J., and Yancy, W. "Uncle Tom and Mr. Charlie: Metaphysical Pathos in the Study of Racism and Personal Disorganization," **American Journal of Sociology** 76 (January 1971), 648-672.

Nobles, W. "African Root and American Fruit: The Black Family," **Journal of Social and Behavioral Science** 20 (Spring 1974), 52-64.

Rodman, H. "Lower Class Attitudes Toward Deviant Family Patterns," **Journal of Marriage and the Family** 31 (May 1969), 315-321.

Scanzoni, J. **The Black Family in Modern Society.** Boston: Allyn and Bacon, 1971.

Sharpley, R.H. "A Psychohistorical Perspective on the Negro," **American Journal of Psychiatry** 126 (November 1969), 645-650.

Stack, C. **All Our Kin: Strategies for Survival in a Black Community.** New York: Harper and Row, 1974.

Stukes, S.P. **Black and White Urban Households and Help Seeking Behavior.** Unpublished doctoral dissertation, University of Michigan, 1979.

Task Panel Reports Submitted to The President's Commission on Mental Health. **Report of the Special Populations Subpanel on Mental Health of Black Americans.** Vol. III Appendix. Washington, DC, 1978.

PACIFIC/ASIAN AMERICAN FAMILIES AND MENTAL HEALTH

BARBARA W. K. YEE
SUMIKO T. HENNESSY

The pervasive myth about Pacific/Asian Americans says that they are the model minority, that they have high educational levels, high economic status, low outpatient rates of mental illness, and low delinquency rates (Sue and Kitano, 1973). The majority of Americans in all levels of society believe this myth. America cannot afford to perpetuate this myth, particularly in the area of mental health. The long-term effects will be catastrophic for Pacific/Asian Americans suffering from mental illness, for their families and communities, and for American society as a whole. The major purpose of this paper is to emphasize the point that Pacific/Asian Americans do have serious mental health problems but their cultural orientation and life experiences in the U.S. may make "mainstream" mental health services inappropriate for their needs, and to suggest potential policy and technical recommendations to meet the mental health needs of the Pacific/Asian people.

Mental Health Status of Pacific/Asian Americans

Pacific/Asian Americans must not only face the daily stresses and strains of living in a culturally nonsupportive environment but must carry the additional burden of being the target of racism. Racism effectively limits the choices one has in life if one is the victim or has been the victim of racism. Seligman (1975) believes that poverty and racism do not allow the victim to feel a sense of control in socially valued areas. The victim becomes "helpless" to control outcomes in his/her life and this sense of helplessness may lead to depression or anxiety. Sue (1977a) and Yee (1977) believe that Pacific/Asian Americans may be exposed to this sort of "uncontrollability" and may become helpless to control their environment. Yee (1979) found that Japanese and Vietnamese elderly women felt more helpless to control things in their lives than Caucasian elderly women. Yee hypothesized that differential exposure to racism may have contributed to this significant difference.

Because of the past limitation of choices by the dominant white society (i.e., effects of racism), the majority of Pacific/Asian Americans have been forced and now prefer to utilize their families first and then indigenous community workers and caretakers (e.g., ministers, prominent community leaders, family physicians) who are an integral part of their daily lives, to help solve problems. Any unresolved problems could be potential stressors which might lead to psychological, social, or emotional breakdowns. Pacific/Asian Americans often choose not to seek professional mental health care except in extreme circumstances. The numerous reasons behind this preference will be discussed below.

When Pacific/Asian Americans do select professional mental health care, their problems are often very serious. Sue (1977b) found that Pacific/Asian clients in Seattle came to the attention of "mainstream" mental health services only at the point of acute breakdown or during crisis situations and had a higher diagnosis of psychosis (22.4%) in comparison to whites (12.7%), Native Americans (17.6%), Blacks (13.8%), or Hispanics (14.5%). Brown et al. (1973) found that Chinese Americans were less likely to utilize existing mental health services but those who did were more disturbed than Caucasian patients. These data suggest that Pacific/Asian Americans do have serious mental health problems and seek help only when the situation becomes critical or when family and community resources have become exhausted. This consistent underutilization of "mainstream" mental health services by Pacific/Asian Americans does not suggest that this population has no mental health problems but rather that those services available are often inappropriate for the needs of Pacific/Asian Americans and that the system itself creates barriers to utilization.

Mainstream mental health services often do not provide bilingual/bicultural staff who could communicate effectively in the native languages of Pacific/Asian clients and who are culturally sensitive to their unique needs. Sue (1977b) found that one of the major reasons for the high dropout rate of Pacific/Asian clients was that they felt they were not getting "relevant" care from the mental health centers. The stigma of mental illness in combination with a conception of a mature person as one who is able to control the expression of personal problems or handle troubled feelings by oneself makes Pacific/Asians reluctant to seek mental health services and be labeled mentally ill and may even lead to the somatization of psychological and emotional problems. In many Pacific/Asian cultures physical illness is more acceptable and recognizable than psychological or emotional illnesses. Therefore, one is more likely to receive care, attention, and treatment if one has a physical complaint than if one talks about emotional problems. Since a significant portion of the Pacific/Asian population is foreign-born and successive generations maintain varying levels of their heritage, certain linguistic and cultural considerations must be acknowledged in the planning and implementation of any services.

In order to fully understand the relationship between mental health and the Pacific/Asian population, one must be fully cognizant of the diversity among various Pacific/Asian groups. Not only do their languages differ but so do their immigration patterns, their treatment by white society, and their cultures and life experiences. The following section briefly covers the history of the various waves of Pacific/Asian ethnic groups.

History of Pacific/Asian Immigration

The history of Pacific/Asian Americans goes back 140 years and could be roughly divided into five major phases. The first phase begins with the arrival of the Chinese in California. Life in the new land was not very hospitable for the predominantly young, single, male Chinese migrants. The influx of inexpensive, "foreign" labor posed an economic and social threat to white workers who believed in the "manifest destiny" of the white race. The white majority retaliated by imposing racist legislation on the Chinese (e.g., Foreign Miner's tax, antimiscegenation laws, Chinese Exclusion Act of 1882). The Exclusion Act of 1882 effectively limited the entry of Chinese to the U.S., particularly women, and prevented the formation of Chinese families--the lifeline and lifeblood of the Chinese (Ling, 1973; Lyman, 1971).

The Chinese Exclusion Act effectively cut off the source of inexpensive labor at a time when American society was undergoing industrial and agricultural expansion. Western farmers and industrialists had to find a substitute labor force and they turned to Japan for help. The 1908 Gentle-men's Agreement effectively limited the number of Japanese male immigrants but did not affect the arrival of "picture brides" from Japan (Yoneda, 1971). This allowed the Japanese to form families--a privilege few early Chinese immigrants had.

In .1924. the U.S. passed the National Origins Act which barred Asians from immigrating to this country. After the Japanese attacked Pearl Harbor, 112,000 West Coast Japanese--two-thirds of whom were American citizens--were forcibly removed from their homes, businesses, and jobs to concentration camps. The relocation of the Japanese during World War II represented a blatant act of racism because neither German nor Italian Americans were forcibly rounded up "en masse" and put into concentration camps (Weglyn, 1976).

The second phase of Pacific/Asian immigration is characterized by the entry of a sizable number of Pilipinos during the 1920s and early 1930s. Since the Spanish-American War, the Philippines had been a U.S. territory. Pilipino immigrants were not regarded as aliens, but they did not have the rights of citizenship, either. Not affected by the National Origins Act, Pilipinos were a new source of inexpensive agricultural labor. Most of the new immigrants were unmarried, younger men and they, like the Chinese, had difficulty establishing a family life because of limits on the immigration of Pilipino women and antimiscegenation laws. Pilipinos inherited the history of negative attitudes already established against Asians on the West Coast (Rabaya, 1971).

The third phase of Pacific/Asian immigration started at the conclusion of World War II because a considerable number of American servicemen married Asian women and wished to return to the U.S. with their new brides. The War Bride Act of 1947 allowed them to do this. Wives of American servicemen present a special challenge for mental health professionals. Unlike early immigrants who came in groups from specific regions of China or Japan, these women came from many geographic regions, from all levels of society, and they lacked the mutual support and assistance of their compatriots. Asian wives of U.S. servicemen settled in many parts of the U.S., rarely in the tight-knit ethnic enclaves like Los Angeles' Little Tokyo or San Francisco's Chinatown. These women suffered from their lack of proficiency in English, limited formal education, isolation from their homeland and culture, and lack of understanding of their cultural values by their American husbands and children (Kim, 1977).

The fourth phase of Pacific/Asian immigration began after the passage of the Immigration Act of 1965 which liberalized immigration laws. Many professionals and intellectuals sought better opportunities in the U.S. and escape from overcrowded homelands. Compared to their earlier counterparts, these better educated immigrants experienced a somewhat easier adjustment to life in the U.S. because they had more urbanized and/or Westernized value orientations and faced less blatant racism against Asians (Melendy, 1972).

The fifth phase of Pacific/Asian immigration began with the fall of Saigon in 1975. Unlike earlier immigrants who made a conscious decision to seek opportunity in the U.S., Indochinese refugees were suddenly uprooted from their familiar social environment, separated from family members, and entered a radically different life with little preparation. The rapid adjustment and success of these refugees have been overrated by the mass media. The earliest refugees were either educated urbanites or worked for the U.S. military. By comparison, more recent arrivals tend to be uneducated, rural people with characteristics which might be less conducive to a smooth adjustment in the U.S. In addition to adjustment and adaptation to a new culture and environment, the Indochinese must also face increasing opposition from other groups who are competing for scarce resources. The current life situation of the Indochinese is not an easy one. Many mental health problems have already surfaced (Aylesworth, 1980). Mental health intervention is needed to ease the transition and adjustment.

The many and varied ethnic groups which make up the Pacific/Asian American population arrived at different historical times, have experienced different reactions by the white majority, and have different languages, cultural values, attitudes, and religions. Some are accustomed to highly complex, urban environments. Others have lived their lives in small tribal villages or in remote parts of their homeland. The diversity and heterogeneity of the Pacific/Asian population must be recognized in every aspect of mental health service delivery and research. In spite of this diversity, there are some common threads which run through many Pacific/Asian cultures. For instance, many Asian nations such as Japan, Korea, Vietnam, Laos, and Cambodia have been influenced by China over the past 2,000 years. The Chinese spread Confucian philosophy to these lands and many traditional Asian values are based upon this philosophy. The following section deals with common family characteristics and coping strategies of Pacific/Asian individuals and families.

Common Family Characteristics

While this section will discuss common characteristics of the **traditional** Pacific/Asian family, in reality each individual family may vary in their degree of acculturation (i.e., relative balance between Pacific/Asian and Western values, attitudes, and behaviors).

Confucian philosophy created the foundation and framework for the traditional Pacific/Asian family. Every man, woman, and child has a definite place in society and a prescribed status. If everyone knows his/her place and acts accordingly, social order is assured (Hsu, 1953). Kitano (1976) calls the Japanese social structure "vertical" because a group (e.g., family) is composed of individuals in varying levels and statuses rather than of peers interacting on a relatively equal basis. A distinctive feature of traditional Pilipino society is that symmetrical, truly equal relationships are rare (Ponce, 1980). Almost all relationships are of the "subordinate-superordinate" type and complementary, such as the leader-follower, teacher-pupil, father-son variety. This pattern is also reflected in the three important social relationships of traditional Vietnamese society: ruler-subject, father-child, and husband-wife (Liem and Kehmeier, 1980). The father in the traditional Japanese family is the indisputable leader and male children, especially the eldest son, have more status than the female ones. Interaction within the family is based upon clearly prescribed roles, duties, and responsibilities rather than on personal affection. The leader of the family, usually the father, has the authority but also great responsibility for the other members of the family (Kitano, 1976).

Women in traditional Pacific/Asian families have a secondary role to men. Since traditional Chinese culture is based on a patrilocal-patriarchal system, authority, control over family possessions and control over family members is passed from the father to the eldest son (Char et al., 1980). The female in traditional Pacific/Asian cultures has to conform to three obediences: (1) to the father until she is married, (2) to her husband, and (3) to her eldest son when she is widowed. These traditional expectations can lead to potential family conflicts when confronted by the more liberated attitudes towards and by women in the U.S. (Liem and Kehmeier, 1980).

Survival in agricultural Asia depended upon a rather large extended family support network. In order to manage and maintain a large group of people, the family leader had to make sure that every decision insured that the needs of the group took precedence over the needs of any given individual. The survival and success of the family was much more important than the success of an individual. Therefore in traditional Pacific/Asian families, individuals learn to suppress their own needs if these conflict with the needs of the family. Behavior, then, is guided by prior approval from authority figures in the family. Also, approval-seeking from authority figures outside the family is an extension of behaviors expressed and socialized within the family. In traditional Pacific/Asian families, individuals learn to act very cautiously because they are representatives of their families and all eyes of the community are upon each individual (Shon,

1980; Harvey and Chung, 1980). If an individual does something bad or deviant, it will reflect upon their entire family and bring "shame" (embarrassment and disgrace) to the family. Therefore, Pacific/Asians learn to be "other-directed," always trying to get feedback from authority figures in order to guide their behavior. In contrast, Western cultures are "inner-directed." Western cultures socialize their children from an early age to be independent, individualistic, and eventually to learn that the guide to behavior should come from internalized standards rather than from authority figures. The life-cycle pattern for Western families is to teach the young how to independently exist apart from the family and, as self-sufficient young adults, to break away from the family. The basic difference between the traditional Pacific/Asian group orientation and the Western individual orientation often creates conflicts for those individuals on the interface between the two, for example, new immigrants, families with immigrant parents and American-born children, or families with mixed marriages.

In order to be able to work the fields of agricultural Asia, Asian families were large and included extended family members. A certain degree of harmony was necessary in order to make that economic unit function effectively and smoothly. Disharmony became very disruptive, especially if one's livelihood depended upon the amount of food produced, so the maintenance of harmony was a survival mechanism. Consequently, the rules of behavior which operate within traditional Pacific/Asian families tend to help maintain cohesiveness. The rules which operate within Pacific/Asian families are also reflected in the way families relate to Pacific/Asian communities and the larger society.

The cohesiveness of the traditional Pacific/Asian family depends upon common expectations, knowledge, and resulting behaviors which are in accordance with those expectations. If all members know how to behave and then behave accordingly, family harmony will be maintained. If on the other hand, either the expectations or behaviors change, then disharmony will probably result. This latter situation often occurs when whole families are transported to a new cultural environment and younger members acculturate faster than older ones, or when there is a mixture of immigrant parents and American-born children in the same family and the different generations have contrasting expectations about "proper" behavior and attitudes (Aylesworth, 1980; Aylesworth et al., 1980; Kitano, 1976; Liem and Kehmeier, 1980; Harvey and Chung, 1980).

There are rules of interaction and mechanisms of social control in the traditional Pacific/Asian family. Because the family is probably one of the most important social structures in Pacific/Asian cultures, harmony and cohesiveness among family members becomes the major goal of socialization.

One mechanism which maintains harmony within the traditional family is each person's extreme sensitivity to the feelings of others. For example, the Pilipino's concept of "pakikisame" underlies the entire structure of Pilipino social relationships. It means to be sensitive to, be aware of the sensitivity of others, and to go through elaborate means to avoid offending

others. This pattern is evident in the use of go-betweens to arrange transactions and marriages, and to settle disputes. There is a deliberate avoidance of direct confrontation, disagreement, and criticism (Ponce, 1980).
The Japanese make constant reference to "kimochi" (feelings). The Japanese handle feelings in seemingly contradictory ways. Feelings may be well
controlled and suppressed in public or on deferential occasions but expressed openly in certain settings (Rogers and Izutzu, 1980). Aggression
and other negative emotions are often repressed. The Vietnamese also
have a well-developed ability to keep their true emotions hidden. Desires
are usually expressed in an indirect manner by hinting or talking around the
subject. Straightforwardness is considered impolite and a sign of lack of
intelligence or lack of courtesy (Liem and Kehmeier, 1980). The extra
sensitivity to the feelings of others helps to insure that no feelings are hurt
which might cause disharmony and break up the family. (One mental health
implication of the above is that, in a therapeutic relationship, a traditionally-oriented Pacific/Asian may not tell a therapist the truth out of a
desire not to hurt the therapist's feelings. Or, a patient may not tell the
truth about their life because it may hurt their family if this information
got outside to Pacific/Asian communities. The suppression and repression
of strong emotions could lead to hypochondrisis, psychosomatic disorders or
substance abuse (Char et al., 1980).)

Intimately related to the avoidance of direct confrontation and hurt
feelings are the communication and verbal patterns of traditional Pacif-
ic/Asian families. Kitano (1976) believes that the most distinctive feature
of the Japanese family is the absence of prolonged verbal exchanges. The
traditional Japanese family believes that few problems are resolved
through open discussion. More importantly, true communication is often
expressed by one's attitudes, actions, and feelings rather than words. A
talkative Japanese person is often seen as a "show-off" and "insincere."
The Japanese socialize their children not to speak at every opportunity
(Rogers and Izutzu, 1980). (Consequently, in a therapeutic relationship, a
traditionally-oriented Pacific/Asian patient may be seen by a therapist
ignorant of Pacific/Asian cultures as a quiet, nonexpressive person who is
resistant to psychotherapy (Shon, 1980). In actuality, the patient may be
emitting important nonverbal cues.)

Another distinctive feature of the traditional Pacific/Asian family is
group loyalty and the encouragement of dependence. Spirits of dead relatives are at the very heart of the family household and they guide the
behavior of each family member. Each individual member of the family
forms a link with past and future generations. Therefore the family must
be held together to maintain this historical continuity (Liem and Kehmeier,
1980). A byproduct of this idea is the filial piety paid to older members of
the family. The rationale underlying filial piety is that older members of
the family will soon be joining their ancestors because they are closer to
death than the younger members of the family.

If family loyalty is to be maintained, then there must be social mechanisms to foster loyalty and dependence on the group. Nakane (1970) believes that Japanese culture fosters loyalty to one system--whether that

system is family, company, or team. The loyalty to a system is not a temporary situation but rather a long-term commitment. The specific social mechanism which helps maintain lifetime loyalty is a system of obligations. For Guamanians, one's social obligations usually supersede the importance of one's own job, schooling, or affairs (Munoz, 1980). For example, if a family member or friend needs help, the fact that you have to take an exam in school is secondary to first helping that person. Pilipinos believe that a voluntary favor must be repaid in the future but cannot be repaid with money. Failure to fulfill such a moral obligation is shameful to both an individual and his/her family. The Pilipino "debt of gratitude" system of obligation ("Utang ngloob") reveals how lifetime loyalties and commitments are made (Ponce, 1980). These obligations are especially strong within the family because many exchanges of favors are made between parents and children, siblings, and extended family members. Char et al. (1980) believe that traditional Chinese customs encourage mutual dependence among family members. More independence is attained by family members when adulthood and marriage occur but not to the extent seen in contemporary Western society.

The Japanese probably have the most elaborate system of obligations. The ascribed obligation system ("on") is based on the vertical hierarchical structure of social units. Interdependence is based on a sense of obligation by younger family members to the whole family and special deference to the family head and on the leader's responsibility for the whole family. There are many other traditional codified norms such as "giri" (contractual obligation), "chu" (loyalty to one's superiors), "ninjo" (humane sensibility), "enryo" (modesty in the presence of one's superiors), and "amae" (need to be loved and cherished) which support the socialization goal of establishing and insuring dependency of the individual on the family or group (Rogers and Izutsu, 1980; Kitano, 1976; Nakane, 1970). (The above discussion has numerous implications for mental health practice. By Western standards, a traditional Pacific/Asian patient might be considered too dependent and immature, but within their own culture they could be perfectly normal. Therefore, a therapist must carefully examine whether the dependence shown by a Pacific/Asian client is causing a problem in his/her milieu or whether some other factor is involved. In addition, the therapist must decide whether guiding the Pacific/Asian client towards more independence would be more adaptable in certain situations (e.g., job promotion in a university setting) but not as adaptable in others (e.g., Japanese family gathering at a Japanese community picnic where an aggressive, independent individual would be perceived as rude and vulgar).)

Another social mechanism for maintaining the cohesiveness and integrity of the traditional Pacific/Asian family are its various forms of social control. A very strong deterrent to the acting-out of socially deviant behaviors is the concept of "shame." By contrast, the Judeo-Christian concept of morality is the sense of guilt or sin. In reality, both shame and guilt occur to a degree in "adequately" socialized members of a culture but are manifested to a different degree in Asian and Western cultures. Guilt is based on the feeling that one is responsible for some offense. There is an active comparison with an internalized standard of good behavior, and one's behavior may be seen as inconsistent with those standards. The fact that other people witnessed or will find out about the deviant behavioral digression is critical to understanding the concept of shame.

Lebra (1976) believes that shame occurs when the appearance, behavior, or performance of a given individual is incongruous with the status of that individual. Shame reflects on that individual and on his/her family. The more status-conscious a person, group, or culture is, the more vulnerable to shame they would potentially become. Lebra contends that the Japanese are thus more sensitive to shame than most Western cultures. Of course this does not imply that the Japanese are guilt-free but rather that shame is a stronger form of social control given their group orientation. Lebra believes that shame results from the revealing of something that undermines or denigrates a claimed status. Status is linked to shame under two conditions: 1) when status is recognizable and identifiable by an audience, and 2) when the status-incongruous behavior is subject to exposure. Since the Japanese are status-oriented and display their status openly they would be very hesitant to display any shame-inducing behaviors. The highly developed gossip system in many Pacific/Asian communities serves to provide an effective feedback system which controls the behavior of members (Kitano, 1976; Liem and Kehmeier, 1980). If there was no danger of exposure, a person would be free from shame but not from guilt over his/her own deviant behavior.

Shame works in the following manner: there is an emphasis in Pacific/Asian cultures on maintaining the family's good name and a high priority is placed on protecting the family from shame in the community. Therefore trouble with the police, diseases, mental retardation, mental illness, and other such problems are treated as family secrets (Rogers and Izutsu, 1980). The traditional Pacific/Asian family maintains extremely tight control over information about itself and its problems. (This situation may create problems for mental health workers, because if a family is identified as having a problem through unobtrusive means, it would probably deny the existence of the problem and not tell an "outsider" their troubles because that would be a very shameful situation.)

Traditionally-oriented Koreans believe that the cause of mental illnes lies in interpersonal disharmony within the family. They consider family care to be the most effective way to treat the mentally ill and will consider hospitalization only when individuals become unmanageably aggressive. Family care consists of a radical reduction in the occupational and social demands placed on an individual. Mentally disordered behavior is seen as temporary and not as possibly progressive if left untreated. That fact, coupled with the resulting shame to the family, strongly discourages traditional Korean families from seeking professional mental health services (Harvey and Chung, 1980). The Hmong view mental illness differently, but they also feel that it brings shame to the family. A mentally ill person is perceived as "crazy" like the village idiot who is unkempt and babbles incoherently or violently (Bliatout, 1980). (If a mental health therapist is cognizant of how shameful being labeled mentally ill is for a Pacific/Asian client and his/her family, then perhaps help might be given in less shame-inducing problem areas such as job employment or housing. Once a trusting relationship has developed--a process which might take longer with Pacific/Asian clients--mental and emotional problems may be discussed.)

In conclusion, the traditional family structures of Pacific/Asian groups served an adaptive function in the past prior to emigration, and the maintenance of traditional structures or some variations probably serve as a buffer against a hostile environment in America. White society repeatedly rejected the majority of early Pacific/Asian groups and only recently has overt racism subsided. Currently, overt racism aimed at Pacific/Asians is lower than it has been in the past while rates of intermarriage are at their highest (Kikumura and Kitano, 1973). This suggests that the barriers to integration (e.g., antimiscegenation practices and social racism) are lower; therefore the maintenance of traditional Pacific/Asian patterns, including marriage within one's own group, are not as necessary as they once were. Some critical questions that can be raised are: What will happen to the family structure and supports with increasing rates of intermarriage? What will happen when social conditions change from low to higher antiAsian sentiments? Will the once adaptive social units (e.g., families and ethnic communities) not be present when they might be needed in the future? These and other questions need to be addressed in any discussion of the mental health of Pacific/Asian Americans.

Three other areas of concern for Pacific/Asian families and mental health should be noted. First, because the family is so important to Pacific/Asian Americans, efforts should be made to insure that those individuals without their own families be given some alternative social supports or help to maintain the support systems they have already established. For example, many single elderly Pilipino and Chinese males in San Francisco and Honolulu have established their own friendship support networks. If it becomes necessary to move them to better housing, efforts should be made to insure that existing support networks are maintained, for instance by moving all friends together to the same location or within walking distance of each other.

Second, intergenerational differences in expectations could potentially be a source of conflict within the family. For example, the immigrant generation may have very traditional expectations and these may conflict with the expectations of their American-born children or the faster acculturating immigrant children. Another potential source of conflict may be the different expectations--concerning, for example, child-rearing patterns, values, attitudes or behaviors--expressed by the partners in an interracial marriage.

Third, it must be recognized that different cultures vary in their definitions and acceptance of mental illness. Pacific/Asians may complain of nonspecific somatic problems (e.g., low energy, backaches, headaches, or general malaise); often these problems could be attributable to underlying emotional problems. Char et al. (1980) believe that traditional Chinese culture considers depression and anxiety to be a part of daily life, so complaints about these kinds of emotional problems do not get special attention. In contrast, complaints about physical illness receive immediate gratification in the form of attention, concern, and care. Traditionally-oriented Pilipinos also have difficulty recognizing and acknowledging emotional factors as the basis for their somatic problems. They find it difficult to comprehend how such intangibles as emotions could result in tangible somatic manifestations such as loss of appetite, loss of weight, or sleeplessness (Ponce, 1980). In many Pacific/Asian cultures, to admit to emotional problems makes one child-like and, for males, less than mascu-line. Thus one would lose face if he/she admitted to having emotional problems and would shame their entire family in the process. These kinds of cultural differences often prevent Pacific/Asian individuals from using "mainstream" mental health services.

The next section outlines policy and technical recommendations for providing mental health services to Pacific/Asian populations. These recommendations recognize that Pacific/Asians have been subjected to racism in the U.S., have unique cultural attributes which might prevent them from seeking "mainstream" mental health services, and have natural family and community support networks which might be used more effectively in helping to maintain mental health, especially in regard to early prevention and the identification of persons in need of professional assistance.

Technical and Policy Recommendations

The following are some technical suggestions for mental health professionals who work with Pacific/Asian clients, families, and communities. These broad suggestions should be used only as general guidelines. (See McDermott, Tseng and Maretzki, 1980; Sue and Wagner, 1973; Endo, Sue and Wagner, 1980 for more details and appropriate bibliographies.) They may not be applicable for all Pacific/Asian clients, for example, American-born Pacific/Asians who are highly acculturated, and it should always be remembered that Pacific/Asians are a heterogeneous population.

1. Assess the individual's level of acculturation and then that of his/her family (e.g., generational level or if immigrant, years in the U.S.; level of English-speaking ability; educational level; occupational status; values, attitudes, and behavioral orientations; socioeconomic level, etc.), his/her own and the family's resources and abilities to cope with problems and stressors, and both the presented problems and other contributing factors (Sue and Sue, 1971; McDermott, 1980).

2. Understand family interaction patterns and social hierarchy and be aware that intervention with an individual will probably change the family as well. Be cognizant of relationships between the individual, family, and larger Pacific/Asian community (i.e., shame-inducing processes and the stigmatizing effect of "mainstream" mental health services) (Char et al., 1980; Bliatout, 1980).

3. Treatment modalities might need to be modified to be consistent with Pacific/Asian cultures or new alternatives might need to be found

(e.g., informal interaction, longer familiarization time period, indirect questioning about problems, role of the therapist as an authority
figure rather than an equal partner in treatment, concrete problem-
solving approaches--job or educational strategies or how to fill out
application forms--rather than talking about the problems, shamanis-
tic healing or herbal treatments) (Ponce, 1980; Rogers and Izutsu,
1980; Harvey and Chung, 1980).

Not only must mental health professionals be sensitive to Pacific/Asian
individuals and their families but they must also advocate for system and
institutional changes which might promote mental **health** in Pacific/Asian
populations. The following are some recommendations concerning broad
social policy and more specific policies dealing with the delivery of mental
health services, personnel and training, and research. These recommendations have been taken from the President's Commission on Mental Health
"Report of the Special Populations Subpanel on Mental Health of Asian/Pa-
cific Americans" (1978) and the U.S. Commission on Civil Rights report,
Civil Rights Issues of Asian and Pacific Island Americans (1980).

SOCIAL POLICY ISSUES

1. Existing and proposed mental health policies should contain specific
   provisions which acknowledge the unique cultures, languages, lifestyles, and experiences of Asian and Pacific Island Americans.

2. The President and Congress should quickly enact an income maintenance program to insure that every human being in the U.S. is able to
   live in dignity because economic insecurity puts undue stress on the
   Pacific/Asian individual and family.

3. Immigration and refugee laws should provide equity and dignity to
   those who want to enter the U.S.

4. Asian and Pacific Island Americans should be appointed to serve on all
   levels (i.e., Federal, state and local) of policy-making bodies concerned with mental health in order to insure that the rights and needs
   of Pacific/Asian Americans have been addressed, monitored, and
   implemented.

DELIVERY OF MENTAL HEALTH SERVICES

1. To insure maximum utilization of mental health services by the
   Pacific/Asian population, provisions must be made for culturally
   relevant modalities of mental health care (including traditional or
   folk medicine), staffing by bilingual/bicultural personnel, contracting
   to Pacific/Asian community-based organizations for the delivery of
   services, integration of health and mental health services with other
   community services, and liaison between Asian and Pacific American
   community organizations and mental health service providing agencies.

2. Existing Federal legislation must be strictly enforced; for example,

Public Law 94-63, subparagraph D, section 206 (c) requires community mental health centers with substantial proportions of individuals with limited English speaking ability to develop plans and make arrangements which are responsive to the linguistic and cultural needs of these individuals.

3. In order to maximize their visibility and impact on service delivery, sufficient numbers of Asian and Pacific Island Americans should be employed to establish mental health teams, especially in areas with high concentrations of Pacific/Asians.

4. Current shortages of licensed and trained bilingual/bicultural personnel require that emergency steps be taken to remediate this situation in mental health services (for example, modifications of training and licensure requirements, development of indigenous paraprofessional employment with built-in career ladder provisions).

5. Administrative, program, and fiscal arrangements must be modified to allow pooling of resources to serve Pacific/Asians in a number of catchment areas.

6. Reimbursement mechanisms for health and mental health services (e.g., Medicare, national health insurance) should include culturally traditional forms of care (e.g., acupuncture or herbal medicine).

7. Pacific/Asian American consumers and service providers must be involved at all levels of the decision-making process in programs which serve the Pacific/Asian population (i.e., governing structures, stages of program development/planning to implementation, ongoing operations).

8. In order to increase knowledge and sensitivity to Pacific/Asian Americans, educational programs for nonPacific/Asian mental health and nonmental health service providers should be required in all areas which serve Pacific/Asian clients.

Murase (1980) suggests that state and local governments can deal with barriers to the utilization of mental health services in the following manner. First, there should be mandatory collection of data on bilingual/bicultural needs and this data should provide a basis for planning and evaluation. Second, there needs to be a mechanism for monitoring compliance with nondiscriminatory statutes. State-level Pacific/Asian American commissions to perform watchdog functions might be such a mechanism. Third, state governments should adopt mandatory bilingual staffing requirements for public contact positions in public service facilities like mental health programs. Such state policies should include a trigger mechanism for enforcement of this requirement (e.g., if at least three percent of the population in their service area is of limited or nonEnglish-speaking ability, then the bilingual staff requirement would be operative). State policies should also include specification of the types of positions to be filled by bilingual staff (e.g., the requirement would not be met by hiring clerical staff). State policies should delineate the procedures for hiring bilingual staff, and bilingual staff should be compensated for using their special language skills more than a specified proportion of their time.

PERSONNEL AND TRAINING

1. Regional Pacific/Asian American multidisciplinary mental health training centers should be developed to render comprehensive mental health services to Pacific/Asian populations. Training should include continuing education, bilingual/bicultural training, field work experience, seminars, curriculum development, recruitment, research and evaluation. These centers should be guided by a board of directors who represent Pacific/Asian Americans.

2. Training programs should include community-based, university-based, as well as self-help groups designed to provide Pacific/Asians with adequate mental health training.

3. Asian and Pacific foreign medical graduates who are already in the U.S. should be provided with orientation programs such as language training, multicultural sensitivity, and preparation for licensing and specialty training because they provide a rich manpower source of bilingual mental health personnel.

These personnel and training recommendations are designed to increase the number of well-trained Pacific/Asian professionals and paraprofessionals in a variety of settings. The rationale behind such recommendations stems from the fact that Pacific/Asians consistently underutilize "mainstream" mental health services for bilingual and bicultural reasons. Therefore, by increasing the number of bilingual/bicultural Pacific/Asians, more Pacific/Asian clients will get "relevant" services in mainstream and specialized mental health facilities.

RESEARCH

1. Research must be conducted on racism at the individual and institutional levels, normative patterns of functioning among and within Asian/Pacific communities, information gaps (census information, current population status, service needs), underserved and high risk segments of the Pacific/Asian population (women, children, refugees, and the elderly), natural support networks, and preventative resources.

2. There must be a development of culturally appropriate and relevant psychological assessment tools and more varied research strategies.

3. In view of past inequities experienced by the Pacific/Asian population, specially earmarked funds should be allocated for research on this population.

These recommendations on research are designed to provide guidelines about critical antecedent factors which impinge on the lives of Pacific/Asian Americans, generate necessary baseline data on underserved and high risk groups, develop culturally appropriate assessment tools and research strategies and suggest that the appropriate information will not be generated unless special earmarked funds are allocated for Pacific/Asian groups. The research recommendations all converge to increase the knowledge base on Pacific/Asian Americans.

Conclusion

As outlined in this paper, Pacific/Asian populations have serious mental health problems and consistently underutilize available "mainstream" mental health services. In order to provide appropriate mental health therapy and service systems, it must be recognized that there are a variety of differences between and among Pacific/Asian groups as well as several common general family characteristics. These common family characteristics point out how natural support systems might be used to facilitate the utilization of mental health services, but also show how cultural patterns might discourage the use of available services. The last section of the paper offers some practical suggestions for practitioners who work with Pacific/Asian clients and policy recommendations to change the mental health system so that Pacific/Asians might be encouraged to exercise their rights and obtain necessary services.

Pacific/Asian Americans are a vital part of this country and could more effectively contribute to the productivity of the U.S. if given psychological, emotional, and social supports during critical periods of their lives. All Americans should seek to aid others reach their full potential in life. Pacific/Asian Americans have a lot to offer all of us.

References

Aylesworth, L.S. **Stress, Mental Health, and Need Satisfaction Among Indochinese in Colorado.** Unpublished doctoral dissertation, University of Colorado, 1980.

Aylesworth, L.S., Ossorio, P.G., and Osaki, L. "Stress and Mental Health Among Vietnamese in the U.S.," in R. Endo, S. Sue, and N. Wagner (eds.), **Asian-Americans: Social and Psychological Perspectives, Vol. II.** Palo Alto: Science and Behavior Books, 1980.

Bliatout, B.T. "The Hmong from Laos," in J.F. McDermott, W. Tseng, and T.W. Maretzki (eds.), **People and Culture of Hawaii: A Psychocultural Profile.** Honolulu: The University Press of Hawaii, 1980.

Brown, T.R., Stein, D., Huang, K., and Harris, D. "Mental Illness and the Role of Mental Health Facilities in Chinatown," in S. Sue and N. Wagner (eds.), **Asian Americans: Psychological Perspectives.** Palo Alto: Science and Behavior Books, 1973.

Char, W.F., Tseng, W., Lum, W., and Hsu, J. "The Chinese," in J.F. McDermott, W. Tseng, and T.W. Maretzki (eds.), **People and Culture of Hawaii: A Psychocultural Profile.** Honolulu: The University Press of Hawaii, 1980.

Endo, R., Sue, S., and Wagner, N. (eds.). **Asian-Americans: Social and Psychological Perspectives, Vol. II.** Palo Alto: Science and Behavior Books, 1980.

Harvey, Y.S.K., and Chung, S. "The Koreans," in J.F. McDermott, W. Tseng, and T.W. Maretzki (eds.), **People and Culture of Hawaii: A Psychocultural Profile.** Honolulu: The University Press of Hawaii, 1980.

Hsu, F.L.K. **Americans and Chinese: Two Ways of Life.** New York: Henry Schuman, 1953.

Kikumura, A., and Kitano, H.H.L. "Interracial Marriage: A Picture of Japanese Americans," **Journal of Social Issues** 24 (1973), 129-148.

Kim, B.C. "Asian Wives of U.S. Servicemen: Women in Shadows," **Amerasia Journal** 4 (1977), 91-115.

Kitano, H.H.L. **Japanese Americans: The Evolution of a Subculture.** 2nd edition. Englewood Cliffs, NJ: Prentice-Hall, 1976.

Lebra, T.S. **Japanese Pattern of Behavior.** Honolulu: The University Press of Hawaii, 1976.

Ling, P. "Causes of Chinese Emigration," in A. Tachiki et al. (eds.), **Roots: An Asian American Reader.** Los Angeles: Asian American Studies Center, Unviersity of California, 1971.

Liem, N.D., and Kehmeier, D.F. "The Vietnamese," in J.F. McDermott, W. Tseng, and T.W. Maretzki (eds.), **People and Culture of Hawaii: A Psychocultural Profile.** Honolulu: The University Press of Hawaii, 1980.

Lyman, S. "Stranger in the City: The Chinese in the Ubran Frontier," in A. Tachiki et al. (eds.), **Roots: An Asian American Reader.** Los Angeles: Asian American Studies Center, Unviersity of California, 1971.

McDermott, J.F. "Introduction," in J.F. McDermott, W. Tseng, and T.W. Maretzki (eds.), **People and Culture of Hawaii: A Psychocultural Profile.** Honolulu: The University Press of Hawaii, 1980.

Melendy, H.B. **The Oriental Americans.** New York: Hippocrene Books, Inc., 1972.

Murase, K. "State and Local Public Policy Issues in Delivering Mental Health and Related Services to Asian and Pacific Americans," in U.S. Commission on Civil Rights, **Civil Rights Issues of Asian and Pacific Americans.** Washington, DC: U.S. Government Printing Office, 1980.

Munoz, F.U. "Pacific Islanders: Life Patterns in a New Land," in R. Endo, S. Sue, and N. Wagner (eds.), **Asian-Americans: Social and Psychological Perspectives, Vol. II.** Palo Alto: Science and Behavior Books, 1980.

Nakane, C. **Japanese Society.** Berkeley and Los Angeles: University of California Press, 1970.

Ponce, P.E. "The Filipino," in J.F. McDermott, W. Tseng, and T.W. Maretzki (eds.), **People and Culture of Hawaii: A Psychocultural Profile.** Honolulu: The University Press of Hawaii, 1980.

President's Commission on Mental Health. "Report of the Special Populations Subpanel on Mental Health of Asian/Pacific Americans," in **Task Panel Reports Submitted to the President's Commission on Mental Health, 1978.** Volume III Appendix. Washington, DC: Government Printing Office, 1978.

Rabaya, V. "Filipino Immigration: The Creation of a New Social Problem," in A. Tachiki et al. (eds.), **Roots: An Asian American Reader.** Los Angeles: Asian American Studies Center, Unviersity of California, 1971.

Rogers, T.A., and Izutsu, S. "The Japanese, in J.F. McDermott, W. Tseng, and T.W. Maretzki (eds.), **People and Culture of Hawaii: A Psychocultural Profile.** Honolulu: The University Press of Hawaii, 1980.

Seligman, M.E.P. **Helplessness: On Depression, Development, and Death.** San Francisco: W.H. Freeman and Company, 1975.

Shon, S.D. "The Delivery of Mental Health Services to Asian and Pacific Americans," in U.S. Commission on Civil Rights, **Civil Rights Issues of Asian and Pacific Americans.** Washington, DC: U.S. Government Printing Office, 1980.

Sue, S. "Psychological Theory and Implications for Asian-Americans," **The Personnel and Guidance Journal** 55 (1977a), 381-389.

_____. "Community Mental Health Services to Immigrant Groups," **American Psychologist** 32 (1977b), 906-910.

Sue, S., and Kitano, H.H.L. (Issue eds.). "Asian-Americans: A Success Story," **Journal of Social Issues** 29 (1973).

Sue, S., and Sue, D.W. "Chinese American Personality and Mental Health," **Amerasia Journal** 1 (1971), 36-49.

Sue, S., and Wagner, N. (eds.). **Asian-Americans: Psychological Perspectives.** Palo Alto: Science and Behavior Books, 1973.

Tachiki, A., et al. (eds.), **Roots: An Asian American Reader.** Los Angeles: Asian American Studies Center, Unviersity of California, 1971.

U.S. Commission on Civil Rights, **Civil Rights Issues of Asian and Pacific Americans.** Washington, DC: U.S. Government Printing Office, 1980.

Weglyn, M. **Years of Infamy: The Untold Story of America's Concentration Camps.** New York: William Morrow, 1976.

Yee, B.W.K. "Asian-American Elderly: A Life-Span Developmental Approach to Minorities and Learned Helplessness." Paper presented at the American Psychological Association Convention, 1977.

_____. **A Life-Span Developmental Approach to Studying the Caucasian, Japanese and Vietnamese Elderly: Cognitive Attributions for Control Over Life Situations and its Relationship to Performance on a Cognitive Task.** Unpublished master's thesis, University of Denver, 1979.

Yoneda, K. "100 Years of Japanese Labor History in the U.S., in A. Tachiki et al. (eds.), **Roots: An Asian American Reader.** Los Angeles: Asian American Studies Center, Unviersity of California, 1971.

THE MEXICAN AMERICAN FAMILY AND INTERACTION WITH SOCIAL SYSTEMS

MARTA SOTOMAYOR[1]

A number of descriptive articles have been written that summarily define the Chicano family as being partriarchal with an authoritarian father, a submissive mother, and children lost somewhere between these two opposing forces. In this type of family, the father is seen as the final authority in all matters while the role of the mother is to be subservient to the father, with an emphasis on her being a good housewife and mother. Family characteristics usually include: "father dominance, masculine superiority, strict disciplining of children, precise separation of sex roles, and an emphasis on submission and obedience to authority figures" (Ramirez, 1978). Family solidarity at most can mean that the family seeks answers to problems within the family itself, obtaining outside help only in extreme situations and as an exception to the expected norms (Edgerton et al., 1970).

However, research which defines the Mexican American family in terms of this simple patriarchal model can reach erroneous conclusions. As Montiel (1970) points out:

> Although numerous studies of the Chicano family purport to be based on empirical evidence, their findings are open to serious question. The concepts and categories used to identify types of families have been developed by theoreticians who are divorced from the population under study.

Montiel explains how the assumptions in such a model have influenced the method of studying the Mexican American family in a variety of relationships. He also notes that: "The psychoanalytic model has been used exclusively in the definition of the Mexican American family, emphasizing the themes of 'inferiority' and 'machismo.'"

Not only is the description of the patriarchal model of the Mexican American family inaccurate, but it also ignores the considerable diversity found in such families (Maldonado, 1977). For example, the extent to which sex roles are adhered to depends in part on the degree of acculturation experienced or adopted by a specific family. The same variations exist in

---

[1]The terms "Mexican American" and "Chicano" are used interchangeably in this paper.

the role arrangements of Mexican American families that exist in families
of other ethnic groups, and many factors can cause these patterns to
change. Although it is important to understand the general arrangement of
roles in order to understand the specific functions of the family unit and its
members, it is more important to be aware of the depth, subtlety, and
complexity of familial relationships and the economic, political, cultural,
and historical factors that determine Mexican American family experiences.

Background

Chicanos originally inherited many patriarchal family patterns from
certain conquered Indian cultures, Spain, and especially Mexico (Ramirez,
1970; Fuentes, 1971). In Mexico, the family institution was defined as the
source of control, protection, economic support, and procreation. Because
of the religious influence of the Catholic church, procreation was ascribed
as the primary function of marriage. Satisfactory, close, warm, emotional
relationships and companionship were relegated to positions of secondary
importance within the marriage.

Clearly distinguished expectations for husbands and wives usually resulted in a clear division of labor within and outside of the home. The husband
made the decisions and the wife was to accept them somewhat passively.
The husband was to provide protection and economic support and the wife
was responsible for household tasks and the bearing and rearing of children. It was from mothering that women were to experience close, emotional satisfactions as well as **las penas mas grandes** (the greatest sorrows)
(Pineda, 1970). Extended kinship networks also provided sources of close,
emotional relationships.

The inclusiveness typical of classic patriarchal families often assumed
extended family expressions in the Mexican traditional family. In preindus-
trial Mexico large extended kinship arrangements could be accomodated
within one household because of the features of the **haciendas** and **ranchos,**
while in modern Mexico the urban **vecindades** (a type of housing project
providing separate residences for kinship groups) serve a very similar
function. Today among the economically well-off, individual residences in
very close proximity are quite common and these allow for frequent and
continuing contacts between kin.

The **compadrazgo** (a voluntary social network which may include blood
kin and others) appeared as an additional kinship arrangement which was
formalized through religious rituals such as baptism, marriage, confirma-
tion, and **fiesta de quince anos** (fifteenth birthday celebration for girls). At
least three pairs of **padrinos** (godfathers and godmothers) could be acquired
at a marriage ceremony. This type of network was further extended
through the relationships between **compadres, padrinos,** and **ahijado** (parents and **compadres** of **compadres).** These practices still exist and variations of them are also found among the nonCatholic groups in Mexico and

the Chicanos in this country (Valle, 1974). The most significant character-istics of **compadrazgo** relationships are reciprocal responsibilities and the sharing of the emotional and physical care of children.

Thus the Mexican traditional family may be characterized by its specific delineation of functions for husbands and wives. Conjugal conflicts and tensions (and those of the children) were diluted through the inclusive extended kinship networks. Emotional and economic needs were shared among kin and within the extensive **compadrazgo** network. The centralized responsibility and control that one would expect the father to have in a classic patriarchal family are in reality shared with members of various social networks.

Within these complex systems of relationships, there was probably no more clearly delineated authoritative role than that of the grandparent. The aged grandparents always had a place of considerable significance in the Mexican traditional family. The grandmother was responsible for much of the nurturing of young grandchildren; it was she who provided for reli-gious education and ritual within the home and encouraged educational achievement (Pineda, 1971). The grandfather assumed the function of transmitter of history, values, and heritage. If, for example, the married sons or sons-in-law did not adequately support their wives and children, it was the grandfather who was supposed to confront them and insure that they met their family responsibilities. In times of crisis, grandparents stood ready to lend necessary support. In turn, a mutual helping relation-ship was expected from grown sons and daughters to provide for the eco-nomic and emotional needs of the grandparents.

It is assumed that the family patterns described above, with Hispanic and Indian influences, was the inheritance that found its way into the rural and urban settlements of Chicanos in this country. The time and sequence of the various migrations as well as the historical circumstances faced by the **Californios, Tejanos,** and **Nuevo Mexicanos** undoubtedly influenced the degree to which these traditional patterns were continued. Ultimately a combination of factors have consigned these peoples to a colonized, ex-ploited, and usually poverty-stricken existence in the **barrios** and **colonias** of cities and rural areas. Thus while Chicanos inherited Mexican family patterns, changes molded by acculturation, urbanization, modernization, discrimination, and poverty could have developed in the structural patterns of Chicano families.

Since relatively little research has been conducted on the Mexican American family, it may be difficult to speculate on changes in family patterns. However, an examination of the role of the elderly and their family interactions might provide one indication of the degree of change.

Recent studies indicate that elderly Chicanos still have a strong familis-tic orientation. That is, for close, emotional social relationships, they place primary emphasis on the extended family instead of nonrelatives. Crouch (1973) and others maintain that there is a traditional, cultural basis for this orientation. Moore (1971) states that the psychological underpinn-ing of this orientation is the fact that elderly Chicanos value interpersonal relationships more than material possessions or competition for material gain.

In a study conducted in San Antonio, Carp (1969) determined that Chicano elderly are strongly attached to the extended family and that they demonstrate a high need for familial affiliation. In Korte's (1978) study of aged Chicanos in rural New Mexico, virtually all respondents had a strong preference for close contact with and mutual support from their extended families. In another study in East Los Angeles, Carp (1969) found that Chicanos who were forty-five and over had a stronger familistic orientation than either Anglos or Blacks. Carp also found that Chicano elderly were most likely to be living as married couples but in the same neighborhood as some of their children with whom there was frequent interaction. A recent study of over 600 Chicano families in three Southern California communities by Keefe et al. (1978) also found these types of living arrangements to be common. Such patterns point to a **modified** extended family structure where the elderly maintain their independence but have close regular contact with their children and grandchildren. These arrangements can include youngsters living in with the elderly; in the East Los Angeles study, 65 percent of the elderly Chicanos (compared to 25 percent of the elderly Anglos) had youngsters living with them (Carp, 1969), while in a Denver study eighty percent of the elderly had young grandchildren living in their homes (Sotomayor, 1973).

Social Systems and the Family

The contemporary Chicano family should be seen as an open system sustaining relationships with other systems in a total transactional field. This approach recognizes the psychological unit of the family with its functional interaction in a variety of combinations and meanings. This approach also gives due importance to the variety and meanings of the family's functions in relating to the multiplicity of systems and subsystems outside itself, and it acknowledges the effects that outside structures can have on the family unit's ability to function.

SOCIALIZATION PROCESS

It is generally agreed that one of the family's primary functions is the socialization of the children, which is usually regarded as the process of transmitting and preserving sociocultural traditions from generation to generation. It is also agreed that the values, beliefs, roles, and functions of individuals and the manner in which they promote the socialization of their children depend in large measure on variations in social conditions.

In this highly technological society with its history of extreme contrasts--a society firmly embedded in a competitive economic system and characterized by constant and sharp changes--the socialization process has become one in which the child acquires skills (not always effective) to deal with abrupt and contradictory change rather than one in which the child is encouraged to promote tradition. As a result, emphasis has been placed on the development of individualistic, personalistic, and polarized values rather than on traditional kinship and group values.

In his formulation of the American national character, Erik Erickson (1956: 247) makes specific mention of a contradiction found in this society that impacts on the socialization process of children. He states that "the baby was not made to feel at home in this world except under the conditions that he behave himself in certain definite ways, which were inconsistent with the timetable of an infant's needs and potentialities and contradictory in themselves." Erickson (1956: 249) also points out that the mother "stands for the superior values of tradition, yet she herself does not want to become 'old.'"

This socialization process in American society, once a purview of the extended family, has been delegated to outside institutions. These institutions are necessary to maintain the social system as a system in order to prevent society from being torn apart by the forces of individual self-interest; institutions, therefore, are essential for maintaining the internal harmony of society and harnessing the individual to community action. Within this context, human society can be viewed as a system of organization in which the individual and his range of needs, at all phases and levels, are both satisfied and held in check. These needs can be met only by the person in social interaction system. This social interaction system is conducted through institutions that are established to meet, repress, or oppress the needs of those individuals that compose them or through those that permit the fulfillment of the potentiality of its members (Goldschmidt, 1966: 58-59).

PARTICIPATION WITHIN SOCIETY

A second function of the family is to participate within society. Through its participation in comunity life and through the support it receives from the community, a family is motivated to adhere to the norms of the community, including norms regarding its own stability (Bell and Vogel, 1968). It is the norms of the community that ascribe status to specific families. It is that status, with all its implications, that becomes the focus of reference for the family and determines not only the economic, political and educational aspirations of the family but also its relationship with society's institutions.

The institutions designed to meet the needs of society and to allow, with their systems of checks and balances, for the maximum development of individual potentiality have failed the Chicano family. Existing institutions have endorsed policies that exclude those who are different and systematically bar admission to educational, health, and welfare systems.

A COLONIZED PEOPLE

If the Chicano family is to be understood, it has to be within the historical perspective of a colonized people in its native country and in this country. In this perspective, Chicanos have many of the characterstics of other colonized peoples, with the majority society relating to them as outsiders. The inferior status of colonized peoples results in damage to self-esteem, the questioning of native cultural traits, the disparagement of certain familial functions and roles, and eventually the loss of social cohesion, due in part to an inability to retain their own cultures (Kardiner and Ovesey, 1962: 47). All of these symptoms have been identified to some degree in a considerable number of Chicano families. There is sufficient evidence of the damage that institutional policies and procedures have inflicted upon Chicanos. Salazar (1970) has summarized the plight of Mexican Americans by stating that:

> The Mexican American has an average of eight years of schooling, (and) a significant number of farm workers who are excluded from the National Labor Relations Act, unlike any other group of workers. Mexican Americans often have to compete for low wages with their Mexican brothers below the border, with limited skills in a highly technological, competitive society. Mexican Americans have to live with the stinging fact that the word "Mexican" is the synonym for inferior in many parts of the southwest. Mexican Americans through their large population are so politically impotent that in Los Angeles where the country's largest single concentration live they have not one representative on the City Council.

Ordinarily the family participates in community activities in exchange for the support of the community. One functional interchange consists of mutual give and take on a daily interaction basis. The extent and quality of the interaction determines the solidarity of bonds between society and the family unit. This daily interaction with the external system has been blocked for many Chicano families, and, as a result, they have often withdrawn from participation in community affairs.

The external community has given the Chicano family an inferior status and has defined that status as one with inferior standards of behaviors and rewards. In a functional society the community gives the family a significant status and identity by means of support and acceptance. The present societal structure has denied the Mexican American family a positive status and identity, excluded it from community activities, and in many instances given it the feeling of alienation, marginality, and anomie.

INTERCHANGES WITH SOCIAL SYSTEMS

The type and quality of the interchanges between the family and the external social system determine to a considerable extent internal family activities and integration. For example, the Mexican American head of household has often been unemployed or underemployed in menial positions that constantly remind him of his inferior status. He has practically no access to the decision-making process that could change his situation, and he has no effective means of making those vital institutions respond to his needs. This damaging, limiting process invariably affects the internal functioning and role arrangements within his family. It has an adverse effect on family leadership, in the maintenance of expected patterns of behavior, and on the integration and solidarity of specific families and their individual members.

Task performances and expected patterns of behavior clearly reflect the family's relationship with external systems. These task performances are regulated in part by the requirements of the interchanges between those systems and the family and the tangible goods obtained from these interchanges. Performance of the expected, assigned tasks in turn affects the quality and integration of the relationships within the family (Bell and Vogel, 1968).

The adequate performance of expected tasks is intrinsically related to other goals of the family. When these goals are limited by decisions of a system over which the individual family has no control, the equilibrium of relationships within the Mexican American family suffers, including the degree of closeness of family bonds and the expected familial leadership. These factors affect the Mexican American father's role as provider, disciplinarian, and protector, roles that traditionally have been important to the Chicano male. To be effective, his position in the home has to be couched in strong, affective bonds.

The patterns of decision-making are thwarted and distorted for many Mexican American families when decisions that involve meeting the basic essential needs of family members are beyond the control of the expected patterns. These conditions have a circular effect in disrupting the family's equilibrium and in preventing the family from reorganizing and mobilizing its internal resources to deal with a rejecting, destructive external system. The pattern is thus perpetuated.

Other forms of dealing with external systems are attempted with no actual opportunity of testing them to discover effects or alternatives. The interchanges afforded other families and the processes learned in the successful completion of those interchanges are not available for many Chicanos because society does not offer them that "testing ground." It is possible that a significant proportion of inmates of correctional institutions, number of narcotic addicts, and percentage of school dropouts among Mexican Americans can be explained not merely on the basis of individual deviancy but more as a result of attempts to achieve some type of interaction with a destructive social system. In many instances, the only knowledge the Chicano has of those institutions outside of his **barrio** is that they repress and oppress him, and the skills he develops to deal with those institutions have to be limited to responding to repression and oppression.

The strong movement of "Chicanismo" within prison walls, the recruitment of Mexican American school dropouts by young Mexican American students, and the involvement of Mexican American addicts in the counseling of other Chicano addicts represent themes typical of the reconstruction of an interactional process that mutually must affect family and society. The following themes appear repeatedly in the Chicano movement: open

and better employment opportunities, changes in policies that have excluded Mexican Americans from the normal activities of society, greater status
for Spanish as a spoken language, respect for the Mexican American as an
individual of value, cohesion and solidarity of a group united by a cause,
pride in the culture and heritage of one's ancestors, and reevaluation of
roles and functions of men and women.

Within this perspective, what is the function of the service provider in
working with Chicano families? This perspective does not totally reject an
intrapsychic approach to helping; in fact there are many Mexican American
families and individuals--particularly those who have achieved considerable
mobility within the majority community--who benefit from aspects of this
traditional counseling approach. The exclusive use of this approach, however, is a narrow one in view of the other factors that dramatically affect
the opportunities for Chicano families to function adequately.

Identifying Supportive Elements

Service providers must be able to identify those elements within the
Chicano family that have given and promoted group cohesion and individual
integration and actively utilize them in every helping relationship. Some of
these elements are briefly described below.

EXTENDED FAMILY PATTERN

As previously stated, one element that appears consistently in the Chicano experience is the extended family pattern. It is a supportive and
flexible structure maintaining a number of functions to deal with the
environment as well as with the emotional and psychological aspects of the
family unit and individuals. The extended family is compatible with the
present Mexican American emphasis on the importance of the group; for
example the Movimiento Estudiantil Chicano de Aztlan (MECHA), the
Mexican Youth Organization (MAYO), and the Crusade for Justice are all
group-oriented and have many of the characteristics of an extended family.

In the Chicano extended family pattern, members often support the head
of a household by sharing their goods to meet the daily needs of the family. The head of the household does not lose face and the extended family
pattern couches feelings of failure. The feeling of isolation often experienced by the nuclear family in similar situations is diluted by the support
and help of the members of the extended family. Various members of the
family assume the physical and affective care of the children when stress
from the external system exacerbates the self-preoccupation of an individual parent. This process is also present at times of internal crisis such as
the birth of a new child when the extended family gives care to the mother
during her convalescence and to the older youngsters.

The **compadrazgo** relationship has many similar characteristics and
functions; relationships assume familial overtones in which the emotional

and physical responsibilities for children are also shared. It is important to note that the ties here are kinlike but with some different interactional rules that might not be found in a familial relationship. In addition to the system of **compadrazgo,** there are the systems of **consejera** and **servidor.** The principal characteristics of these networks include: 1) ties based on linkages established between individuals and not between group members; 2) the absence of any formal governing structures based on either written or unwritten constitutions; and 3) the career specialization of linkperson natural helpers along with the specialization of their voluntary helping activity (Valle and Mendoza, 1978). The key characteristic of these networks is the provision of services in which the element of mutuality is highlighted. Equally important is the notion of **el deber** or obligation as an element in the helping interaction among members of networks (Korte, 1978).

RESPECT FOR THE AGED

As noted earlier, the elderly are greatly respected among Mexican Americans. Positions of authority are assigned to them regardless of their sex. Through the continued participation of the elderly in family decision-making processes, the issue of authority is diluted among extended family relationships. Chicanos have strong convictions that commit them to taking care of aged parents and grandparents.

FAMILY ROLE PATTERNS

Contrary to generalizations regarding the valueless position of women in the Chicano cultural experience, the mother is given a significant position within the family. Respect for the mother is expressed symbolically through her children's use of her family name in conjunction with that of the father. This custom is prevalent in Latin America but is totally overlooked in the United States with the usage of only the father's last name.

The participation of the oldest son and oldest daughter in the parental function in relation to younger siblings continues to exist. This pattern is often interpreted by service providers as overdependency and great efforts are made to "emancipate" these family members from their "unfair" burden of family responsibility. The notion of **el deber** is a strong component in understanding the role of older children in the raising of younger siblings.

THE BARRIO

The **barrio,** like the ghetto, has become a negative concept. It is often destroyed by urban renewal projects or the construction of freeways that methodically disperse **barrio** residents. For a group of people who have been consistently rejected by the environment and who value the group and tend to cluster in familial and neighborhood arrangements, the **barrio** has offered a feeling of belonging and cohesion. The **barrio** serves as a kind of coping mechanism, in effect an extension of familial support systems in response to an impersonal or threatening society outside.

The negative aspect of the **barrio** is not the clustering of Chicanos but the almost total lack of resources coming into the confined community to meet the needs of its residents. With limited opportunities to reach out of the **barrio,** there are relatively few alternatives for the expression and development of the potentiality of the Mexican American.

Conclusion

Effective social intervention requires the careful assessment of areas that require change and areas that should be preserved, encouraged, or supported. The sociocultural strengths of the Mexican American family therefore need to be closely identified, evaluated, and supported. More often than not, the positive features of the Chicano family have provided the only strengths available in the life experiences of the Mexican American people. The internal functioning of the family as a system does not have to be minimized; however, given the degree of the negative effect of the external system on the integration of the family unit, a significant priority is intervention to change those destructive external forces.

If effective services are to be given to Chicano families, intervention has to take place at many levels and in many areas requiring institutional change. New models of decision-making have to be supported. Accompanying rearrangements of power need to be made to bring about more equitable resource allocations which will not only strengthen the **barrios,** but will also bring the decision-making power to the individuals who are directly affected and who hopefully are more responsive to the needs of the Mexican American.

References

Bell, N., and Vogel, E. "Toward a Framework for Functional Analysis of Family Behavior," in N. Bell and E. Vogel (eds.), **A Modern Introduction to the Family.** New York: Free Press, 1968.

Carp, F. "Housing and Minority Group Elderly," **Gerontologist** 9 (1969), 20-24.

Edgerton, R., Karno, M., and Fernandez, I. "Curanderismo in the Metropolis: The Diminishing Role of Folk Psychiatry Among Los Angeles Mexican Americans," **American Journal of Psychotherapy** 24 (1970), 124-134.

Erickson, Eric. **Childhood and Society.** New York: Norton, 1950.

Fuentes, C. **Tiempo Mexicano.** Mexico City: Editorial Joaquin Mortiz, S.A., 1971.

Goldschmidt, W. **Comparative Functionalism: An Essay in Anthropological Theory.** Berkeley and Los Angeles: University of California Press, 1966.

Kardiner, A., and Ovesey, L. **The Mark of Oppression: Exploration in the Personality of the American Negro.** New York: Meridian, 1962.

Keefe, S., Padilla, A., and Carlos, M. "The Mexican American Extended Family as an Emotional Support System," in J. Casas and S. Keefe (eds.), **Family and Mental Health in the Mexican American Community.** Los Angeles: Spanish Speaking Mental Health Research Center, 1978.

Korte, A. **Social Interaction and Morale of Spanish-Speaking Elderly.** Unpublished doctoral dissertation, University of Denver, 1978.

Maldonado, D. "La Familia Mexico Americana and the Elderly," in **Aging Research Utilization Report,** vol. 4, no. 1. Austin: Texas Department of Public Welfare, 1977.

Montiel, M. "The Social Science Myth of the Mexican American Family," **El Grito** 3 (1970).

Moore, J. "Mexican Americans," **Gerontologist** 9 (1971), 30-34.

Pineda, F. **El Mexicano, Psicologia de sus Destructividad.** Mexico City: Editoral Pax-Mexico, S.A., 1971.

Pineda, F. **El Mexicano, Su Dinamica Psicosocial.** Mexico City: Editoral Pax-Mexico, S.A., 1971.

Ramirez, M. "Identification With Mexican Family Values and Authoritarianism in the Mexican American," **Journal of Social Psychology** 30 (1978).

Ramirez, S. **El Mexicano, Psicologia de sus Motivaciones.** Mexico City: Editoral Pax-Mexico, S.A., 1971.

Salazar, R. **Los Angeles Times,** February 6, 1970.

Sotomayor, M. **A Study of Chicano Grandparents in an Urban Barrio.** Unpublished doctoral dissertation, University of Denver, 1973.

Valle, R. **Amistad-Compadrazgo as an Indigenous Webwork Compared to the Urban Mental Health Network.** Unpublished doctoral dissertation, University of Southern California, 1974.

Valle, R., and Mendoza, L. **The Elder Latino.** San Diego: Campanile Press, 1978.

PART THREE

SERVICE DELIVERY

This section discusses the development of various mental health service delivery policies and practices for minority group populations. In the first article, Barbara Solomon proposes a modification of current theoretical models of behavior in order to better explain the mental health problems of minority groups. Her framework takes into account the significance of an individual's sociocultural context and uses a systems approach with power as the central concept. Solomon explores the implications of this framework for service intervention strategies.

In the next article, Armando Morales examines mental health problems in the Mexican American community related to police practices, riots, gangs, and substance abuse which tend to be viewed and handled as strictly law enforcement issues. Meeting such problems necessitates changes in traditional methods of service delivery. Morales makes specific suggestions for approaches that can deal with this more complete range of mental health needs.

In the third article, June Jackson Christmas details six features which should characterize appropriate mental health services for minority groups. These features are cultural relevance, a holistic orientation, a structure that supports coordination, priority attention to certain target populations, use of community support systems, and minority group involvement in decision-making, accountability, and quality assurance. Christmas also presents recommendations for the implementation of these six features.

A THEORETICAL PERSPECTIVE FOR DELIVERY OF
MENTAL HEALTH SERVICES TO MINORITY COMMUNITIES

BARBARA BRYANT SOLOMON

The behavioral science foundations of the major mental health professions are unsurprisingly similar in content. Psychiatrists, social workers,
psychiatric nurses, clinical psychologists, and other mental health practitioners have all been exposed to Freud's psychosexual view of human development; Erikson's epigenetic principle and eight stages of psychosocial
development; the learning theories of Watson, Skinner and Bandura; the
humanistic theories of Maslow and Fromm; and the ego psychologies which
have contributed such concepts as coping, adaptation, and mastery. The
therapeutic technologies emerging from these theoretical perspectives
have met with varying degrees of success. However, nowhere have our
theories of behavior or our theories of practice been more intensely criti-
cized than inside minority communities. The past decade has witnessed the
splintering of professional organizations in the mental health field into
minority counterparts as well as the establishment of the Center for Minority Group Mental Health Programs in the National Institute of Mental
Health. However, the initial spurt of activity aimed at producing new
sensitivities to minority issues in mental health appears to be waning, and
it therefore may be a propitious time to examine the extent to which they
have influenced the actual delivery of mental health services to minority
communities, for better or worse.

There has been a strong conviction expressed by many mental health
professionals that our theories of human behavior are in fact universal and
acceptance of a common humanity is a sufficient base from which to manage a therapeutic encounter with clients regardless of their race or ethnicity. Others have argued as strongly that our traditional theories of human
behavior and practice do not take into account the realities of minority
group experiences, either in assessing the sources of problem-producing
behavior or in managing the processes of therapeutic change. In turn, these
dissidents have been accused of resorting to rhetoric with nondocumenta-
tion.

There is considerable evidence, some circumstancial rather than quantitative or statistical, which suggests that minority persons do have problems
of mental health which are **different** from those of the Anglo middle class
which has been the sole model in many cases for the normative behaviors
described in our traditional theoretical formulations. Thus, the focus of

this paper will be on: 1) an appraisal of the unique mental health problems which minority propulations have in common; 2) the assessment of current theoretical models in regard to their utility for addressing these problems; and 3) the proposal of a modification of current theoretical models in order to improve services to minority client systems.

Mental Health Services and the Minority Client

There is often an exceedingly thin line between stereotyping and cultural awareness. Each time that a group is identified as demonstrating some characteristic to a greater extent than other groups, there is a tendency to want to utilize this information in interactions with a single group member. Unless the group in question is completely homogeneous in terms of the characteristic, it may be a serious mistake to attribute the characteristic to the individual. This is perceived as a danger in many cultural awareness-types of programs, that such programs merely attempt to trade positive stereotypes for negative ones. However, to insist that minority populations by virtue of their common experience of racism and their membership in stigmatized collectives have developed unique mental health problems is not a case of stereotyping minorities as pathological entities, but rather reflects an awareness and sensitivity to minority experiences in the United States. It is in fact the insensitivity to the significance of cultural factors in diagnosis and treatment which has characterized the mental health system, perhaps out of a mistaken notion that theories of human behavior are culture-free. For example, psychodynamic theory suggests that depression is usually precipitated by the experience of a loss that typically involves prestige, esteem, material goods, or an ambivalently loved person. However, the significance of a particular kind of loss, for example loss of honor or loss of youth, may be different from culture to culture. Also, one may certainly question whether the precocious maturity of many ghetto youth implies acceleration, distortion, or even inhibition of the process of identity formation as described by Erikson and other ego psychologists.

Let us consider the case of Mr. Lee and Mr. Wong:

Mr. Wong and Mr. Lee came to this country during the wave of importation of Chinese laborers to work on the railroad. They were both young men, but of course were prohibited from bringing wives or families. They worked very hard for several years and saved enough money to open a small grocery store in a low income neighorhood in Los Angeles. The neighbors were predominantly white--mostly first and second generation immigrants from Eastern Europe, a few Spanish-speaking residents, and only a scattering of Asians who were for the most part single men in rooming houses.

Mr Wong did not learn to speak English well, but Mr. Lee, the more out-going of the two, was able to speak English rather well and served as a connecting link between the world and Mr. Wong. There were at times references made to "dirty Chinks" by a few young neighborhood bullies, but most people in the neighborhood were neither hostile nor particularly friendly.

The years went by as Mr. Wong and Mr. Lee worked hard, took a trip to New York, visited infrequently with friends in Chinatown-- mostly friends from the railroad days--and did not complain about their lives in a country that remained somewhat alien. Then one day when Mr. Lee was 66 and Mr. Wong was 68, Mr. Lee died of a heart attack. After the simple funeral, Mr. Wong went inside their store-home, and for three weeks no neighbors saw him and the store remained closed. Finally a neighbor attempted to call him from the bolted front door but received no response. Worried, she called the police who entered to find Mr. Wong lying on the floor near his bed, unconscious and suffering from malnutrition.

Mr. Wong was taken to the county hospital where he was given good medical care and soon regained consciousness. However, he never asked where he was or why, remained apathetic, and kept his face to the wall most of the time. He never talked to the doctors or other hospital staff and finally, one evening after dinner, attempted to sever an artery with his dinner knife. The physician immediately requested psychiatric consultation and an evaluation of Mr. Wong for possible transfer to a psychiatric service.

One might immediately speculate as to the potential for an effective response to Mr. Wong from the mental health system. The contention here is that the system is not designed to be able to make an effective response. First of all, the likelihood of a Chinese-speaking mental health professional being on the staff of the hopsital is remote. Even if present, the flexibility of that system to permit the exploration and involvement in the life space of Mr. Wong outside the walls of the hospital is unlikely. This is reinforced by the probability that the mental health practitioner would have no intervention model for such exploration and involvement.

The remainder of this paper will seek to identify a theoretical framework which will take into account the significance of the sociocultural context in assessing the mental health problems encountered in minority populations and the nature of the intervention strategies which are suggested by that framework.

A Theoretical Framework

The world has changed dramatically from the relatively simple structure of Freud's Austria; yet the treatment models he developed for dealing with certain types of mental health problems remain the most frequently encountered ones today. However, contemporary society, moving rapidly toward the twenty-first century, is infinitely more complex, the social milieu infinitely more varied and dynamic; thus a systems approach for explaining human behavior in that kind of social environment is mandatory. I almost hesitate to use the term "systems approach" since it has been a popular approach to write about, to promote, and even to indicate as having been incorporated into models of behavior and practice. We have in fact given greater attention to the person-in-situation, the person in interaction with significant suprasystems of family, schools, community, work organizations, other families, neighborhood, etc. However, it has rarely been explicated as to how or by what process one actively intervenes in multiple systems in order to bring about positive change in problem-producing behavior. So we often express our recognition of the way that society and its institutions impinge negatively upon minority persons but have little notion of how any direct intervention can be made in the larger social systems to circumvent that negative force. Having no such notion, we generally fall back to those systems in which we can intervene--person, family, or group. This is reminiscent of the analagous situation in which a gardener has only one tool--a rake; therefore, any problem in the garden naturally calls for the rake to solve it.

The systems approach, however, makes possible the development of new tools by introducing new concepts for use in explaining human behavior and developing strategies of practice. The kingpin concept is power. Anderson and Carter (1978) suggest that the basic stuff of all living systems is energy or power. Freud's conceptualization of the person-system utilizes the same notion as psychic energy, and its transformation is the basis of his psychodynamic theory. What occurs in a social system are transfers of energy or power between persons or groups of persons. This power derives from a complex of sources including the physical capacities of the persons that make up the system; social resources such as loyalties, shared sentiments, and common values; and resources from the environment including not only material resources but information, ideas, and manpower. This power permits a system to maintain itself and to effect desired changes.

It is not unimportant to note that an underlying theme that seems to be evident in analyses of minority-majority group relationships is the ubiquitous experience of powerlessness among minority groups. Power is a concept which is present in almost any discussion of human relationships-- whether from a psychological, economic, political, or philosophical point of view. Thus it can be an integrative concept in the effort to obtain an understanding of those forces which shape relationships in a social system. It can also be utilized as a basis for problem-solving when it is conceived as the necessary element required to obtain adequate solutions to social and psychological problems. Powerlessness, therefore, is defined as the inability to obtain and utilize resources to achieve individual or collective goals. Moreover, the powerless person is characterized by an inability to manage emotions, knowledge, skills, or material resources in a way that makes possible effective performance of valued social roles so as to receive personal gratification. The powerlessness that is described here is institutional powerlessness; in other words, powerlessness is a consequence of negative valuations of minority collectives and of individuals based on their membership in those collectives.

There are some individuals or groups whose exposure to negative valuations have been so intense that they accept these valuations as "right" or at least as inevitable and therefore make no effort to exert power at all. These are the individuals or groups within minority communities who are most often the targets of "outreach" efforts. The powerlessness that they exhibit can be considered "power absence" rather than "power failure." It is interesting to note that the push of minority racial and ethnic groups for greater power (i.e., greater opportunities to achieve desired personal and social goals) succeeded in raising the consciousness of other groups that traditionally have been negatively valued--the handicapped, women, homosexuals, etc.--and they too have begun to push for reduction of their powerlessness.

Some negative valuations do not result in powerlessness because strong family relationships or strong cohesive group relationships provide a cushion or protective barrier against the negative valuations from the larger society. Despite these negative valuations, some minority persons for example are able to obtain and utilize a broad range of personal, interpersonal and technical resources to achieve goals effectively. Not all minority group members are powerless! As a matter of fact, the shift in emphasis from assessing the psychodynamics of the individual to assessing the power flow between persons or groups of persons makes it possible to discern much more complex determinants of individual behavior. We are much less likely to fall into the trap into which Grier and Cobb (1968) fell when they ascribed feelings of self-hatred and low esteem to all Blacks as an inevitable consequence of living in an oppressive society. A systems approach would have gone beyond the narrow perspective of the individual responding to "society" to include other important transactions.

Strategies of Intervention With Minority Clients

If power is perceived as the kingpin concept in explaining human behavior in a multiracial and racist society, then empowerment is both the goal and process of the mental health professional who must deal with social and emotional problems created or exacerbated by membership in a stigmatized collective. Empowerment refers to a set of activities aimed at reducing institutional powerlessness, the powerlessness stemming from the experience of negative valuation and discrimination. These activities are particularly aimed at counteracting the negative valuations. Furthermore, the success or failure of empowerment is directly related to the degree to which the service delivery system itself is an obstacle course reinforcing the negative valuation or an opportunity system in which the inherent power potential of the indiviudal to direct his life becomes actualized.

The empowerment process involves the following:

1. Helping clients to perceive "self" as a causal agent in solving the problems they bring to an agency. In particular, those persons who have been subjected to systematic and pervasive negative valuation must be helped to perceive of themselves as causal forces capable of

exerting influence in a world of other people and capable of bringing about some effect which they desire. It should be made clear that this does not deny the power and the significance of external forces in the creation of their problems or problem situations; however, it does place an overarching emphasis on the limitations of "giving up" and on the latent potential in minority individuals and minority communities to deal more effectively and more creatively with the sources of their distress. Thus this conceptualization of the individual as a causal force emphasizes those forces which will influence change rather than those forces which created the problem.

2. Helping clients to perceive of practitioners as having knowledge and skills which they can use. There is no automatic status received in most minority communities by those mental health professionals who become certified "help-givers." Help-seeking behavior is not similar to that of whites, even at identical socioeconomic levels. Most persons, minority or white, do not see mental health professionals as resources in times of trouble, and professionals are much more likely to be seen as a source of help for others rather than as a source of help for themselves. But there is considerable evidence that the proportion of minorities who perceive psychosocial therapy as a resource when in trouble is even less than the proportion of whites. Relatives and friends are often called upon to help, even more so than among whites; ministers, faith healers, and fortune tellers are also looked upon as a source of help in times of trouble. It is not surprising, then, that the majority of persons who come for help to mental health agencies in minority communities have been sent by social control agencies such as the police, the probation department, or the schools. Sometimes persons may come because a friend has told them that they can get pills or medication for their "bad nerves." Establishing expertise, then, becomes a crucial first step in the engagement of minority clients in a psychosocial helping process.

3. Helping clients to perceive of practitioners as peer collaborators or partners in the treatment process. If this is to occur, it requires a different definition of the relationship between therapists and clients. The negative valuation from society and the reinforcement of dependency patterns by major social institutions does not provide much opportunity for minorities to feel a sense of their own worth or a conviction that they are able to make the important decisions that affect their lives. The therapist-client relationship is most often seen as another superior-inferior relationship in which the power is unequally distributed, and low self-esteem is, in fact, reinforced. Therefore, it is important, with the clear goal of increased self-esteem, to have a different kind of relationship. In this different kind of relationship the therapist and client are partners, combining forces in the problem-solving work, and there is an increased probability of success based on their combined strength. In this kind of relationship, the therapist is clearly the employee of the client in the same way that a lawyer may be the employee of his prestigious corporation. There is no message that either side is inferior to the other.

4. Helping clients to perceive the "power structure" as multidimensional with varying degrees of rigidity at various times (i.e., it can be open to influence). Of course, this presupposes that we have an accurate perception of the suprasystem but our training often does not provide us with that knowledge or an understanding of how to get it.

We are all too keenly aware of the messages that we should intervene effectively in the system that has led to negative impacts in our clients' lives (not to mention our own). The "how to" of that intervention has for the most part escaped us. We have tried and are still trying indirect approaches to mental health delivery but without results that can be pointed to as indicators of significant impact. It may very well be that our own education was not so much deficient in theoretical perspectives on individual growth, development, and the dynamics of change as in principles of community organization and how to operate at social system levels. For those practicing in the mental health field in minority communities, competence in influencing complex organizations is equally as important as sensitivity to the complexities of intrapsychic functions. This is not as relevant for mental health practitioners in white communities where the contingencies are different.

It should be noted that the dynamics of family processes which generate behavior have been thoroughly studied. The family processes that are associated with the development of problem-producing behavior have been the focus of research in psychology, sociology, etc. for years. Yet the organizational processes also related to the development of problem-producing behavior of individuals have scarcely been touched upon.

It should also be pointed out that community mental health professionals are usually seen as being in the business of applying knowledge but not building knowledge. This is an unfortunate misconception of scientific practice. The fact is that we **are** in the business of knowledge building. It is extremely important that we not only make the assessment of the effects of social institutions on individuals who come to mental health agencies for help, but also that we document and count so that we can begin to amass the data necessary to gain increased understanding of the individual-system dynamics. For example, our data could begin to help us pinpoint more precisely the nature of the school experiences which influence the development of particular attitudes and behaviors in youngsters with which set of personal and familial characteristics. Again, our data could help us to identify with greater conviction the extent to which the lack of job opportunities for unskilled persons generates attitudes and behaviors which lead to what set of consequences for which individuals with what set of personal and familial characteristics.

Summary

In summary, then, the delivery of mental health services in minority communities is at a point where the challenges are severe but the opportunities are great. The challenge is to move from the level attained during the 1960s, when the goal was, appropriately, entry into a system from which minorities had been excluded, to the reformation of the system with a broader perspective on theory and practice which is inclusive.

References

Anderson, R., and Carter, I. **Human Behavior in the Social Environment: A Social System Approach,** 2nd ed.   Chicago: Aldine Publishing Co., 1978.

Grier, C., and Cobbs, P. **Black Rage.** New York: Basic Books, 1968.

THE NEED FOR NONTRADITIONAL MENTAL HEALTH PROGRAMS IN THE BARRIO

ARMANDO MORALES[1]

The traditional mental health training model was designed by and for the use of the middle class. This model is able to successfully train practitioners to meet the mental health needs of this group; however, there is evidence that this model has not succeeded in training practitioners who can adequately meet the mental health needs of Mexican Americans, the majority of whom are a part of the lower socio-economic stratum of our society (Hollingshead and Redlich, 1958; Srole et al., 1962). In turn, Mexican Americans have tended to underutilize mental health facilities. Becoming cognizant of as well as concerned about this underutilization, mental health practitioners over the last 10 years have directed their efforts toward making their services more accessible to the Mexican American. Although an increase in utilization was the expected outcome of such efforts in Los Angeles County, where 23 percent of the population is Mexican American, the fact of the matter is that the Mexican American for varied reasons continues to underutilize traditional mental health facilities (Keefe, 1978; Newton, 1978). This underutilization might be construed by some as an indication that the mental health needs of Mexican Americans are less than those of other groups. The available literature and personal observations provide evidence to the contrary (Karno and Edgerton, 1969; Keefe, Padilla, and Carlos, 1978). The fact is that Mexican Americans experience many of the same mental health needs, although to varying degrees, as do other groups in this country.

On close examination of the facts, it is apparent that the prevalent patterns of underutilization are primarily the result of culturally irrelevant services which are being provided to the Mexican American (Burruel and Chavez, 1974). Available statistics provide support for this explanation. For instance, there is evidence that specific mental health programs which provide culturally relevant services tend to show an increase in the rate of utilization by Mexican Americans and, more astonishingly, in some instances there is evidence of overutilization. Such overutilization is present in East Los Angeles, a community in which persons of Mexican descent comprise more than 70 percent of the population.

---

[1]Reprinted by permission from J. Casas and S. Keefe (eds.), **Family and Mental Health in the Mexican American Community.** Los Angeles: Spanish Speaking Mental Health Research Center, 1978.

There are three major mental health facilities in East Los Angeles: the Los Angeles County-University of Southern California (LA-USC) Psychiatric Outpatient Clinic, the East Los Angeles Mental Health County Regional Office, and Metropolitan Psychiatric Services, Inc. Out of these three, the LA-USC Clinic is underutilized by Mexican American patients who comprise only 15 percent of this clinic's caseload. The other two facilities are overutilized by Mexican Americans. In both of these facilities, Mexican Americans represent 90 percent of the caseload. Apparently the basic reason for the difference in utilization between these facilities is the fact that a large percentage of the staff at the East Los Angeles Mental Health County Regional Office (50 percent) and Metropolitan Psychiatric Services, Inc. (80 percent) have bilingual and bicultural capabilities. In contrast, the LA-USC Clinic has only three staff members with such capabilities (Yamamoto, 1977). A reasonable assumption is that by providing culturally relevant services, these overutilized clinics are beginning to effectively meet some of the basic mental health needs of Mexican Americans.

However, even if there continues to be an increase in the utilization of clinics so as to reflect and even surpass the ratio of Mexican Americans in the population, it is of the utmost importance that efforts also be made to acknowledge, understand, and subsequently meet some needs which are presently not being met. The needs to which I refer are those which are the result of violence (barrio-police relations) as well as those which are dysfunctionally expressed through destructive behaviors directed externally (riots, gang wars) or internally (alcohol and drug abuse). If these needs are to be adequately met it will be necessary to break away from the traditional delivery model of mental health services. It is the intent of this paper to provide an understanding of these often ignored mental health needs and subsequently to delineate possible modifications which might make the traditional model more sensitive toward training nontraditional practitioners who can more effectively meet all of the mental health needs of the Mexican American.

Mental Health Implications
of Police Practices in the Barrio

POLICE COMMUNITY RELATIONS

A March 1970 report of the United States Commission on Civil Rights (1970) reveals that a poor relationship exists between Mexican Americans and law enforcement agencies in the Southwest. By necessity, the Commission report was somewhat general as it was concerned with police-community relations in the Southwest as a whole. However, a more recent in-depth study of this problem pertaining to Mexican American perceptions of selected law enforcement policies and practices was conducted in 1972 by the author in East Los Angeles (Morales, 1972b).

For this study interviews were conducted in randomly selected census tracts in East Los Angeles by 10 university students having bilingual and bicultural capabilities. The questionnaire had several core questions pertaining to "language," "roust and frisk," "stopping and searching cars," "searching homes," and "unnecessary force" in "arrest," "custody," or "riot" law enforcement practices. The questions were asked in four different contexts: 1) Does it happen in this area? 2) Has it happened to you? 3) Have you seen it happen? and 4) Has it happened to someone you know? Sixty-five to eighty percent of the sample believed that law enforcement officers in East Los Angeles were using "insulting language," "rousting and frisking citizens," "stopping and searching cars without cause or a good reason," and using "unnecessary force" in arrests, custody, and in handling riots when they involved Mexican American citizens. Thirty-three to forty-two percent of the sample reported that three of the foregoing practices had actually happened to them, 62 to 71 percent reported that they had observed four of these law enforcement practices in East Los Angeles, and 50 to 62 percent reported that six of the seven police practices had happened to someone they knew.

The fact that well over half of the Mexican American respondents believed that the various forms of law enforcement practices were happening in East Los Angeles, had observed them, or knew they had happened to someone known by them, and that one-third or more of the respondents actually experienced some of these practices, should cause serious concern and speculation regarding the future of police-community relations in the Mexican American community. These findings should be interpreted by law enforcement agencies as a criticism of their services to the community. One major factor responsible for the development of these critical perceptions by Mexican Americans of law enforcement behavior was the general lack of explicit policies and guidelines within and between law enforcement agencies for officers to follow. This has the effect of granting the officer in the field the freedom to apply a "general rule of thumb" approach in his work in the community (Morales, 1972b).

Exploring in depth the perceptions of Mexican Americans regarding law enforcement behavior is only the first step in understanding the incidence and prevalence of the problem. Careful attention should be given to other related aspects of conflict in police-community relations which have direct implications for mental health research and practice. For instance mental health practitioners must realize that they have the responsibility to help individuals and their families who are the victims of police malpractice. From past professional experiences it is fair to say that, in addition to physical suffering, police abuse may be one of the most painful psychological experiences that a human being can experience. These experiences can be of such intensity as to inflame violence in individuals, groups, and communities. When this occurs, as happened in East Los Angeles in the early 1970s, it then behooves mental health practitioners to work closely (if possible, on an ongoing basis) with both the community and the police force in order to open up channels of communications, relieve tension, and subsequently develop a plan of action which may be mutually beneficial. In order to be effective in this aspect of community work, law enforcement personnel could benefit from training in group work, crisis intervention, and in the theory and practice of community organization. On the other hand, graduate students working closely with law enforcement agencies could learn much about the institutional difficulties and constraints encountered by the police.

Because mental health practitioners with established minority community sanctions might be looked upon with suspicion by that community if they meet with law enforcement agencies on a regular basis, it might be preferable and perhaps more effective to have other representatives, such as graduate students and faculty, meet with law enforcement agencies to find ways of dealing with the sensitive and complex issue of training in police-community relations. Sessions on group work, crisis intervention, and community organization theory and practice would be of value to law enforcement personnel and graduate students who together could learn much about the institutional difficulties and constraints encountered when a law enforcement organization, working within the requirements of the law, attempts to relate to the minority community in progressive and flexible ways. Along these lines, faculties might further explore ways in which graduate students from varied disciplines could enter into joint research projects with law enforcement agencies in order to gain a richer understanding of the field of police-community relations. A recent example of graduate students gaining some exposure to problems in police-community relations is exemplified by the study "Perceptions of the Police in a Black Community," in which students of the University of Maryland's School of Social Work conducted all of the interviews (Wallach and Carter, 1971). The present polarization between minority communities and law enforcement agencies, as described above, makes these reciprocal approaches almost mandatory.

DRINKING AND DRIVING

A second aspect of police practices in the barrios is the tendency to assign more police to patrol the Mexican American community than the white community. More police in any community increases the likelihood of police observing certain kinds of behavior such as curfew violations and drinking behavior. Consider the following example.

Drunk and drunk driving arrests account for a little over 50 percent of all offenses in the Mexican American East Los Angeles community. The East Los Angeles area, with a population of 259,275, has an average of 9,676 drunk and drunk driving arrests per year compared to the 95 percent white West Valley area with a population of 260,832, which has an average of only 1,552 drunk and drunk driving arrests per year. One might conclude that the larger number of arrests in the Mexican American community is due to a greater incidence of alcoholism in that community, but this simply is not the fact. The Division of Alcoholic Rehabilitation of the California Department of Public Health reports identical ratios of alcoholism to population--8,143 alcoholics per 100,000 population--for both areas. It is apparent that the answer lies in the large number of police that are assigned to the Mexican American community--375 officers averaging 13.5 officers per square mile as compared to 151 officers averaging 3.5 officers per square mile in the white community. Looking at this problem from a treatment perspective, it is also apparent that with the exception of three or four Alcoholics Anonymous groups and a modest public health satellite service in East Los Angeles, there are no detoxification or professional services available for Mexican Americans with drinking problems. The major "treatment" facility continues to be the Los Angeles County Jail where Mexican Americans comprise 40 percent of the jail population for offenses mostly related to drinking. In other words, the affluent are tracked into the medical system and treated for their drug and drinking problems whereas the poor are tracked into the criminal justice system and receive no treatment.

These practices in the deployment of law enforcement personnel have several mental health implications. First of all, the 9,676 persons arrested each year in East Los Angeles for drinking offenses are mostly males between the ages of 30 and 45. Most are married fathers with an average of four to six children. The economic status of the family is threatened if the father has to pay bail or a fine or go to jail. His job is jeopardized. Marital and family emotional stability is threatened if the father loses his job, or goes to jail and subsequently loses his job. If he goes to jail this will affect the school performances of his children; younger children will be more affected than older children, and daughters will be more affected than sons (Friedman and Esselstyn, 1965). In short, this police deployment is not just affecting the 9,676 persons being arrested each year but rather 48,000 people in one community when their families are included. This is a community mental health problem and one which requires an approach far beyond that of traditional case-by-case clinical intervention.

RIOTS AND THE MEXICAN AMERICAN COMMUNITY

In 1975 the Los Angeles Times reported that the Los Angeles Police Department was beginning a program of training to control possible food riots ("LAPD Begins Training," 1975). Police Commander Fred Brittell, who previously had been in charge of the "Special Weapons and Tactics" (SWAT) force, said that the special training had been ordered by Ed Davis, the Chief of Police. More than 500 police supervisors went through the program, and plans called for all of the 7,200 officers on the force to go through riot-control drills at each station house. The nation's declining economy and major unemployment prompted the police to take this action. More recently, police intervention in the Boston school integration riots are an indication of what must be in store for Mexican American communities confronting the same issue.

Should riots be a mental health concern? Are they a concern in mental health practice? The answer to the first question should be "yes," and the answer to the second would have to be "no." The 1969 report of the National Commission on the Causes and Prevention of Violence (1969) revealed that the United States ranked number one in riots among the 17 Western democracies, primarily as the result of police action. The United States had four times more riot casualties because of police intervention—48 per million compared to 12 per million in the other 16 Western democracies.

Just as Watts spearheaded Black riots in the 1960s, East Los Angeles spearheaded Chicano riots in the 1970s (Morales, 1972a). Approximately 40 riots took place in Mexican American communities between 1970 and 1972 in various parts of the Southwest, and in East Los Angeles, in particular, there were eight destructive riots during 1970-1971.

Whether riots are the result of racism and police brutality as in the East Los Angeles riots of the early 1970s, food riots as were anticipated in 1975, or rioting crowds in defense of minority children being attacked by whites who oppose school integration, mental health practitioners must not continue to be passive observers. Humanitarian values demand that mental health practitioners obtain knowledge of a practical nature in this area. In order to ensure the attainment of this knowledge, mental health educators will have to expand the curriculum and adopt relevant texts which focus on sociology, anthropology, and political science as well as on law and the criminal justice system. In addition, mental health practitioners must develop skills and experience in working with groups and community organizations and in working with the media.

There are a variety of ways in which mental health practitioners can apply their skills to riots. On a preventative level, once mental health workers have established meaningful working relationships with the political power structure, the police, and minority community groups, they can serve as mediators, consultants, and advocates of minority interests with these groups. These efforts can serve to relieve tensions, especially if community people feel that some progress is being made regarding their grievances.

Once a riot has started the amount of force used by law enforcement can greatly affect the course of the riot. Overreaction in law enforcement has proven to be counterproductive and has even escalated riots. In the early stages of a riot the mental health practitioner's role would be to encourage restraint in law enforcement while simultaneously involving the more responsible community groups in policing their own community. This has been found to be very effective. The deployment of volunteer attorneys to monitor and record law enforcement and community behavior encourages restraint and professionalism in law enforcement and communicates to the local people that others are concerned about their treatment.

During the more intense stages of rioting, law enforcement must be discouraged from using deadly force in handling rioters. The excessive use of deadly force has led to riot escalation and even the initiation of new riots. Such was the case in the East Los Angeles community which experienced eight riots during a 21 month period in 1970 and 1971. Rather than deadly force, the utilization of tear gas, water hoses, or harmless plastic bullets should be recommended.

Following the conclusion of a riot, feelings of anger fill the air. Law enforcement personnel, in particular, have been found to develop even greater negative attitudes toward the minority community after a riot; overly aggressive patrol which violates community civil rights is not uncommon in the riot's aftermath. Discretion in patrol coupled with community support for sensitive police patrol should be encouraged.

Riots have also had their impact on human service and mental health agencies. Staffs of these agencies have many times developed conflicts along ethnic lines. As they become immobilized with guilt, anger, and frustration, human services to the minority population cease. Mental health practitioners in the role of consultants could help staffs in conflict to resolve their differences and facilitate their work in meeting clients' needs.

Finally, mental health practitioners can be of direct clinical assistance to psychological victims of the riots. Children in particular may require counseling since there is evidence that children exposed to riots have their fears aroused, often exacerbating preexistent inner problems.

Mental Health Implications for Youth in the Barrio

INTERVENTION APPROACHES WITH GANGS

The "gang" label has a negative connotation and has been applied to what is generally considered a unique lower class phenomenon. Rarely are middle class adolescent groups referred to as gangs, regardless of their similarity to their lower-economic class counterparts. Such groups are more commonly referred to as peer groups, cliques, or clubs. For the purposes of this paper, however, a gang will be defined as a peer group of adolescents in a lower, middle, or upper class community who participate in activities that are significantly harmful to themselves and/or others in the community.

There are numerous Mexican American adolescent groups in all barrios in the Southwest, and in some barrios one will find evidence of gangs. Currently in Los Angeles, for example, gang violence against the community as well as between gangs is on the increase. There has been a rising number of youth killings of which at least half are attributable to intergang violence. Society has developed different approaches in dealing with gangs which are oftentimes related more to the economic and political climate than to the needs of the gang and barrio. The interventive approaches may have varied effects upon the gang, but most of these approaches are short term remedial measures which are at times of some limited social-recreational value to the gang or the agency attempting to break up the gang. There are at least eight interventive approaches that are applied in attempts to solve the gang problem: the social-recreational approach, competitive sports, law enforcement, institutionalization, street workers, the community organization approach, clinical approach, and the psychosocial awareness approach. These will be briefly summarized and evaluated here.

1. **The Social-Recreational Approach.** This traditional approach views the gang as a group of unhappy adolescents who lack social and recreational outlets. Attempts are made by social-recreational agency

representatives to give the gang a positive identity as a result of their
hard work in planning and having dances and other social-recreational
activities. Likewise, through various fundraising efforts, they may
work toward the purchase of lettered jackets for themselves. This
approach simply uses group processes to transform group values and
behavior.

On the other hand, there is evidence that gang-group cohesiveness
and delinquency are related; thus factors increasing gang cohesiveness, such as group programming, will lead to increased gang recruitment and delinquency (Klein, 1972). This suggests that the detached
street-worker approach should be severely modified or abandoned.

The main problem with this approach, however, is that it is super-
ficial and does not deal with the basic causes of the gang. As soon as
one rides the current wave and calms the symptom, another wave
comprised of younger brothers is on the horizon.

2. **Competitive Sports.** Some researchers believe that the underlying
force in the gang is aggression (Singer, 1971). It would seem logical,
according to this perspective, to channel the aggression into more
positive outlets, such as boxing. Some gang youth prefer boxing over
what they consider to be less masculine team sports such as baseball
and football. The main drawback with this approach is the same as
with the previous approach. That is, it only deals temporarily with
the symptom. It also communicates to the youngster that this is all
he will ever be good for: to beat someone or to be beaten.

3. **The Law Enforcement Approach.** This approach has as its theoretical
basis good versus evil. The gang is seen as evil and hence something
that has to be destroyed. The gang will be harassed and intimidated
by the police, the intent being to discourage the gang members from
associating with each other. They will be frequently arrested for
even minor offenses until there are sufficient arrests to warrant
institutionalization. A special effort is usually made by police,
parole, and probation officers to rid the gang of the "leader," the
theory being that if one takes away the leader of the gang, the
gang--in its confusion--will dissolve. These tactics are rarely, if ever,
successful and might be considered counterproductive as a youngster's
path toward criminalization is accelerated.

4. **Institutionalization.** Gang youth in the barrio are frequently placed in
juvenile detention facilities for their gang behavior. This delinquent
behavior usually involves "joy-riding," curfew, drinking, drugs, and
misdemeanor and felony assault offenses. Chicano gang youth respond very well to the requirements of an institution, and a study by
the author (Morales, 1963) revealed that they hold the highest positions of authority in various probation camps. They are experts at
group processes and often manage to "run" the institution. Following
graduation from an institution, however, most gang members (75
percent) were returned within three months. There was rarely any
carryover of what was learned in camp, and once they returned to the

same oppressive conditions that were a major cause of their initial downfall, old patterns were resumed.

5. **Street Workers.** Street workers attempt to develop close, trusting relationships with gang members and, as their friends, attempt to redirect individual gang members toward socially constructive goals using various community resources. They help them get a job or get back to school. They become their advocate within limits and help them adjust to rather than change their environment. This approach is similar in its limitations to the other approaches in that primary intervention as to the core causes of the problem are rarely, if ever, addressed.

6. **The Community Organization Approach.** The Los Angeles County Department of Community Services' pamphlet recommends that community organization efforts be directed at the basic problems--educational, economic, and cultural--which are the underlying reasons for gangs (Los Angeles County Department of Community Services, 1972). Yet no substantive suggestions for initiating a community organization approach are offered. How is this to be done? Who will do it? It would appear naive to believe that a government agency would attack basic problems that might in any way endanger the status quo. Perhaps this is the reason that the gang as a symptom has continued to exist for over 50 years in the barrio.

7. **The Clinical Approach.** Within the framework of the clinical approach the individual is believed to be a member of the gang because of psychological problems. His delinquent behavior is perceived as a reaction to a combination of physiological, social, and psychological stresses. A typical case might involve "acting out" on the youngster's part because of an inconsistent home environment and anger incited by a strict father. In another case there might be elements of an unresolved Oedipal situation and consequently the boy runs with the gang to ward off feelings of anxiety, unconsciously seeking punishment (i.e., affection) from father figures such as the police for his delinquent behavior. Armed with this formulation, the therapist helps the gang member and his family understand the psychological dynamics of their behavior. Through such understanding, the gang member is supposed to abandon the gang and delinquent behavior, return to his family and begin a new life.

The clinical approach is also limited because it ignores the basic causes of the gang and because it assumes all gang members are psychologically disturbed. This is not to say that a few gang members might not require psychotherapy. But are mental health practitioners clearly able to distinguish between those gang members and their families that require treatment and those that do not? Is the adjudication of a petition by the juvenile court and subsequent referral to a treatment agency of an "involuntary client" the main criteria for treatment? Fischer (1977) found, for example, that deterioration occurred in nearly 50 percent of the involuntary clients referred for treatment. This would represent the **iatrogenic** effects of psychotherapy (Morales and Sheafer, 1977). Mental health practitioners must consider the ethics of administering psychotherapy as a social control function to a gang member and family who may be well-adjusted in relationship to the situation in which they find themselves.

8. **The Psychosocial Awareness Approach.** As a graduate student, the author was taught the clinical approach in the school of social work for dealing with gang members and discovered that, by and large, it was ineffective. Over the years the author has learned about gangs from gang members themselves. They are extremely cohesive units and members have a dedication to each other that often surpasses their commitment to their families. They will actually die or kill for one another. Such powerful cohesion which gang members need for survival in a hostile, racist environment can be positive if, with approval of the gang, it can be directed toward efforts that will improve the barrio. This may be called the psychosocial awareness approach.

Using this approach, the gang first develops an understanding of the different ways in which the gang and the barrio are exploited and oppressed. In order to put this approach into action, social and mental health agencies could initially hire older gang members who would be sensitized socially by the intellectuals and political activists of the barrio. These respected veteran gang members in turn could then go to the gangs in the barrio to work with them. As gang members become aware of the absence of community representation on various boards or agencies that are supposed to serve them, they could direct their efforts toward assuming decision-making positions on these boards or agencies and subsequently have a direct hand in improving their community.

There is a precedent for this approach. In the Woodlawn areas of Chicago in the late 1960s, the Blackstone Rangers, a black gang numbering 1,800 members, were responsible for a 25 percent reduction in crime in their community. This gang was successful in signing treaties with other gangs and, in so doing, helped to prevent riots in their area. As a result of this accomplishment, they were soon thereafter courted by political forces. Of equal if not greater importance is the fact that this gang developed an awareness of their power base which they could use to good ends; in turn, they were able to organize businesses and obtain grants for projects which could benefit the community. Amazingly enough they accomplished these objectives even in the face of an unremitting policy of harassment by a task force of the Chicago Police Department (Dumont, 1968).

A similar phenomenon occurred in numerous barrios throughout the Southwest in the late 1960s and early 1970s. Mexican American gang members of an organization called the Brown Berets politicized their communities, protected them from police harassment, and in some barrios established "free clinics." As psychiatrist Matthew Dumont (1968: 153) has said, "The line between destructive and constructive activism is much finer than the line between activism itself and passivity." Few would disagree that a crucial element of mental health is a sense of environmental mastery, a feeling that some part of the environment, however small, is subject to the control and manipulation of the individual.

This approach does not destroy the gang, but rather changes and redirects its activities and energies toward doing something about its environment. It begins to attack the basic cause of the gang. As the gang participates in political activities, it is no longer participating in activities that are harmful to the gang and/or others in the community and can no longer be defined, therefore, as a "gang."

SUBSTANCE ABUSE

Citing statistics from a 1972 national survey, the second report of the National Commission on Marijuana and Drug Abuse states that inhalation of glue and other vapors such as those from spray paint cans has tended to be a youth phenomenon which, in general, appears to be subsiding (Abelson et al., 1972). A more recent nationwide survey by Response Analysis Corporation (1976) involving 12 to 17 year old subjects reveals that nine-tenths of one percent used inhalants, 12.3 percent used marijuana, and 32.4 percent used alcohol "last month."

The situation among Mexican American barrio youths is several times more serious than the national picture and definitely should be a mental health issue and concern. During the summer of 1976, the author and his colleagues, working with the UCLA Spanish Speaking Mental Health Research Center and Youth Opportunities Unlimited, Inc., conducted a glue and paint sniffing survey among children and adolescents ranging in age from 9 to 17 in five East Los Angeles housing projects. The results of the study revealed that 13.1 percent of respondents had used inhalants "last week" (Padilla et al., 1977). This is almost 13 times higher than the percentage for the national sample. With reference to marijuana, 28.7 percent of the East Los Angeles sample reported it was "used last week," or a little over two times the percentage for the national sample. Had the national sample reported whether the substance was "used last week" as did the local sample, the differences between the two would probably be even greater. The use of alcohol in the local sample, on the other hand, approached the incidence of use in the national sample as follows: "used last month"--28.9 percent versus the national sample's "used last month"--32.4 percent. The "used ever" category was 50.8 percent of the East Los Angeles sample versus 53.6 percent for the national sample.

Generalizing the findings of the study to the nine to 17 year old universe in the housing projects, they would indicate that about 170 children and adolescents had been inhaling glue and spray paint, 373 had been using marijuana, and 376 had been using alcohol within a reported period of "last week." The mental health implications of these findings are enormous.

These is no question that children and adolescents may develop a severe psychological dependence on all of these substances, but in the case of glue and paint sniffing, the habit is dangerous for two reasons. First of all, there is a risk of tissue damage--particularly to the bone marrow, brain, liver and kidneys. Furthermore, death may result from respiratory arrest (Grinspoon, 1975). In 1970, Millard Bass reported 110 hydrocarbon sniffing fatalities in the West Coast (Bass, 1970). Secondly, children and adolescents intoxicated on these solvents appear to be more aggressive and impulsive and at the same time exhibit impaired judgment, a combination which can lead to any number of dangerous and sometimes life-threatening behaviors and activities. Studies have shown that sniffers are uniformly depressed, do not care about brain damage, and want to feel better. The underlying depression of these users is marked. There is no doubt that some of these factors may also be found among child and adolescent users of marijuana and alcohol.

Children and adolescents living in the housing projects using inhalants, marijuana, and alcohol are definitely in need of various social, recreational, and mental health services. It would be totally unrealistic to expect the poorest and largest families in East Los Angeles to conform to a traditional delivery system and travel to a mental health agency for services. Rather, the community-satellite mental health model observed in El Paso and San Antonio should be considered for East Los Angeles. Mental health services will have to be provided in each of the housing projects in East Los Angeles. Failure to do this will not only be inhumane from the standpoint of deaths and the loss of the creative potential and contributions of hundreds of young people in East Los Angeles, but in the long run it will be extremely expensive considering welfare, crime and delinquency, police, and court costs.

Conclusion

Although there is growing evidence that the few mental health facilities which provide culturally-appropriate help are being effectively used by Mexican Americans, there is still a great need to acknowledge and understand that Mexican American mental health needs extend far beyond a traditional case-by-case model of clinical intervention. Community organization and comprehensive planning is still required in order to solve mental health problems generated by police deployment practices related to drinking offenses. Furthermore, because of the all-pervasive effects which riots have on a community, they should also be a community mental health concern. As such it would be helpful if mental health concepts and principles developed for natural disasters were also applied to such manmade disasters such as riots. Techniques must also be developed to reduce conflict between police and minority communities. In addition, mental health practitioners must receive training in order to deal effectively with mental health problems provoked by police-related social conflict.

Until now the police have been the main agency concerned with barrio youth gangs. Most approaches for dealing with gangs are not working, and in fact the prevalence of gangs continues to increase. From all perspectives, it is apparent that mental health agencies have a responsibility in dealing with this problem area especially with respect to the development of effective methods of working with gang members. Likewise, the incidence and prevalence of inhalant, marijuana, and alcohol abuse by Mexican American children and adolescents provide further evidence of the need for developing nontraditional mental health programs which would entail a comprehensive plan focused on a variety of social, recreational, and mental health services.

Finally, the problems identified in this paper and the accompanying recommendations will require a new, pioneering breed of mental health practitioners and agencies not bound by rigid, traditional models of clinical practice. Schools of psychiatry, psychology, and social work are faced with the necessity of making their training more relevant to minority mental health needs and realities. Otherwise, they will continue to produce mental health practitioners who are primarily trained to meet the mental health needs of the white middle class. As it stands, therefore, the challenge is to provide nontraditional mental health practitioners and services which can effectively meet the diverse mental health needs of the Mexican American.

References

Abelson, H., Cohen, R., Schrayer, D., and Rappaport, M. "Drug Experience, Attitudes, and Related Behavior Among Adolescents," in National Commission on Drug Abuse (eds.), **The Technical Papers of the Second Report, Vol. I.** Washington, DC: U.S. Government Printing Office, 1972.

Bass, M. "Sudden Sniffing Death," **Journal of the American Medical Association** 12 (1970), 2075-2079.

Burruel, G., and Chavez, N. "Mental Health Outpatient Centers: Relevant or Irrelevant to Mexican Americans," in A.B. Tulipan, C.L. Attneave, and E. Kingstone (eds.), **Beyond Clinic Walls.** University, AL: University of Alabama Press, 1974.

Dumont, M.P. **The Absurd Image.** New York: The Viking Press, 1968.

Fischer, J. "Is Casework Effective? A Review," in A. Morales, and B.W. Sheafor (eds.), **Social Work: A Profession of Many Faces.** Boston: Allyn and Bacon, 1977.

Friedman, S., and Esselstyn, T.C. "The Adjustment of Children of Jail Inmates," **Federal Probation** 29 (1965), 59.

Grinspoon, L. "Drug Dependence: Non-Narcotic Agents," in A.M. Freedman, H.L. Kaplan, and B.J. Sadock (eds.), **Comprehensive Textbook of Psychiatry.** Baltimore: Williams & Wilkins, Co., 1975.

Hollingshead, A.B., and Redlich, F.C. **Social Class and Mental Illness.** New York: John Wiley & Sons, Inc., 1958.

Karno, M., and Edgerton, R.B. "Perception of Mental Illness in a Mexican American Community," **Archives of General Psychiatry** 20 (1969), 233-238.

Keefe, S., Padilla, A., and Carlos, M. "The Mexican American Extended Family as an Emotional Support System," in J. Casas and S. Keefe (eds.), **Family and Mental Health in the Mexican American Community.** Los Angeles: Spanish Speaking Mental Health Research Center, 1978.

Keefe, S. "Why Mexican Americans Underutilize Mental Health Clinics: Fact and Fallacy," in J. Casas and S. Keefe (eds.), **Family and Mental Health in the Mexican American Community.** Los Angeles: Spanish Speaking Mental Health Research Center, 1978.

Klein, M.W. **Street Gangs and Street Workers.** Englewood Cliffs, NJ: Prentice-Hall, Inc., 1972.

"LAPD Begins Training to Quell Possible Food Riots," **Los Angeles Times,** January 23, 1975, Part I, pp. 1; 30.

Los Angeles County Department of Community Services. **A Program to Combat Gang Problems in Los Angeles County.** Los Angeles: LAPD Department of Community Services, 1972.

Morales, A. **A Study of Recidivism of Mexican American Junior Forestry Camp Graduates.** Unpublished master's thesis, University of Southern California School of Social Work, 1963.

_____. **Ando Sangrando (I Am Bleeding): A Study of Mexican American-Police Conflict.** La Puenta, CA: Perspective Publications, 1972a.

_____. **A Study of Mexican American Perspectives of Selected Law Enforcement Policies and Practice in East Los Angeles.** Unpublished doctoral dissertation, University of Southern California School of Social Work, 1972b.

Morales, A., and Sheafor, B.W. **Social Work: A Profession of Many Faces.** Boston: Allyn and Bacon, 1977.

National Commission on the Causes and Prevention of Violence. **The Progress Report of the National Commission on the Causes and Prevention of Violence to President Lyndon B. Johnson.** Washington, DC: U.S. Government Printing Office, 1969.

Newton, F. "The Mexican American Emic System of Mental Illness: An Exploratory Study," in J. Casas and S. Keefe (eds.), **Family and Mental**

Health in the Mexican American Community. Los Angeles: Spanish Speaking Mental Health Research Center, 1978.

Padilla, E., Padilla, A., Ramirez, R., Morales, A., and Omedo,E. **Inhalant, Marijuana and Alcohol Abuse Among Barrio Children and Adolescents.** Occasional Paper #4. Los Angeles: Spanish Speaking Mental Health Research Center, 1977.

Response Analysis Corporation. **Nonmedical Use of Psychoactive Substances.** Research report prepared for the National Institute of Drug Abuse. Princeton, NJ: Response Analysis Corporation, 1976.

Singer, J. **The Control of Aggression and Violence.** New York: Academic Press, 1971.

Srole, L., Langer, T.S., Michael, S., Opler, M.K., and Rennie, T.A.C. **Mental Health in the Metropolis: The Midtown Manhattan Study. Vol. 1.** New York: McGraw-Hill, 1962.

United States Commission on Civil Rights. **Mexican Americans and the Administration of Justice in the Southwest.** Washington, DC: U.S. Government Printing Office, 1970.

Wallach, I., and Carter, C. **Perceptions of the Police in the Black Community.** McLean, VA: Research Analysis Corporation, 1971.

Yamamoto, J. (Director of the Los Angeles County-USC Medical Center Psychiatric Outpatient Department). Personal communication, February 17, 1977.

TRYING TO MAKE IT REAL: ISSUES AND CONCERNS IN THE PROVISION OF SERVICES FOR MINORITIES

JUNE JACKSON CHRISTMAS

To acknowledge the complex interrelations among the social environment, interpersonal relationships, and the inner emotions of individuals who happen to be members of racial and ethnic minorities, it is necessary to be aware of certain factors which are significant in their lives. These factors include the historical determinants of present-day minority life, the social reality of that life, and the psychological effects of poverty, segregation, discrimination, and deprivation--conditions imposed by the majority upon minorities. Awareness of these factors helps direct attention to the totality of the life situation of minorities.

This paper will not attempt to deal in depth with the varieties of individual and group experiences both among and within minority groups. Their past histories are too varied, and their current lives have their own group-specificity. The historical determinants of the lives of minorities in this country still influence them today, for example: the near-annihilation of Native Americans and their restriction to reservations; the exclusionary immigration practices against Asians and the all too recent herding of Japanese Americans into concentration camps; the past and present colonial mentality directed toward Hispanic Americans; and the inhumanity of 300 years of slavery and its vestiges (e.g., lynching, Jim Crow, and **de facto** segregation) imposed upon Afro-Americans. The characteristics of present-day life differ, not only from group to group, but within each of these peoples, for example: the varieties of Indian tribal life and the differences between Native Americans in cities, rural areas, and on reservations; the dissimilar backgrounds of Hispanic Americans, depending upon their place of origin in Mexico, Puerto Rico, other parts of the Caribbean or South America; the cultural and racial differences among Spanish-speaking people, depending upon the degree to which their roots are African, Indian and/or European; the great social and economic differences among Afro-Americans and the cultural differences between Blacks of Latin, West Indian, or continental United States background; and the differences in national origin among Asians from Japan, China, India and, more recently, the Pacific Islands, and the differences in philosophy between Asians who are old immigrants and those who are new.

Yet, there are commonalities which are present, with certain notable exceptions, among most members of these minority groups. As colored peoples they have experienced the racism, discrimination, and prejudice of past and present life in the United States. The attitudes and behaviors which characterize racism have in recent years no longer been accepted with suppressed anger but have been turned against the aggressor, most

constructively in civil rights activism. With the awakening of consciousness in these groups, their pride as minorities has become a tool for change,
and they have pointed to their past traditions and their cultures as evidence
of their strength for survival and as an opportunity to enhance the richness
of American life.

On the other hand, minority groups share the common experience of
being relatively powerless, politically weak, and overrepresented among the
poor, the undereducated, and those in poor health. For some, alcoholism,
drug abuse, and psychiatric illness are commonly expected. With few
exceptions, minority groups do not have the mental health resources available in the quantity or quality that they are available to members of the
dominant society. With few exceptions, they have not had the access to
higher education that would produce mental health professionals; those
professionals who do exist generally do not serve their own communities.
The mental health services to which minorities have turned are fragmented, uncoordinated, and often inappropriate for their needs. Barriers to
utilization exist, and control is generally in the hands of the white majority
for whom those services were developed.

Thus to describe those characteristics of comprehensive services appropriate to meet the needs of minorities, this paper will discuss certain
features which are considered applicable to **most** members of these minorities rather than focusing on the individual variations of service best suited
for each group. For many years minorities were the forgotten men and
women of the mental health literature. Even today it is difficult to find
articles that deal in any depth with these groups. Not only does that literature not refer to minorities to any great extent, but it also tends to be
descriptive rather than analytic and to not report efforts to evaluate the
efficacy or effectiveness of comparative approaches to service.

This paper will discuss six features which should characterize appropriate mental hygiene services for minorities: cultural relevance, a holistic
orientation, an organizational structure that supports coordination, priority
attention to certain target groups, the use of community support systems,
and minority involvement in decision-making, accountability, and quality
assurance. Recommendations will follow the presentation of each feature. The overarching concern for a second financial base will be discussed
in closing.

Cultural Relevance

Racial and ethnic differences have generally been overlooked, denied, or
used to justify discriminatory acts on the part of the dominant majority
(Christmas, 1977a). Since racial pluralism and ethnic diversity are persistent and real factors in American life, mental health and other human
services should not only acknowledge racial and ethnic characteristics but
also become sensitive to them in a positive way that builds appropriately
upon this diversity. This implies biculturalism and sensitivity to the cultur-

al dimensions of groups--their lifestyles, language, and interactional patterns (Bullough, 1972; Knoll, 1971; Martinez, 1973).

The need for cultural relevance and the development of services which
take into account race and ethnicity are of particular significance. Specific social and cultural mores, ethnic group values, and varied familial
patterns are among the aspects of culture-specific services which ought to
be addressed in program design and operation. This means that programs
must not only be in but of a particular group. They must take into account
the values that a particular groups holds--the way it defines health and
illness, who its caretakers are, who it turns to in time of trouble. Programs
must consider, for example, that behaviors such as heavy drinking may be
culturally syntonic but the complications that result from these acts, while
destructive, may not necessarily be recognized as related to the value
system which a group holds. This example is cited particularly in regard to
the heavy drinking among Blacks and the difficulties in the Black community of acknowledging heavy drinking as a symptom of alcohol dependency
rather than solely as a social custom.

When social factors are taken into consideration this should not occur in
a way which tends to devalue them per se. On the other hand the connec-
tion must be made between reliance upon alcohol in its utilitarian role--or
the reliance primarily on corporal punishment of children as a means of
discipline or the shame of admitting mental illness--and the possibility of
problems. Each of these culturally acceptable behaviors may lead to
difficulties.

Culture-specific models of service delivery should be developed which
integrate the positive, constructive values of traditional helpers into the
more conventional treatment modalities with appropriate modifications to
meet the needs of minorities. Drawing upon traditional medicine men or
women of Indian peoples, the curanderos of Hispanic communities, and the
healers in Black neighborhoods in a way that allows them to complement
Western approaches to health and mental health services may increase the
utilization of services by minorities who customarily turn to these helpers
(Belcourt, 1977).

The subject of culture and the need for biculturalism become particularly important when related to the need for bilingualism. It is not enough to
have intake staff who are bilingual and able to interpret for a new immigrant in his or her particular language or dialect. It is essential to have
services, particularly in the "talking therapies," that are conducted in the
language in which clients are versed, comfortable, and able to express
feelings, ideas, and wishes. Communication is an essential vehicle particularly in counseling services for emotional problems (Sue and McKinney,
1974).

Beyond this is the need for actional, group counseling, and group therapy
approaches conducted in the language and style of particular minority
groups. These may be more feasible when coupled with the creative use of
minority professional and paraprofessional staff. The use of group approaches with multiple interdisciplinary team leaders, composed of some

persons who understand the culture of the clients, not only assists the clients to participate more actively but may also be a vehicle for broadening the cultural awareness of the nonminority team professionals. (The shortage of minority professionals should not doom minorities to continue to wait without services until this inequity can be redressed, nor should it be assumed that nonminority staff can play no role in the provision of services to minorities. Yet the importance of knowledgeable minority staff in service and in leadership positions can enhance the cultural relevance of programs, provide role models, and increase the understanding of nonminority personnel.)

When there are large numbers of minority persons, it is possible to design services that are characterized by the cultural practices of a particular group and to provide those services within the ethnic community on a geographic base for a defined population. But this is not so likely in those situations where smaller numbers of minority persons live--on the edge of or in the midst of communities where services are developed for a predominantly white majority (Ho, 1976; Huang, 1977; Kitano, 1973). In those instances, culturally relevant services may have to be developed on a regional basis with services shared by several catchment areas.

There is another element to cultural relevance based on the fact that minority groups live within a wider majority society which significantly influences their lives. The force with the greatest impact upon minorities is the existence of racism with its negative effects on growth and development and its restrictions on the ability of individuals and groups to function fully and constructively in society. From a consideration of the social and economic factors that racism, discrimination, and prejudice impose upon minorities and from a consideration of their responses to such oppression come efforts to develop program settings which include ways of coping constructively with these stresses. Thus additional recognition is given to the need to appropriately incorporate social action to deal with oppression, socioeconomic discrimination, and the triple jeopardy imposed when one is mentally disabled and economically deprived, as well as a member of a minority in a racist society.

RECOMMENDATIONS

1.   The rights of minority patients in health, mental health, alcoholism and drug abuse programs should be duly recognized, particularly as they relate to their unique cultural, linguistic, and ethnic characteristics and to their historical and life experiences.

2.   Mental health policies should contain specific provisions which acknowledge the unique cultures, languages, and lifestyles (including immigration experiences) of minorities and reflect the cutural, racial, and ethnic differences among minorities.

3.   Culture-specific and relevant models of service delivery should be developed and implemented which integrate traditional or folk medicine, values, and support systems of minorities with conventional treatment and rehabilitation modalities.

4. Agencies must hire minority bilingual/bicultural staff at the service, support, administrative, management, planning, and supervisory levels.

5. Indigenous paraprofessionals from minority communities should be accepted for training, employment, and upgrading in the mental hygiene field with career ladders and lattices for upward and lateral mobility. Recognition should be given to traditional healers, medicine men and women, and other folk healers as helpers for those with emotional, mental, and physical disorders.

6. Mechanisms for reimbursement for health and mental health services (e.g., national health insurance, Medicare, Medicaid, etc.) must include culturally traditional forms of assistance.

7. Research funds should be allocated for the purpose of demonstrating the effectiveness of traditional medicine as a part of comprehensive programs of treatment and prevention.

8. The Federal government should give direction to training programs so that they develop curricula that will produce professionals who recognize, understand, and utilize the dynamics of individual and institutional racism and who are sensitive to and knowledgeable about the varieties of culture and ethnicity.

9. Local, state and Federal agencies should develop and implement mental health training programs that provide learning environments and curricula congruent with the various cultures and mental health needs of minority Americans.

10. Training funds specifically designated for the development of minority mental hygiene paraprofessionals and professionals to serve minority communities (and other communities) must be increased.

11. Mental health training programs must be established that will provide for the teaching of cultural differences and the psychology of minority men and women from a positive frame of reference.

12. Educational programs for nonminority mental hygiene service providers must be required in all areas that serve minority American clientele in order to increase knowledge and sensitivity to those clients.

13. Accreditation agencies for service and training should be mandated to include in their evaluation reviews the quality and quantity of recognition of and responsiveness to cultural factors in regard to minority populations.

The Holistic Approach to Service

In the holistic orientation, an individual is seen not as an isolated entity separated from society or living within a vacuum but as a human being related to other individuals and interacting with family and society. The whole person is the subject of consideration and programs must address the human totality. From this point of view, a psychosocial approach is developed which takes into account psychological, social, and behavioral referents. The interrelationships of these referents are particularly significant for persons who occupy positions of low or marginal social status, who experience continuing deprivation, or who occupy a devalued social position as do members of racial or ethnic minorities. The usual therapeutic interventions directed separately at individual psychiatric or social conditions or individual conditions of health or disease without multiple coordinated and sustained efforts are of reduced effectiveness (Christmas, 1972).

Persons who suffer the disadvantages of poverty, discrimination, and mental illness need to cope not only with the symptoms and effects of mental disorders but with environmental stresses as well. Appropriate and effective services should recognize the significant transactions between the individual and the environment. These services are directed not only at individual pathology but toward individual and group strength, not only toward easing inner tensions but toward coping with environmental stresses that may themselves have been among the determinants of illness.

In the holistic approach, the goals go beyond restoring a previous state of equilibrium, handling symptomatology, or dealing solely with reality problems. They encompass helping an individual achieve his or her own potential, improve social functioning, and relate more effectively to the familial and social environment. The holistic approach seeks to develop innovative measures that not only strengthen integrative intrapsychic and interpersonal forces but also circumvent and alter external forces which impinge upon the lives of individuals and groups. The approach further seeks to encourage the development of competence and power by persons who have been denied these attributes by virtue of factors such as psychiatric labeling, race, and social or economic position (Cameron and Talavera, 1976).

In the holistic approach, emphasis is placed on prevention, on mobilizing the potential for health, strength, and drives toward growth, autonomy, and self-actualization. This emphasis is based on the fact that human beings grow, change, and develop under manifold circumstances. The ability of most minority people to survive the stresses of life in a racist society is striking. Psychosocial strategies--addressed to the strengths and resources of persons living with both success and failure and under conditions of chronic poverty, discrimination, and societal rejection--may result in their functioning more effectively and with greater effectiveness if these strategies are utilized as change efforts. In addition the knowledge acquired from observations of individuals and groups striving toward social articulation within a society which has rejected them because of their race, social class, physical handicap, or psychiatric diagnosis can contribute to an understanding of the developmental tasks occurring at critical stages of life and of the transactional relationships between human beings and the environment.

Recognition is given here to the existence of racism, economic inequities, and prejudice and discrimination in the lives of most minorities. Institutionalized racism is one of the social factors that must be taken into account in the content of services. Thus the line is not always clearly drawn between socio-therapeutic interventions and social action. Service directed toward changing and improving the individual and familial situation are related to those directed toward social change (Lightfoot, 1970).

The holistic orientation implies that the interconnections between the psychological, social, economic, and interpersonal aspects of the life of an individual or a family must be dealt with in ways that are appropriate to them. Acknowledgement is given to psychodynamics in regard to intrapersonal conflicts but, at the same time, greater attention is paid to interpersonal and societal factors. A coordinated total service approach with a multifocused range of services is interdisciplinary in its staffing (when part of a formal program) or it addresses multiple needs through linkages among varied programs. Continuity of service and care are critical in providing comprehensiveness.

The concept of empowerment of individuals and groups serves to provide the link between this orientation and the creative use of community institutions as social supports. Whereas social science has generally considered minorities from the vantage point of superiority-inferiority and has developed concepts based on a model of deficiency, the holistic approach looks for the strengths within the individual, the family, and significantly in the minority group. The recognition of strengths addresses the fact that minorities have within their social structures and histories abilities to not only survive societal pressures and oppression but to develop coping mechanisms which might well be adapted to social and therapeutic situations (McAdoo, 1977).

From the holistic viewpoint emerges the further idea that minority persons who have themselves functioned with some degree of success may engage in helping transactions with those more damaged or less successful in their functioning (Taber, 1970). Experience has shown that trained paraprofessional mental health personnel recruited from the local minority community can provide an added dimension to the services delivered by professionals. The development of such new roles and the related modifications in services may lead to improvements in the nature and quality of services. Moreover the use of a previously untapped human resource may contribute to the solution of the minority manpower shortage. Beyond these factors, there exists another basis for using human service workers drawn from the ranks of the minority disadvantaged--the use of the product of a social problem to cope with, alter, and resolve that problem.

RECOMMENDATIONS

1. Preventative services in mental health programs must be an integral component of a range of mental health planning, services, and research.

2. Federal, state and local mental health programs should be flexible to allow and encourage the implementation of innovative models of

service delivery appropriate to the needs of minorities in different settings.

3.   Research funds should be made available to encourage and support innovative service delivery approaches and their evaluation.

4.   Human services should be delivered to minorities in available and accessible multiservice centers providing acceptable health, mental health, social welfare, educational, economic, and legal services based upon the context of the minority family and community.

5.   Family resource centers should be developed to include systematic comprehensive family support services as part of a national urban policy.   State and local health and welfare policies should support such centers.

6.   Minority staff should be employed in sufficient numbers and assigned so as to maximize their visibility and influence upon the service delivery system.

7.   In areas where there are large numbers of minority individuals, programs should be designed to provide specialized services to those minorities needing bilingual/bicultural services (with appropriate staff).

8.   Priority should be given to funding the development of innovative social and residential programs in minority communities as alternatives to traditional medical institutions providing mental health services.

9.   Funding and policy should encourage the development and evaluation of alternative mental health service delivery models for community social institutions, self-help groups, neighborhood service programs, and "school-as-community" programs.

10.   A clearinghouse should be established for information on promising model programs so that minority communities can benefit from the experiences of other similar communities.

11.   A technical assistance program to consult with community groups that wish to start mental hygiene programs should be established and staffed by knowledgeable professional staff.

Organization for Coordination and Linkages

From the holistic orientation emerges the view that creative use should be made of community-based programs and the transactional relationships between individuals, families, and the community to enhance, support, and assist the processes of growth, recovery, or rehabilitation. In this view, the stresses of the social environment can be used to aid individuals and groups in developing techniques of mastery, strengthening effective coping mechanisms and acquiring social learning, and altering one or more of the social systems in which they participate. Thus the harsh realities of economic and social stress are not viewed simply as interferences to be eliminated so that orthodox treatment or rehabilitation can take place; they are, rather, significant aspects of the lives of people, aspects to be understood and dealt with as forces for growth. Indeed, the helping process should be considered as necessarily including involvement in learning to deal with the environment, altering the damaging aspects of reality, reinforcing the strengths of individual groups, and enhancing social networks.

This implies the need for coordination with other health and human service organizations and the development of services that are accessible and available to individuals. Access is defined not only as physical access but as the creation of an atmosphere which makes a program inviting to an individual or group and in fact reaches out to bring that person or group in. Cultural relevance becomes important when certain subtle or overt signs are given to minority groups that they are not wanted, for instance, by the location of the program, the hours a particular service is offered, the physical structure, or the lack of minority persons in positions of power and/or visibility. Availability includes the idea that services are not only offered but that they are economically and financially within the reach of the minority individual.

The concept of comprehensiveness includes not only the provision of services that deal with the social, economic, and cultural factors referred to above, but the importance of effective linkages with other human services. This integration can take many forms. Contracting to minority community-based organizations for the delivery of services wherever they exist is one model. Another is the integration of existing services such as mental health with other community services which have more widespread acceptance such as youth programs, family and child care services, senior citizen centers, and social clubs. There are two relevant general approaches, each with its advocates. One approach is that mental health and alcoholism services should be offered in specialized kinds of settings (community mental health centers, alcoholism treatment centers) with linkages to other human services such as education, employment, and social services. This approach is based on the need for a high degree of internal specialization. The other view is that the stigma of receiving services for mental disabilities is so great that it may be better to provide these services within the general health care system (Bullattee, 1972) or, alternatively, within the general human service system (in social welfare agencies) or the educational system. There is no evidence to suggest that either approach has an advantage over the other. However, in those communities where numerous organizations, civic associations, lodges, and clubs abound, few linkages may exist to service programs for persons with mental disabilities and substance abuse problems. Nevertheless, there is a base to build upon where coordination and linkages could exist and where easier access to services could come about if action were taken to arouse the interest of community organizations and leadership.

It is apparent that human service agencies are not themselves coordinated and that the services with which people have to deal are frequently provided under a multiplicity of auspices by agencies whose staff rarely talk to one another. Not only does fragmentation exist in the service system but individuals are forced to move from one agency to another to maneuver in a service system without having a sense of the whole. In the prime of the New Careers movement, paraprofessionals played the linking, expediting role quite effectively long before the term "case manager" became chic. Indeed, the case manager role was well played by paraprofessionals from minority communities during the heyday of the War on Poverty. Although used extensively in the rehabilitation services provided at the Harlem Rehabilitation Center (Christmas and Daniels, 1978), the community worker/expediter role seems to have vanished in many instances--a victim of fashion in mental health and a lack of Federal funding.

An alternative approach for the integration of services can be seen in the development of interagency coordinating councils. But this requires the presence of several programs, some of which may not be as acquainted with the needs of minorities as others. The danger here is that the agencies and their new superstructure might become another bureaucracy rather than an aid to individuals maneuvering through the service system.

RECOMMENDATIONS

1.   There should be flexibility in the organizational arrangements for the provision of services so that coordination, availability, and accessibility can be fostered in a service system that takes into account minority sociocultural characteristics in staffing and programming.

2.   Programs designed to provide human services to minority Americans should provide for closer liaison with mental health service delivery systems and personnel.

3.   Liaisons should be established between community organizations and mental health services.

4.   Contracting with minority community-based organizations for the delivery of services should be encouraged.

5.   Integration of existing mental health services with other community services (such as youth services, family services, services to children, services to the aged, services for developmentally disabled, etc.) should be one model that is developed and evaluated.

6.   Mental health services should be made available, as an alternative model, within the context of primary health care programs so that no illness is so radically different that "special" isolation is necessary.

7.   Aftercare and rehabilitation programs should be developed and implemented within the context of comprehensive human services that coordinate community resources to provide social and cultural support throughout the rehabilitation period.

8.   Administrative, program, and fiscal arrangements must be made to

allow minorities who are few in number in an area to be served across catchment boundaries when appropriate services do not exist in their own catchment areas. In catchment areas with small populations two or more areas should pool resources whenever feasible.

Priority Attention to Target Populations

Although minorities on the whole are served poorly or inappropriately by human services, some segments are especially at risk, including children and youth, the elderly, and women. Similarly, there are certain problems and disorders among minorities which warrant special attention (La Vietes, 1974; Harper, 1976; McNickle, 1968). The overrepresentation of minorities in state psychiatric hospitals reflects the failure to apply known rehabilitation techniques to minorities. Suicide and alcoholism among Indians; alcoholism among Mexican Americans; and alcoholism, homicide, and suicide among young Black males are tragic indicators of the lack of successful intervention to alter self-destructive behavior (Faulkner, 1975; Paine, 1977; Resnik, 1971; Shore, 1972). While overall policy should be directed toward the minority population at large, these target groups and problems require the priority attention.

RECOMMENDATIONS

1.   Priority attention should be given to the needs of minority children through national policy and through the funding of services, training, and research directed toward helping them cope with the damage caused by poverty, malnutrition, and poor education.

2.   It is imperative for human service workers along with minority youth to plan--with governmental leadership, support, and financial assistance--programs of prevention, treatment, and rehabilitation for the mental health problems of minority adolescents and for their integration into socially constructive work, school, and family roles.

3.   Special attention needs to be paid to the unique role of minority women, their contributions to the improved mental health of minority people, and the stressful life situations in which they find themselves.   The particular sociocultural stresses faced by minority women should be studied and the findings used to develop and implement counseling programs and other interventions designed to prevent emotional disorders and to build upon their coping skills.

4.   Monies should be granted for the development of alcoholism and drug abuse treatment centers for minorities which take into account the breadth of age, sex, and cultural diversity within these groups.

5.   The needs of the minority elderly warrant special attention through Federal, state and local programs.   Minority elderly should participate in decision-making roles in such programs.

6. Mental health services to minorities who are incarcerated in local, state, and Federal institutions should be developed. The Justice Department and the Federal Bureau of Prisons must assume leadership in developing guidelines for health and mental health care in correctional institutions and for minimum standards of health and safety. Public and private rehabilitation programs for ex-prisoners should include mental health components among their services.

7. Federal policy should give priority to the rehabilitation of the chronically disabled. The Federal government should insure that specific plans for deinstitutionalization are developed and implemented.

8. Deinstitutionalization plans should clearly provide for the retaining of state hospital personnel with detailed means for dealing with seniority rights and the establishment of career ladders and lattices to insure upward and lateral mobility upon retraining for new careers more appropriate to the delivery of community-based services.

9. Current sociopsychiatric rehabilitation techniques should continue to be developed and utilized. Federal funds have previously gone into developing pilot programs to train service providers in these techniques; such programs should be expanded throughout the country.

10. The Federal government should take the leadership in developing funding and program development mechanisms which would encompass all the separate systems needed to sustain the chronically mentally disabled in the community. This would mean bringing together, with an emphasis on deinstitutionalization, such Federal agencies as the Department of Labor, the Department of Housing and Urban Development, the Rehabilitation Services Administration, and the various Department of Health and Human Services agencies related to social services, mental health, developmental disabilities, and education for the handicapped. The Federal government should encourage models in which the multiple needs of the mentally disabled could be addressed through funds provided by various agencies.

Community Support Systems

If service programs are judged not to be helpful to minorities, this may occur in part because programs do not address themselves to the settings in which minorities find themselves. To be effective, services have to take into account group cultures, priority needs, and the use of existing community support systems (Sotomayor, 1971; Sue, 1977).

A social support system has been defined as a means of continuing interaction among individuals which provides ways that a person may know that he or she is cared for and loved, esteemed, and a member of a network of mutual obligations. These three critical functions which community support systems may potentially fulfill relate to basic social needs for trust, nurturance, and intimacy (i.e., emotional support); a sense of being valued by others (i.e., esteem support); and a sense of belonging to a community and being part of a group in which there are shared values, interests, and obligations. In the past, many of these needs were met by the support system of the nuclear or extended family. The pressures of urbanization and other factors have contributed to a decreased ability to rely upon the family or even neighbors and friends for these supports. But social support remains necessary to aid individuals with coping processes and in dealing with critical life transitions (Christmas, 1977c). Thus, social supports may have to come, to a greater degree than in the past, from community institutions to which people have traditionally turned for guidance, strength and comfort--organized religion, the health care system, and the community caretakers whose personal talents and empathy mark them as a source of solace or assistance.

Increased knowledge of the interrelationships between social and environmental stresses and physical and mental illness has led to the creation of preventive approaches to enhance personality development and mental health. Here, community support systems have a vital role to play, particularly as human services are called upon to move away from an overemphasis on and preoccupation with the "sickness model" and treatment to the much needed areas of prevention and rehabilitation.

This leads to the second area of innovation in which community support systems can contribute. The chronically mentally disabled have been among the expendables of society. They are fast being joined by others for whom mental health and other human services have failed: children going through the harrowing experience of learning to be criminals in the juvenile justice system; abusers and child and adult abuse victims; the discarded and neglected elderly; and the alienated, underemployed, and rejected racial minorities. For these populations, the functions of social support systems related to improving adaptive competence (i.e., dealing with critical life transitions and with long term challenges and stresses) can be called into play in the service of rehabilitation. Community support systems can also contribute to a sense of well-being and competent functioning and thus be preventive. They can aid in reducing the negative consequences of stressful life events and thus connect treatment and rehabilitation with prevention. They can provide the ongoing source of skills in living and interpersonal relationships so needed by the chronically mentally ill in the course of rehabilitation (Christmas, 1969). By building on constructive social institutions, support systems help to identify the strengths of minorities including the survival skills they have developed over time to cope. This approach can foster the collection of potentially useful information for the helping professions (Thorton, 1975; Tuck, 1971).

Three theoretical principles underlying community mental health are relevant here. The first is that of the promotion of health as opposed to the remediation of disease. Support systems can help develop coping, mastery, and problem solving skills. The second principle is that services are directed toward populations at risk. The third principle is a commitment to use all resources within various localities rather than focusing only on professional clinical services. The emphasis here is to help people where they are--whether at home, school, work, or neighborhood--or where they turn for help. This emphasis should assist in breaking down barriers to help because it also implies drawing upon whatever culturally appropriate institutions exist and in seeing how they could contribute to social support.

Another underlying principle relevant here is that of helping people to help themselves. This is based on the idea that coping efforts are strengthened by helping relationships in which the mutuality of the support process results in the helper being helped. Helping people where they are and assisting them to help themselves allows their entry into the help-giving and receiving system without requiring that they be labelled as "patients" or as "sick." This may help with the significant problem of stigmatization as a barrier to care.

There is a personal gain for people as they help themselves and decrease their sense of powerlessness and thus enhance their mutual help through a greater sense of competence and greater actuality of control. Building on natural strengths not only with individuals but within community networks and institutions will mean helping those institutions discover their unused resources and make appropriate linkages with those who need these resources.

Even if they were desirable, professional mental health services would be able to cope with only a small number of the people who have immediate pressing psychological disorders. Thus the above approach can help complement and supplement clinical services that aim to reduce socially induced stress.

Among the approaches with great potential are those related to self-help. But there is also an opportunity to revive the New Careers movement and to see how indigenous community leadership can be used not only in clinical mental health services but in new community services which minority neighborhoods so strongly need (Gullattee, 1972).

RECOMMENDATIONS

1. Services should be delivered within the context of a minority group's own definition of its community.

2. Funding should be made available to settings that are part of a minority community's natural support systems.

3. Comprehensive support services must be available in order to adequately implement mental health programs.

4. A flexible public housing policy should be instituted that would permit and encourage extended family households.

5. Viable alternatives to schools as they now exist must be established for minority youth in addition to a reorganization of educational systems that fail to achieve their socially designated missions. Reorganization would include the creation of governing structures that involve administrators, parents, teachers, and children in decision-making.

6. Efforts should be addressed to the education of teachers serving in minority communities. Teachers need to understand "problem" behavior as lags in social and psychological development capable of being modified. Minority children need to have successful experiences in school as a deterrent to dysfunctional social behavior.

7. Action-oriented research must be supported to assess the strengths and survival strategies of minorities and to determine ways and means of fostering the development and support of these assets.

8. Coping skills that have enabled minority group children and adults to survive should be understood and this knowledge applied to programs of human development.

9. Consultations and educational programs, sponsored by community mental health agencies, should be established for minority group service providers and community organizations.

10. Preventive programs of consultation and education should be established and expanded which would impart bilingual/bicultural mental hygiene information to minority families, individuals, community organizations, and service providers.

11. Bilingual/bicultural mental health education programs should receive high priority at the local, state, and Federal levels. Such programs should be planned and implemented by minority group members to insure their relevance and sensitivity.

12. Training funds should be specifically designated to deal with the special needs of the minority American with developmental needs in order to train more bilingual/bicultural staff and support the growth of consumer and self-help groups.

Minority Participation, Accountability,
and Quality Assurance

If programs are to be developed which are culture-specific, address the needs of minorities in a holistic framework with linkages to other human services, and build upon the autonomy and growth-enhancing and empowering abilities of natural support systems within local communities, then there must be a foundation of participation by minorities in the conception, planning, delivery, and evaluation of these services. The literature suggests that this type of participation has not previously taken place. Several specific examples may be cited.

The Health Systems Agencies (HSAs) created by the National Planning and Resource Development Act have inequitable patterns of minority group representation. In large cities such as New York with sizable Hispanic and Asian American populations, the representation of these particular groups on policy-making boards is minimal; the representation of other minorities including Blacks remains grossly inadequate while Native Americans are virtually ignored (Kalish and Moriwaki, 1973). The HSAs have a vital role to play in determining the direction of the health care delivery system through relationships established with organizations responsible for planning mental health services. It is essential that they include minority group participation.

One critical area that has to be given attention is the role of state psychiatric hospitals in the future provision of community mental health services as the trend toward deinstitutionalization continues across the nation. Since, with the exception of Japanese Americans, minorities are overrepresented in state hospitals, consideration of the role of these institutions ought to involve minorities along with others. Thus there needs to be greater involvement of minorities on state hospital planning and policy setting bodies as well as local and state government boards, hospital advisory bodies, and community mental health center governing boards.

To finance and deliver services requires not only policies set at the national and state levels but also their implementation at the county and local levels. Here as well there is an underrepresentation of minorities. This situation prevails in many programs even in areas of direct service. In spite of the fact that it became fashionable in the 1960s under the guise of the New Careers movement to train minorities for mental hygiene work, with the decrease in Federal funds and the lack of emphasis on the New Careers movement, many minority group persons find themselves out of work. The roles that a minority paraprofessional New Careerist could play would add to the expediting of services and the enhancement of therapy. Well-trained paraprofessionals can not only be helpful to minority group clients in service programs but they may also allow the more efficent use of professional staff for consultation and administration. The effectiveness of this approach is dependent upon the skill, training, and appropriate deployment of both professional and paraprofessional staff according to client/patient needs. For programs which see paraprofessionals as a "cheap" source of labor, the quality of service provided may well be low. There should certainly not be an automatic assignment of paraprofessionals to minority patients; nor on the other hand should there be an assumption that white, middle-class professionals lacking a holistic approach and knowledge of a particular minority community must be better by virtue of their professional educations.

For minorities a serious concern is the shrinking Federal commitment to funding for professional as well as paraprofessional training. With the decrease in funding for professionals in psychiatry and other professions the problems that derive from past and current racial discrimination still remain. For instance, there are too few professionals of Native American, Hispanic American and Afro-American background. Even for Asians, among whom there are a relatively large number of certain types of health professionals, the majority of those who have been educated and trained are not Asian Americans from this country nor are they serving Asian American communities (Berk and Hirata, 1973).

The need of minorities to be involved as program staff is accompanied by their need to be involved as citizens in advisory roles to agencies monitoring the quality of care. Thus it is essential in bodies such as professional standards and review organizations that minorities not only be among those professionals who comprise peer review groups but also among the service providers and consumers who work and serve on various committees. Considering the scarcity of certain minority group professionals (for example, fewer than a dozen Native American psychiatrists in the country), quality assurance may have to come through advisory groups to such bodies. Again, there must be citizen participation on each level of planning and service delivery (Christmas, 1977).

Discussion of quality assurance leads to the problem of the evaluation of services and the thorny issue of how confidentiality can be maintained in a situation that requires accountability to public agencies. The need for mechanisms to bring about the effective referral of individuals from one agency to another and to assist them through a maze of agencies may best be met with a multiservice center. This might however require an information system, a single set of records, or a case manager. How can this be accomplished without breaching confidentiality? The problem is also difficult when the multiservice approach is carried out through several agencies acting in a consortium.

The issue of confidentiality becomes particularly important in minority communities when paraprofessional mental health workers, for example, are drawn from those communities and must work side by side with people who might (at least in smaller communities) be their neighbors. This issue must be addressed in a way that recognizes both the supportive role which friends and neighbors can play and the different role which volunteer and staff should play and must distinguish between the responsibilities and constraints that devolve upon each.

With regard to data-sharing and program evaluation, concerns that minorities hold about being "researched to death" are not groundless. Fears that information about their civil rights activities will be put into a computer or that their names will be placed on government lists are genuine. Yet, data collection and research are necessary.

Little evaluation has taken place comparing the efficacy of various approaches for services to minorities in the mental health fields. If such studies are to include reference to culture variables, then the pool of culture-sensitive researchers has to be greatly expanded (Sue, 1972). In order to collect the kind of evaluation data that have not been collected in the past, it is essential that more objective outside bodies be able to conduct evaluations of both the more traditional and the newer more innovative programs. This kind of evaluation might involve not only professional agency staff but, in the interest of accountability, citizens from neighborhood mental health councils who might participate in selected parts of site visits and program audits. The consumer viewpoint is critical for quality assurance. If concerns are raised, for example, as to why Chinese Americans underutilize the few services available to them, their views must be sought on the functioning of existing services. In some instances this can be done through the participation of minorities as staff on mental hygiene administrative and supervisory organizations as, for example, the Patient

Care/Client Service Committees of providers and consumers in New York City.

RECOMMENDATIONS

1. Minority Americans (consumers and service providers) must be included at all levels of the decision-making process in programs which serve minorities.

2. Minority Americans must be appointed to serve on Federal, state, and local governmental boards, review committees, commissions, councils, and policy-making bodies especially where substantial numbers of minorities are affected.

3. Minority representation on HSAs must be mandated and such representation be reflective of the populations over which HSAs have jurisdiction; this representation should be a condition of Federal funding.

4. Professional standards and review organizations should be mandated to include minorities on peer review groups, committees, and advisory bodies; this inclusion should be a condition of Federal funding.

5. Boards composed of minorities should be established to review and monitor hospitals, agencies, and other health facilities to insure compliance with Department of Health and Human Services regulations as they affect minorities.

6. Comprehensive investigations should be conducted to assess the quality and quantity of services provided to minority Americans by the Veterans Administration, the Social Security Administration, the Department of Labor, the Bureau of Indian Affairs, and other governmental bodies.

7. The Alcohol, Drug Abuse and Mental Health Administration should allocate a portion of its research budgets (intramural and extramural) for: a) the development of normative data on minorities, b) the development by minority researchers of culturally relevant assessment instruments, c) the development of standards for service delivery, d) a review of the geographical/political/social locations of community mental health centers and effects on service, e) action-oriented research, and f) an evaluation of service approaches.

8. There needs to be strong, vigorous, and immediate action on the part of the Federal government to insure quality, community-based, holistic, and integrated helping services for minority Americans; these services must be based on local needs, planning, and decision-making structures and include health, social service, employment, educational, and economic programs.

9. The Federal government should take a more active role in providing incentives for training minorities as professionals and paraprofessionals. Such training programs should take into account the bar-

riers institutionalized racism imposes on effective treatment. Minority group professionals in mental health are critically needed not only to provide direct services but as mental health administrators and managers dealing with policy, fiscal, informational, and programmatic issues.

Financing

Basic to the service characteristics which have been discussed above are recommendations for a sound fiscal base. The elements of appropriate services for minorities cannot exist without a fiscal base that ensures that funds are available for innovative linkages with community organizations, new types of personnel, traditional folk medicine as well as Western medicine, and public education of communities in regard to individual and institutional responsibilities.

If the parameters of mental health, drug abuse and alcoholism services are to be broadened to include the social elements which are a part of a holistic orientation, then there must be funding that draws not only from the health care system but also from other sources such as social services. Consistent with this is the need for funding to come to the local level where services should be integrated. There is, further, the necessity for less reliance on categorical funding (not to eliminate it, for it may be the only way of reaching certain target groups who are overlooked) and to lengthen cycles for funding so that innovative programs do not have to endure the annual stress of proposal writing and project refunding, efforts which divert energies from service (Christmas, 1977b).

RECOMMENDATIONS

1. The Federal government should consider establishing minimum standards for care and treatment for all states receiving Federal funding. This may be difficult if Federal authority is limited to the boundaries of a particular funding program. However, the Federal government should give consideration to imposing its presence more specifically in terms of the care and treatment received by the mentally disabled who are also minorities.

2. The Department of Health and Human Services should adequately fund mental health delivery systems serving minority communities. In addition, much needed consultation and education services and research and development programs which are not reimbursable as direct treatment services must be maintained.

3. Adequate and stable funding should be provided to continue the operation of community mental health centers or networks of community mental health services. Implicit in this recommendation is the need for a firm and stable shared commitment on the part of Federal and State governments to the continued funding of mental

health services and to flexibility in design and sponsorship.

4. Where community mental health centers serve large Medicaid care populations, Federal initiatives should ensure reasonable coverage of ambulatory psychiatric services under Medicaid care. Where centers serve a working poor population not eligible for coverage, mechanisms for long-term funding must be established.

5. The Federal government should act through funding restrictions and guidelines within Federal authority to prohibit discriminatory state and local practices with respect to providers and recipients of service.

6. A related problem is the undue influence which is often exerted by the provider arm of a state government. Federal standards should consider mandating a separation within a state between the provider arm, if one has to exist, and that agency which engages in standard-setting, the awarding of agency contracts, and revenue distributions. An independent oversight agency might be mandated to insure this separate functioning.

7. If mental hygiene funds are allocated as part of larger social services funding schemes, it is critical that the Federal government include careful definitions of care and treatment programs and minimum percentages for the funds to be required for such programs.

8. Mechanisms must be developed at the Federal level to secure strict enforcement of and compliance to existing legislation pertaining to all mental health facilities and the participation by minorities in the implementation of such procedures.

9. Each community mental health facility must be held accountable to serve all minority groups within its area of coverage.

10. Public Law 94-63 Title III "Community Mental Health Centers" should be amended to identify minority group populations as target populations for this legislation. It should also be amended to ensure the establishment of a sufficient number of mental health delivery mechanisms so that minorities have true access to quality mental health services.

11. Training and license requirements must be reexamined and modified to take into account the shortage of bilingual and bicultural licensed personnel of certain minority group backgrounds.

12. A bill should be enacted to establish a Division of Minority Group Health Programs to include Asian and Pacific Americans, Blacks, Hispanics, and Native Americans.

References

Belcourt, Gordon. "Traditional Native American Healing in Contemporary Western Society's Mental Health Programming." Paper presented to the President's Commission on Mental Health, 1977.

Berk, B., and Hirata, L. "Mental Illness Among the Chinese: Myth or Reality," **Journal of Social Issues** 29 (1973), 149-166.

Bullough, Bonnie. "Poverty, Ethnic Identity and Preventive Health Care," **Journal of Health and Social Behavior** 13 (1972), 347-359.

Cameron, D., and Talavera, E. "An Advocacy Program for Spanish-Speaking People," **Social Casework** 57 (1976), 427-431.

Christmas, J.J. "Socio-psychiatric Rehabilitation in a Black Urban Ghetto: Conflicts, Issues and Directions," **American Journal of Orthopsychiatry** 39 (1969), 651-661.

_____. "Cultural and Social Factors in the Delivery of Alcoholism Services to Minorities: Training Issues and Concerns." Paper presented at the Annual Conference of the National Council on Alcoholism, 1977.

_____. "Unresolved Governance Issues as Barriers to Care." Paper prepared for the Technical Conference on Barriers to Mental Health Care, President's Commission on Mental Health, 1977.

_____. "Some Remarks on Community Support Systems." Presentation to the President's Commission on Mental Health, 1977.

Christmas, J.J., and Daniels, M.S. "A Socio-psychiatric Approach to Rehabilitation in a Low Income Community," in A. Tulipain (ed.), **Psychiatric Outpatient Centers and Low-Income Populations.** Oil City, PA: Psychiatric Outpatient Centers of America, 1968.

Faulkner, A.O., Heisel, M.A., and Simms, P. "Life Strengths and Life Stresses: Explorations in the Measurement of the Mental Health of the Black Aged," **American Journal of Orthopsychiatry** 45 (1975), 102-110.

Fuji, S. "Elderly Asian-Americans and Use of Public Services," **Social Casework** 57 (1976), 202-207.

Gullattee, A. "Mental Health Planning and Evaluation for the Black and the Poor," **Journal of the National Medical Association** 64 (1972), 134-138.

Harper, F., and Dawkins, M. "Alcohol and Blacks: Survey of the Periodical Literature," **British Journal of Addiction** 71 (1976), 327-334.

Ho, Man Keung. "Social Work with Asian-Americans," **Social Casework** 57 (1976), 195-201.

Huang, K., and Pilisuk, M. "At the Threshold of the Golden Gate: Special Problems of a Neglected Minority," **American Journal of Orthopsychiatry** 47 (1977), 701-713.

Lightfoot, O., and Foster, D.L. "Broadened Definitions of Community Psychiatry," **American Journal of Orthopsychiatry** 40 (1970), 751-755.

Kalish, R.A., and Moriwaki, S. "The World of the Elderly Asian-American," **Journal of Social Issues** 29 (1973), 187-209.

Kitano, H. "Japanese-American Mental Illness," in S. Sue and N. Wagner (eds.), **Asian Americans: Psychological Perspectives.** Palo Alto: Science and Behavior Books, 1973.

Knoll, F.R. "Casework Services for Mexican-Americans," **Social Casework** 52 (1971), 279-284.

La Vietes, R.L. "Crisis Intervention for Ghetto Children: Contraindications and Alternative Considerations," **American Journal of Orthopsychiatry** 44 (1974), 720-727.

Leon, R. "Some Implications for a Preventive Program for American Indians," **American Journal of Psychiatry** 125 (1968), 232-236.

Martinez, C. "Community Mental Health and the Chicano Movement," **American Journal of Orthopsychiatry** 43 (1973), 595-601.

McAdoo, H. "Family Therapy in the Black Community," **American Journal of Orthopsychiatry** 47 (1977), 75-79.

McNickle, D. "The Sociocultural Setting of Indian Life," **American Journal of Psychiatry** 125 (1968), 219-223.

Paine, H. "Attitudes and Patterns of Alcohol Use Among Mexican Americans," **Journal of Studies on Alcohol** 38 (1977), 544-553.

Resnik, H., and Dizmang, L. "Observations on Suicidal Behavior Among American Indians," **American Journal of Psychiatry** 127 (1971), 882-887.

Shore, J., and Von Fumetti, B. "Three Alcohol Programs for American Indians," **American Journal of Psychiatry** 128 (1972), 134-138.

Sotomayor, M. "Mexican-American Interaction with Social Systems," **Social Casework** 52 (1971), 316-322.

Sue, S. "Community Mental Health Services to Minority Groups," **American Psychologist** 32 (1977), 616-624.

Sue, S., and McKinney, J. "Asian-Americans in the Community Mental Health Care System," **American Journal of Orthopsychiatry** 45 (1974), 111-118.

Sue, D., and Sue, S. "Ethnic Minorities: Resistance to Being Researched," **Professional Psychology** 3 (1972), 11-17.

Taber, R. "A Systems Approach to the Delivery of Mental Health Services in Black Ghettos," **American Journal of Orthopsychiatry** 40 (1976), 702-716.

Thornton, C., and Carter, J.H. "Improving Mental Health Services to Low Income Blacks," **Journal of the National Medical Association** 67 (1975), 167-170.

Tuck, S. "Working with Black Fathers," **American Journal of Orthopsychiatry** 41 (1971), 465-472.

PART FOUR

MANPOWER DEVELOPMENT

This section is concerned with mental health manpower development issues as they affect the delivery of services to minority group populations. In the first article, William Denham traces the history of the National Institute of Mental Health's manpower development programs. He shows how they moved from simple efforts to increase the number of trained mental health professionals, through a closer matching of manpower to actually needed skills and knowledge, to a redirection of priorities in light of reduced funding. Current policies emphasize the preparation of manpower to meet the needs of unserved and underserved populations, including minority groups.

In the next article, Madison Foster and Louis Ferman point out that while a large proportion of mental health service recipients are members of minority groups, nonminorities tend to be the service providers and to determine mental health policy. A general lack of practitioner familiarity with minority group cultures often leads to misdiagnoses of culturally influenced behaviors as pathological and failure to use indigenous community support systems. Minority group representation in mental health policy-making and service delivery must be increased to improve the relevance and acceptability of services.

In the final article, Rodolfo Sanchez argues for increased minority group participation in the politics of mental health manpower development. He identifies major processes and actors in manpower policy-making, training, and regulation. Minority groups are late arrivals to this political arena and need to mobilize a strong constituency in support of necessary legislation, funding, and regulatory and policy changes.

133

FEDERAL TRENDS IN MENTAL HEALTH MANPOWER PROGRAMS

WILLIAM H. DENHAM[1]

In the thirty years of their existence, National Institute of Mental Health (NIMH) manpower programs have evolved through roughly four stages: 1) the beginning period, 1948-1960; 2) the Camelot Era or period of expansion, 1960-1969; 3) the period of retrenchment or the Ice Age, 1970-1975; and 4) the period of reassessment and redirection, 1975 to the present.

The Beginnings, 1948-1960

At their inception in 1948, the basic thrust of NIMH clinical manpower programs was to enlarge the national pool of professional specialists and to build the national capacity of educational institutions to provide quality training, particularly in the core fields of psychiatry, clinical psychology, social work, and psychiatric nursing. When this policy was first initiated there was an enormous need for clinically-oriented personnel. The emphasis was on increasing the numbers of professionals and improving the quality of training at the graduate level. Modest support for research training at both the undergraduate and graduate levels was also provided through the research fellowship program of the National Institutes of Health.

Subsequently it became apparent that there was a need to expand the scope of mental health training programs to include other than generic training in the core disciplines. Consequently, beginning in 1953, several new types of projects were developed. They included: pilot training projects in mental retardation, juvenile delinquency, alcoholism, and aging; improvement of teaching methods and curriculum for communicating mental health information to lawyers, dentists, theologians, etc.; a career investigator support program to prepare qualified individuals for careers in research and training; an undergraduate nursing program to equip nurses to deal with the emotional aspects of illness and death; and a career teaching program to initiate more effective teaching procedures and to encourage

---

[1]The opinions expressed in this paper are those of the author and do not necessarily reflect the official views or policies of the National Institute of Mental Health, the Alcohol, Drug Abuse and Mental Health Administration, the Department of Health and Human Services, or the officials therein.

people to enter mental health teaching careers.

In 1957 the efforts of prominent mental health advocates such as philan-thropists Mary Lasker and Florence Mahoney and Congressional supporters such as Senator Lester Hill, Chairman of the Senate Labor and Public Welfare Committee, and Representative John Fogarty, Chairman of the House Appropriations Subcommittee, resulted in a twofold increase in the appropriation for mental health, from $5.9 million in fiscal year 1956 to $11.5 million in fiscal year 1957. Additional new programs were initiated including senior stipends to train selected invididuals with advanced stand-ing in teaching, research, and administration; part-time stipends for psy-chiatric internships for medical students; and grant support for the devel-opment of research training programs in epidemiology, biometry, and other basic and applied sciences.

The Camelot Era or Period of Expansion, 1960-1969

The report of the Joint Commission on Mental Illness and Mental Health in 1961, the passage of the Community Mental Health Centers (CMHC) Act in 1963, and the CMHC amendments of 1965, while reconfirming the origi-nal policy emphasis on correcting professional shortages, also called for an effort to relate manpower production to the actual skills and knowledge required by the service system. There was also a demand for the develop-ment of new supplementary sources of personnel such as psychiatric aides and other varieties of technical or paraprofessional workers. These events, together with such other factors as the considerable influence and interest of the Kennedy Administration and family in mental health and mental retardation programs, the successful lobbying of the mental health consti-tuency in Congress for increased appropriations, and the generally excep-tional receptivity nationally for mental health programs, resulted in what has been referred to as the "Camelot Era" in NIMH manpower programs in terms of program scope and budgetary support.

In rapid succession, programs in experimental and special training, continuing education, and paraprofessional training were established. The budget, heavily influenced by these events, continued to increase to a peak of approximately $120 million in 1969.

The Ice Age or Period of Retrenchment, 1969-1975

During the next decade, funding for mental health manpower programs was either decreased or maintained at previous levels of support, which is in essence a decrease when inflation is taken into consideration. The real "Ice Age" in NIMH manpower programs occurred during the "Nixon years" and was highlighted by the Nixon Administration's announcement in 1973 to get out of the training enterprise by phasing out support for the core disci-plines and the CMHC program (ostensibly because it had proven to be a successful experiment and could now be supported and financed by the states). NIMH lived on the precipice of phaseout through 1975. Court actions, constituency pressure, and Congressional overrides temporarily removed this "sword of Damocles," but appropriations never returned to the apex of 1969. Thus the stage was set for a reevaluation of the Institute's role in manpower and training within a context of declining resources, inflation, and a sympathetic but increasingly cost-conscious Congress.

The Period of Reassessment and Redirection,
1975 to the Present

Reassessment of personnel policy was initiated in 1975 by the former NIMH Director, Dr. Bertram Brown. Dr. Brown established an NIMH Services Manpower Task Force which was directed to study and reevaluate manpower policy and programs in light of the prospect of continued declining resources and the emergence of several complex and unresolved issues such as manpower maldistribution by specialty and geographic area, inadequate mental health preparation of primary health care personnel, and poor access to health and mental health care by unserved and underserved populations (i.e., children and youth, the aged, the chronically ill, minorities, and women).

Two phases of this Task Force plus the NIMH Forward Plan proposal for 1977-1982 lead to the first step towards a new manpower policy. That step was primarily based on the assumption that the focus of manpower production through training and education must be relevant to, and derived from, the manpower needs of service agencies. This interrelationship between manpower and service delivery was reflected in the identification of four service priorities:

1. Community-based mental health services.
2. Services to special target populations and geographically unserved or underserved areas.
3. Service alternatives to long-term care.

Tentative manpower initiatives which relate to these service priorities were identified. They included:

1. The targeting of professional disciplinary training to the aforementioned service priorities.
2. An accelerated manpower development program focused on state and local manpower planning and capacity building.
3. Creation of a research and development manpower training and development program which encompassed the previous experimental and special training program.
4. Acceleration of support for innovations and demonstrations in the mental health training of primary health care personnel.

This policy conception was still under review by the Alcohol, Drug Abuse and Mental Health Administration (ADAMHA), the Public Health Service, and the Executive department levels when two subsequent events occurred:

1. The establishment of the President's Commission on Mental Health by President Carter in February 1977, powered in no small measure by the First Lady's special interest in mental health.
2. A policy analysis of all ADAMHA manpower programs was mandated by Dr. Gerald Klerman, ADAMHA Administrator, in December 1977 as a component of a broader health manpower policy analysis being undertaken by the Office of the Assistant Secretary for Health in preparation for legislative renewal of the Health Professions Educational Assistance Act of 1976 (P.L. 94-483).

The focus of both the ADAMHA manpower analysis and that of the President's Commission were essentially the same, namely to identify the major policy issues and problems affecting clinical/services manpower in mental health, evaluate options for addressing these issues and problems, and make recommendations for future Federal manpower policies and programs. Similarly, the outcomes of both policy assessments showed a significant degree of agreement on future policy directions. Furthermore, both assessments tended to legitimize the interim or "ad hoc" manpower initiatives which NIMH subsequently undertook in the 1978 and 1979 fiscal years.

The philosophical bedrock of the new policy rests on the principle of service to the unserved and underserved and the concomitant development of personnel through training and other devices to complement this emphasis. The specific objectives of this policy as articulated in the report of the President's Commission on Mental Health are:

1. To encourage mental health specialists to work in areas and settings where severe shortages exist.
2. To increase the number of qualified minority personnel in the mental health professions and the number of mental health personnel trained to deal with the special problems of children, adolescents, and the elderly.
3. To assure that the skills and knowledge of mental health personnel are appropriate to the needs of those they serve.
4. To develop mental health sensitivity and appropriate skills and knowledge of personnel in the health care sector.

Finally, to achieve these objectives, the President's Commission recommended an approximately 15 percent increase in the appropriations for clinical and services manpower and training programs to $85 million in fiscal year 1980.

ADAMHA was given lead-agency responsibility to develop a plan for implementing the President's Commission's recommendations beginning with the 1980 fiscal year legislative cycle. Preliminary proposals called for: 1) increasing the number of specialists in the mental health of children and the aged and the number of minority professionals; 2) sensitivity training of nonminority personnel to make them more sensitive to minority needs; 3) encouraging mental health specialists to work in areas and settings where severe shortages exist; 4) linking mental health training and services more closely to health and community systems; and 5) improving manpower data systems as an aid to planning.

Implications for the Future

I have briefly traced the evolution of Federal mental health manpower policy over the past 30 years. I have also tried to identify the general directions of policy for the immediate future beginning in fiscal year 1980. Now I want to conclude with a reference to three of the major themes of this future policy in terms of their conceptual and programmatic implications. These themes are : 1) the services-training linkage; 2) manpower maldistribution; and 3) manpower research and development.

SERVICES-TRAINING LINKAGE

The concept of linking mental health training more closely with health and mental health service systems implies a broadened concept which calls for attention by educational institutions to manpower as well as training concerns. Manpower, in contrast to training, is a systems concept which includes such elements as personnel supply and demand considerations, personnel maldistribution, and personnel utilization viewed from the perspective of differential staff role and functional configurations.

The addressing of such manpower components by the mental health education field is based on at least three important assumptions:

1. An increased interaction and exchange between mental health educators' and the policy and planning levels of service delivery systems at the local, state, and regional levels.
2. The identification of institutional mechanisms in the core professions and the paraprofessional field which could assume responsibility for such interaction on behalf of mental health education either for the field as a whole, individual schools, or consortia of schools.
3. The development of manpower information systems by the core professions for educational planning purposes.

The manpower orientation is a relatively new and uncharted arena for educators of mental health professionals and raises a number of complex issues. For example, how can training and service delivery system interaction be developed so as to avoid incursions into the areas of academic freedom and prerogatives? Can educational planning and manpower planning be coordinated? What lead roles should major gatekeepers of the core professions play in such interaction? What is the nature and locus of the manpower intelligence system(s) that must be developed in the core professions to provide the data base for manpower and educational planning? What will such systems cost and how will they be financed?

PERSONNEL MALDISTRIBUTION

Maldistribution is one of the most popular and frequently cited manpower concepts in health and mental health. Frequently it tends to be referred to more by rhetoric than operational definition. Nevertheless, maldistribution is the centerpiece of the President's Commission's personnel recommendations and those of the ADAMHA policy analysis. What the term conveys in its current official usage is that manpower or personnel resources are **inequitably** distributed geographically and in terms of populations in need. The assumption that follows is that such inequities can be corrected by manipulating the training/education variable. What is missing in this conception are at least two major determinants: 1) the free marketplace choice of individuals to select the locus of their employment; and 2) the broader context in which personnel are employed, trained, and utilized, namely the service environment. Until these factors are interwoven into policy, it will remain somewhat ambiguous and one-dimensional. Still, we must respond to that one dimension, namely education and training. In this regard it is important to keep in mind that research data are lacking on the strength of the training variable as a factor in where people choose to work.

Among the major initiatives which will need to be developed in the training area to influence maldistribution are efforts to:

1. Direct new supplies of manpower to shortage areas. This will involve: a) revision of authorizing legislation for the National Health Service Corps to include the full range of mental health professional manpower (e.g., psychiatrists, clinical psychologists, social workers, and graduate level nurses); or b) modification of the Health Professions Educational Assistance Act or Section 303 of the Public Health Service Act to implement the principle of payback so that students who receive Federal support for their training would be required to repay this aid through a period of service in designated geographic areas or facilities where there is a shortage of personnel.
2. Target education or training programs to shortage areas especially the inner city and rural areas and to the most unserved or underserved population groups, namely children and youth, the aged, and minorities.
3. Increase mental health-related content in the training of primary health care givers.

MANPOWER RESEARCH AND DEVELOPMENT

The education process in mental health has not been a subject for systematic investigation. By and large what has been offered as educational research and development, such as innovative or demonstration training projects to develop new sources of manpower, do not meet the criteria of systematic generation, testing, and replication of knowledge and needed technology on the educational process itself. The training of minorities or the training of nonminorities for serving minority populations is a striking example of an area of educational policy which has been influenced relatively exclusively by political and social justice factors. Policy in this area certainly would be strengthened if it was informed by systematically de-rived knowledge. Similarly, there are a variety of other training areas where we are literally "flying by the seat of our pants." For example, many of us will argue that one of the most effective strategies for impacting the maldistribution problem is to train people or develop training facilities in underserved or unserved geographic sectors. Adequate evidence is lacking to support this thesis.

Then there is the area of manpower utilization. At the beginning of this paper, I alluded to this as of central importance in clarifying the boundaries of mental health practice and education among the mental health profes-sions. Illustrative of the urgent need for research on this problem is a recent exploratory study of job functions and credentialing of 812 workers in 17 community mental health centers in seven states (Steinberg et al., 1976). This study produced an array of 17 functions performed by commu-nity mental health center professionals in which a substantive degree of functional overlap among the various professionals occurred at the direct service provision level. An earlier study by Berg et al. (1972) resulted in a similar finding. Both studies also inferred a substantial degree of overlap between the so-called medical as opposed to social welfare oriented treat-ment functions.

Conclusion

In conclusion, I have attempted to set forth some of the mental health policy trends and the major issues confronting mental health and mental health personnel education. In my judgment they add up to a critical benchmark in terms of the way mental health manpower has been generat-ed in the past in contrast to the way it must be generated in the future. NIMH recognizes that abrupt change is neither possible nor desirable. What is expected and hoped for is that the field will creatively and forthrightly address the new policy iniatives in terms of the goal we all share, namely better preparation of manpower to maximize the delivery of services to those in need.

References

Berg, L. et al. **Social Workers in Community Mental Health.** Chicago: University of Chicago School of Social Science Administration, 1972.

Steinberg, S. et al. **Survey of Manpower Utilization, Functions, and Cre-dentialing in Community Mental Health Centers.** New York: Univer-sity Research Corporation, 1976.

MINORITY POPULATIONS AND MENTAL HEALTH MANPOWER DEVELOPMENT: SOME FACTS OF LIFE

MADISON FOSTER
LOUIS A. FERMAN

Minorities and Mental Health

The salient anomaly in the field of mental health is that much of the population being served, notably in public institutions, is composed of minority group members while the service providers are nonminority group members. Furthermore the few minority mental health workers that do exist are primarily represented in the allied health positions which are lower in professional status and pecuniary rewards. These two conditions are further compounded by the general underutilization of the available mental health services by most minority communities. For example the Chicano community, second only to the Native American community in its extreme scarcity of conventional mental health personnel and resources, underutilizes mental health services when compared to nonminority communities (Acosta, 1977; Barrera, 1978; Gibson, 1978). Minorities in general and Native Americans and Hispanics in particular are among America's most neglected groups in terms of mental health services.

As stated above, when minorities do manage to receive mental health services, the service provider is generally found to be of nonminority background. This anomaly is best viewed against the general fact that there is a paucity of personnel in the mental health field. Resources and governmental commitment to train mental health workers have been steadily declining over the last decade. Since 1969, the Federal government has phased out financial support for programs in psychiatry, psychology, nursing, and social work. For example between 1969 and 1976, the National Institute of Mental Health (NIMH) reduced its financial support for mental health training and research by $34.9 million; the 1969 commitment of $120 million diminished to a low of $85.1 million (Sanchez, 1979). This shortage of mental health personnel is a national dilemma.

But for America's minorities the reduction of financial support for mental health services is an acute problem. The consequent shortage of mental health practitioners impacts most on minority communities primarily because they are the least likely to have access to conventional mental health resources. This impact is intensified by the fact that there is a dearth of minority group providers to tend to the special needs of the minority group client and community at large. It is important to note here that these issues are exacerbated by the decreasing social policy interest in ethnic minorities since the height of minority protest during the turbulent 1960s.

The popular approach to the delivery of quality mental health services continues to be the "medical model" as practiced by psychiatric personnel. Psychiatric personnel in America are overwhelmingly of nonminority descent and cultural origin. Consequently it is nearly impossible for a significant number of minority persons to receive psychiatric service from mental health personnel who have lived-experience within the cultural and linguistic context of minority life. Nonminority students of psychiatry, psychology, and nursing receive scant academic or experiental exposure to the varied cultures and languages of America's minorities. Furthermore most psychiatric residents themselves do not make independent efforts to study or understand minority cultures (Nellum, 1975). Therefore minority communities are left with only a handful of psychiatric practitioners who know and are sensitive to their languages and cultures.

Table 1

Race/Ethnic Background of American Psychiatric
Association Members and Nonmembers

Race/Ethnicity	Members		Nonmembers		Total	
	N	%	N	%	N	%
Native American	19	.08	0	0	19	.06
Mexican	38	.15	8	.13	46	.15
Puerto Rican	36	.15	15	.25	51	.16
Spanish (Other)	323	1.30	66	1.08	389	1.26
Pilipino	237	.95	29	.47	266	.86
Asian Indian	642	2.59	98	1.60	740	2.39
Asian (Other)	411	1.66	20	.33	431	1.39
Black	344	1.39	78	1.27	422	1.36
Other Minority	20	.08	1	.02	21	.07
Other Nonminority	22,755	91.65	5,805	94.85	28,560	92.29
TOTAL	24,825	100.00	6,120	100.00	30,945	100.00

Table 1 dramatically illustrates this phenomenon: psychiatric service by minorities in America is virtually nonexistent as indicated by the numbers of minority physicians trained in psychiatry. Table 1 reveals that although the Federally identified minority groups--Afro-Americans, Hispanics, Asian

Americans and Native Americans--represent between 17 and 20 percent of the American population, they represent only 8.35 percent of the American Psychiatric Association (APA) membership. If one includes members and nonmembers (psychiatrists not holding APA membership) the estimated percentage of minority psychiatrists in this country is reduced to 7.7 percent.

This scarcity of minorities in psychiatry is possibly more severe than indicated in Table 1. For example many Hispanic members of the APA are not representative of America's indigenous Hispanic cultures (Ruiz, 1971). Cerando Martinez, Jr. of the University of Texas Health Science Center, after reviewing APA Hispanic membership figures, concluded:

> First of all, there are several hundred Spanish-speaking psychiatrists in the American Psychiatric Assocation. It must be noted, though, that the majority of these psychiatrists are Mexican, Puerto Rican, and South/Central Americans. There are very few Chicanos!

A second example further illustrates the problem. Figures in Table 1 indicate that the Native American has fewer indigenous psychiatrists than any other minority group in America. At first glance it appears safe to assume that all Native American psychiatrists are by definition indigenous to America and are therefore able to provide mental health service in the context of Native American life. However, two factors might reduce the already low number of 19 Native American psychiatrists:

1. The heritage, geographic, cultural, and linguistic variations among native American groups might render it difficult for a given Native American psychiatrist to deliver mental health assistance to all the diversified and distinct tribal groups. There are more distinct Native American groups (i.e., Navaho, Chippewa, and so forth) than there are individual Native American psychiatrists in America.

2. Informal reporting by mental health professionals interested in identifying psychiatrists who possess a sense of tribal heritage can come up with no more than ten Native American psychiatrists. Stanley W. Boucher and Faye U. Munoz, Associate Directors of the Western Center for Continuing Education in Mental Health of the Western Interstate Commission for Higher Education, stated recently that their Native American associates have identified seven or eight psychiatrists in a national search for consultants and practitioners with lived-experience and heritage in Native American culture. The APA figure of nineteen psychiatrists may be explained by noting the tradition among Americans of claiming Native American heritage even when there are only remote cultural, linguistic, and phenotypical ties to persons of Native American ancestry.

The percentage of minorities in mental health professions other than psychiatry is not significantly different. Table 2 clearly illustrates that although minorities represent 17.5 percent of the general population, they are not adequately represented in any of the major mental health professions. Once again, Native Americans have the lowest representation of all minority groups in all of the mental health professions reviewed.

Table 2

Minority Representation in the Population
and in Mental Health Professions

Race/ Ethnicity	U.S. Population	Psychiatry	Psychology*	Social Work	Licensed Nursing
		(1978)	(1976)	(1975)	(1972)
Black	11.1%	1.4%	0.9%	7.6%	3.3%
Hispanic	5.3	1.5	0.4	1.6	0.4
Asian	0.7	4.9	0.7	1.9	0.9
Native American	0.4	0.1	0.1	0.3	0.1
TOTAL MINORITY	17.5%	7.8%	2.1%	11.4%	4.7%

*Ph.D. health service providers only.

The social work profession has the highest representation of minority mental health manpower. In Table 3 one observes that the percentage of minority social work graduates in 1977 was 17.2 percent, only 0.3 percent less than the estimated 17.5 percent of minorities in the American population. However, if one considers the reality of American social work as an urban occurrence where minorities often comprise more than 50 percent of a city's population, the 17.2 percent minority graduates in social work is clearly inadequate--not only in terms of population distribution but also in terms of quality social welfare and mental health services.

Table 4 indicates, based on the present enrollment of students and including psychiatric residents, that America is unlikely to have adequate minority mental health manpower in the foreseeable future. Even if this country had 60,000 minority psychiatrists, or more than twice the APA reported number of 28,560 (Table 1), it would still have a severe and critical scarcity of minority psychiatrists.

Significantly, Table 4 also documents the stark reality that minorities will show only small employment gains in these higher status health professions with the exception of social work (and Asian psychiatrists). Minorities are primarily relegated to allied health positions which, as mentioned earlier, are lower in professional status and pecuniary rewards. Rarely do minorities move from these low status positions in various public agencies to the better paying, more secure, and higher status positions that are held by nonminority mental health workers.

Table 3

Minority Representation in the Population and Among
Degree Grantees in the Mental Health Professions

Race/ Ethnicity	U.S. Population	Psychiatry	Psychology Ph.D.*	Social Work - MSW	Nursing B.S.
			(1977)	(1977)	(1975)
Black	11.1%		4.1%	10.7%	5.2%
Hispanic	5.3	Not	2.0	4.3	1.8
Asian	0.7	Appropriate	0.8	1.8	1.3
Native American	0.4		0.9	0.4	---
TOTAL MINORITY	17.5%		7.8%	17.2%	8.3%

*Clinical and counseling only.

Table 4

Minority Representation in the Population and Among
Students in Training in the Mental Health Professions

Race/ Ethnicity	U.S. Population	Psychiatric Residents	Psychology Ph.D.*	Social Work MSW	Nursing B.S.
		(1977-78)	(1976-77)	(1977-78)	(1975-76)
Black	11.1%	3.6%	6.5%	10.3%	7.1%
Hispanic	5.3	5.1	2.2	4.4	1.7
Asian	0.7	24.4	1.0	1.6	1.0
Native American	0.4	0.1	0.3	0.46	---
TOTAL MINORITY	17.5%	33.2%	10.0%	16.9%	9.8%

*Clinical and counseling only.

An underlying assumption in this section on minorities and mental health
is that mental health practitioners grounded in the cultural and linguistic
heritages of minorities would better serve and provide for minority com-

munities. Although we cannot "prove" this **per se**, our reasons are three-fold:

1. Many nonminority practitioners, unfamiliar with minority cultural expressions, tend to explain their unfamiliarity in terms of significant pathology in their minority clients' behavior (Marcos, Alpert, Urcuyo, and Kesselman, 1976). This tendency reflects one of the most popular and pejorative models of minority culture in American social science literature and research--namely that minority communities are anomic or pathological (Foster, 1978). In fact James Ralph (1974) reported that over 50 percent of the NIMH research on minority groups was conceptualized from the deficient or pathological model of minority life and culture. Furthermore, the Afro-American community continues to be a common target for researchers and practitioners using the pathological model in spite of the fact that there is strong evidence that blacks are not anomic and very likely have strong support systems for personal well-being (Aptheker, 1971; Foster and Perry, 1977; Walsh, 1975).

2. Minority communities very likely have support systems which can be utilized to bolster efforts to deliver quality mental health services, but these systems tend to be invisible to nonminority professionals.

3. Available and orthodox mental health services are possibly underutilized because they conflict, ignore, or simply misunderstand minority languages, values, and heritages as well as prevailing community support systems.

The Political Economy of Mental Health Manpower

As we have observed, most of the minority group personnel in the mental health field are crowded into allied health services. Therefore the major problem for the manpower development of minority group workers is that most of them are subject to manpower and policy decisions beyond their control. What this means is that **other** professional groups influence and control their opportunities for access to training, conditions of work, access to certain kinds of practice or treatment situations, and mobility/career opportunities. We can specify six areas in which external control is exercised:

1. **Licensing and Certification by Physicians.** The world of minority group paraprofessionals is largely controlled by the medical profession in several ways. First, physicians write the professional standards and licensing requirements for a wide variety of medical personnel. They do this through their overrepresentation on state licensing boards where they exercise legal power to define the tasks of allied health workers and the mechanisms through which certification is determined. In licensing and certification procedures there is a strong emphasis on written examinations and formal educational training criteria. These frequently pose a formidable barrier for minority

group workers in the mental health field. One problem is that the determination of competency is not based on performance in a job but rather performance on verbal and written tests where minority group individuals can be at a disadvantage. These tests often reflect mastery of educational materials rather than competency in a job. The emphasis on formal training and education obviously screens out many minority group members who cannot afford the time or money for such an educational investment.

Second, even where physicians do not exercise direct control on licensing boards, they can exercise indirect veto power. Since physicians set standards for hospitals and clinics where the main business of mental health practice takes place, they are in a position to "advise" allied health service groups that work there as well as organization administrators as to what is acceptable practice, what preparation is necessary, and what models of practice should be used. Physicians are not only in a unique position to rule on what is professionally acceptable but also to veto new models of mental health practice that might enhance the professional opportunities of minority paraprofessionals.

2. **Third Party Payments.** Mental health care is expensive, so expensive that an increasing number of citizens depend on some form of medical insurance reimbursement to pay for such care. Personnel in the allied health professions that cannot receive third party payments are in fact excluded from a considerable number of practice opportunities. Two points should be made about third party payments. First, there is a tendency to want to limit such payments to members of the medical professions because the "medical model" has become identified in the popular mind with legitimate and quality mental health care and any other model is suspect. Second, members of the medical profession are overrepresented on medical insurance boards and are in a unique position to further their own professional interests and at the same time to lobby against the interests of others. For most paraprofessional groups in the allied health services, obtaining access to third party payments is an uphill struggle. Finally, members of the allied health professions are almost always the early victims of cost-containment in third party payments. Whenever insurance carriers seek to contain costs, they usually restrict or eliminate payments to other than the most highly certified personnel in the mental health field (e.g., psychiatrists and clinical psychologists). Cost-containment is usually rationalized as an attempt to focus financial resources on "quality service" with the implication that the excluded practitioners somehow give less than quality service. Although the restriction of third party payments to allied health service professionals has been a fact of life in the larger conventional health insurance programs, there has been far less restriction in health insurance programs sponsored and administered by the large labor unions (e.g., United Mine Workers, United Automobile Workers). Therefore it is disconcerting to the cause of allied health service that recent decisions by the United Automobile Workers are in the direction of restricting pay-

ments to "professionals who give quality care"--psychiatrists and social psychologists. If other union health plans follow this lead, we can only see further restrictions of practice opportunities for minority group members in the allied health services.

3. **Public Investment in Professional Development in the Field of Mental Health.** The granting of financial aid for professional development by public agencies has worked against minority group personnel in mental health. In the 1960s, the period of greatest spending, the tendency was to overinvest in research rather than in practitioner training grants for minority group members who were entering the field. This was particularly true of the National Institute of Mental Health. The logic here was to build up a research information base by minority group researchers on the behavioral and mental health problems of minority group peoples. To some extent this was an attempt to correct the previous decade's overinvestment in nonminority researchers studying minority group problems. However laudable this goal was, the end result was to restrict the number of minority group members who could enter the practitioner training system. The shortage of minority group practitioners undoubtedly reflects this misinvestment. This shortage was reinforced in the 1970s by a shift toward postgraduate training with sharp cutbacks on funds for preprofessional and graduate training in mental health. The result has been to advance further the training of practitioners who had already traversed the training system (predominantly nonminority personnel) and to restrict further the access to preparatory training for professional positions. Thus, predoctoral and paraprofessional support has declined with an adverse effect on the development of minority group practitioners.

4. **The Medical Model of Mental Health Treatment.** In the mental health field there has been a traditional reliance on the "medical model" of practice. This has meant an emphasis on diagnostic routines, surgical or drug therapy, hospital care, and individualized treatment. In most cases the client is perceived as an individual in a vacuum rather than as an individual that is part of a larger context--family, work place, and neighborhood.   The evaluation of mental health personnel is frequently an assessment of how well they are able to take a role within the medical model. Personnel who have demonstrated competencies in tasks outside of the medical model may be excluded or rated negatively.   The failure to emphasize **alternative** models in mental health (monitoring, counseling, health education) means that significant barriers are raised for allied health workers who may not have the task competencies required by the medical model. Since minority group members tend to be competent in nonmedical models, the current emphasis works against their practice participation in the mental health field.

5. **Union-Management Labor Contracts.** As the health services become increasingly unionized (a trend that is already apparent), the union contract will become an important instrument in job definitions

(specification of training, definition of job prerogatives, and specification of working conditions). Such contracts frequently freeze and rationalize the employment status quo rather than laying the ground for hybrid jobs and innovative task performance. In such a situation it is difficult to develop new models and forms of practice. In this respect, the minority group worker finds himself at a further disadvantage.

6. **Affirmative Action Planning.** A great deal depends on the extent to which affirmative action programs are developed and implemented to affect the entry and career development of minority group practitioners. The pressures generated by professional associations are also a significant factor. At the upper levels of the mental heath field (e.g., psychiatrists and clinical psychologists) affirmative action planning and implementation has been less than satisfactory. Several factors are responsible for this state of affairs. First, since minority group representation at these levels is small, nonminority group members plan and implement affirmative action programs based on their own values and precepts with little input from minority group communities. This means that the nonminority group gatekeepers of the system produce plans without any realistic information about the needs, competencies, and attitudes of minority group professionals. Second, in the medical and mental health field there is a tendency to "water down" affirmative action in favor of assuring quality care. Affirmative action and quality service are frequently seen as opposing concepts with the assumption that one must be sacrificed to assure the other. Finally, affirmative action surveillance by government agencies has declined in the 1970s partly as a result of the leveling off of the overt civil rights protests of the 1960s and the "cooling down" of overt protest in the urban ghettos. The consensus of civil rights leaders is that affirmative action machinery is in place but that it has no real impact.

This is, then, what we mean by a political economy of mental health manpower. The power and decisons are outside the control of minority groups themselves. The gatekeepers of the system are mainly nonminority persons and are only vaguely aware of the problems of minority group practitioners. The result is a significant number of barriers for the development of minority group manpower in the mental health field.

Manpower Development of Minority Group Practitioners
in Mental Health

In the mental health field the phrase "manpower development" is relatively new. There has been no philosophy, logic, or plan of manpower development in the field. There has been only a laissez-faire situation guided by the laws of supply and demand. In this context, minority group manpower has been ignored or relegated to the lowest paid and unskilled jobs. We can give no quick answers on how to remedy the situation. But we can outline a strategy of minority group manpower development that has worked in other fields and which might work in mental health.

We begin with two basic assumptions about the manpower development of minority group workers. First, manpower development not only requires a strategy for effective training but also a strategy for effective job retention. There already exist a series of effective training technologies to assure that almost anyone can be trained to do something. But once placed in a job, minority group workers, because of situational pressures, frequently have real problems in retaining the job. Thus manpower development must mean training **and** retention.

A second assumption is that manpower development means not only training the workers but frequently also altering the conditions under which they work. Jobs may have to be simplified or restructured or redesigned to give a real opportunity for access and advancement. The redesign of the work situation is difficult and is at loggerheads with the basic prerogatives of management, but it is a necessary condition.

The strategy for manpower development of minority group workers in mental health involves the following six steps.

1. **Needs Assessment.** Manpower development must start with some inventory of the needs in the mental health field. The manpower development strategy will be different if the need is for counselors than if it is for mental health educators. The question "what is needed?" can only be answered by the people working in the field--not only the "top dogs" but also middle-line managers and front line practitioners. There will be differences of opinions on needs but it is important to identify, prioritize, and gain consensus on them. This is a critical starting point.

2. **Identification and Study of Technologies.** The needs assessment leads to an identification of prevailing and needed technologies. Such technologies may involve mental health education, counseling, or client-tracking, but in each case components must be identified and factored into identifiable behaviors.

3. **Identify Job Tasks.** Patterns of behavior identified from the technologies must be grouped into a series of related routines and behaviors or "job tasks." These are the irreducible and standardized routines that must be carried out day-to-day if the objectives of an agency are to be met.

4. **Identify Skills and Competencies.** The job tasks, in turn, must be factored into a series of skills and capacities that are needed for performance. These must be obtained either directly or indirectly from personnel who have been effective in performing these job tasks. Each skill and capacity must be translatable into real behavior (i.e., it must be identifiable as behavior that can be routinized and translated into a training program).

5. **Establish Training Standards and Contents.** Again using the people who do the job tasks well it should be possible to specify norms and values that are identified with effective job performance and to identify the content of the job for training programs. It is crucial to answer the question, "what training (institutional or on-the-job) should be given to make sure that practitioners have acquired these job standards and technical information?"

6. **Develop Consensual Basis for Certification.** Identifying job tasks, job standards, and even relevant training programs is not sufficient. At some point there must be a concern with the legitimization of the practitioners and particularly their acceptance in the field by peers. This is the problem of certification. Three points should be stressed. First, the certification must be consensually based. In other words there must be agreement among peers and gatekeepers in the field as to what are realistic and acceptable certification procedures. A basic step is to obtain this agreement. Second, the certification does not need to be based on only the successful completion of training. It may combine classroom training with on-the-job training or with written tests or with supervisor ratings. What is important is that the certification procedures demonstrate job-performance competency. Finally, one must revise or modify certification procedures if the needs of a job change require it. It is important to have the perspective that nothing should be frozen into concrete and that openness for change is a cardinal virtue.

Summing Up

We have been dealing with some facts of life that restrict meaningful health care for minority group members and circumscribe professional opportunities for minority group practitioners in the mental health field. Our argument is that the service-giving situations would be optimized if minority group members could be attended by practitioners who come from the same cultural background and share the same cultural heritage. This is a situation that does not exist at the present time. Rather, the bulk of minority group members are attended by practitioners of nonminority background. We have pointed out some of the facts of life that sustain this situation. What can be done to remedy this situation? We would suggest the following four strategies that should be regarded as starting points:

1. Some action must be taken to build up the participation of minority group members in the upper echelons of mental health practice. This involves giving them better access to the credentialing process (i.e., graduate study and training). Given the situation at the present time, we see the need for a "Marshall Plan" for minority group practitioners where a massive sum of money would be invested to develop upper echelon minority group practitioners. We also see the necessity for a program of sponsored mobility (or quotas) to target investments for minority groups where there is a substantial shortage. A first prereq-

uisite would be more financial aid for graduate study and development of non-bachelor's degree admissions procedures where undergraduate degrees would not be the primary criterion used to select students for graduate study.

2. Special efforts must be made to include minorities in the higher levels of the mental health professions (especially psychiatry). Of particular importance is the need to create opportunities in administration and research for minority group members in order to raise the consciousness of these professions in regard to minority group content.

3. Curricular changes need to be made in mental health training with more attention given to the nature of minority group life in America. These changes should be incorporated into all mental health programs for minority and nonminority students and interns.

4. We must increase our efforts in recruitment and retention in the mental health field. We are not getting enough minority group candidates and we are not keeping all of those that we get. We must be particularly sensitive to attrition based on retirement, death, and career change. The need for innovative recruitment that beats the bushes for candidates in out-of-the-way places is necessary.

The goal in increasing minority group participation in the mental health field is not simply to expand the employment opportunities for minorities. Rather, the major objective is to provide inputs from minority group perspectives that would add considerably to the effectiveness and quality of service delivery for minority group peoples.

References

Acosta, F.X. "Ethnic Variables in Psychotherapy: The Mexican American," in J.L. Martinez, Jr. (ed.), **Chicano Psychology.** New York: Academic Press, 1977.

Aptheker, H. "Afro-American Superiority: A Neglected Theme in the Literature," in R.L. Goldstein (ed.), **Black Life and Culture in the United States.** New York: Academic Press, 1971.

Barrera, M., Jr. "Mexican American Mental Health Service Utilization: A Critical Examination of Some Proposed Variables," **Community Mental Health Journal** 14 (1978), 35-45.

Foster, M. "Black Organizing: The Need for a Conceptual Model of the Ghetto," **Catalyst** 1 (1978), 77-90.

Foster, M., and Perry, L. R. "Black Self Valuation." Paper presented at the Center for Afro-American and African Studies Lecture Series, The University of Michigan, 1977.

Gibson, G. "An Approach to Identification and Prevention for Developmental Difficulties Among Mexican American Children," **American
Journal of Orthopsychiatry** 48 (1978), 96-113.

Marcas, L., Alpert, M., Urcuyo, L., and Kesselman, M. "The Effect of
Interview Language on the Evaluation of Psychopathology in Spanish
American Schizophrenic Patients," **American Journal of Psychiatry**
130 (1973), 549-553.

Nellum, A.L. and Associates, Inc. "Training Mental Health Professionals to
Serve Minority Groups." Paper prepared for the Center for Minority
Group Mental Health Programs, National Institute of Mental Health,
1975.

Ralph, J.R. **An Analysis of NIMH Efforts with Respect to Minority
Groups.** Report to the National Health Advisory Council, The Center
for the Study of Minority Group Mental Health Programs, National
Institute of Mental Health, 1974.

Ruiz, R.A. "Relative Frequency of Americans with Spanish Surnames in
Associations of Psychology, Psychiatry and Sociology," **American
Psychologist** 26 (1971), 1022-1024.

Sanchez, R.B. "The Politics of Mental Health Personnel and Its Impact on
Minority Group Mental Health Services." Paper presented at the
Second Annual Rocky Mountain Mental Health Conference on Minori-
ty Groups, 1979.

Walsh, E.J. **Dirty Work, Race and Self Esteem.** Ann Arbor, Michigan: The
Institute of Labor and Industrial Relations, The University of Michi-
gan-Wayne State University, 1975.

THE POLITICS OF MENTAL HEALTH PERSONNEL AND ITS IMPACT ON MINORITY GROUP MENTAL HEALTH SERVICES

RODOLFO B. SANCHEZ

Introduction

How do the "politics" of mental health personnel impact on minority group mental health services? Obviously, the quality of services depends ultimately on the knowledge, skills, and sensitivity of those who provide them. Assuring the quality of services depends, in turn, on what is planned and carried out across a broad spectrum of related issues. These issues include such questions as:

1. How are personnel to be developed and trained, by whom, where, and for how long?

2. How and to what degree is responsibility for supporting personnel development and training shared by the public and private sectors?

3. What methods should be used to distribute personnel more equitably by geographic area and by specialty?

4. How should personnel be recruited, utilized, licensed, certified, and reimbursed?

5. How should their effectiveness be evaluated?

On all of these issues there are many differences of substance, emphasis, and style. These differences are what make up the content of the "politics" of mental health personnel.

Usually, however, when we talk about the "politics" of mental health personnel, we are referring to the process involved. We are referring to how competing interests affect the understanding and resolution of these issues. In essence, we are talking about the process through which personnel roles and resources are allocated in society to safeguard and promote a vital public interest, namely the health, well-being, and productive functioning of people in their personal and social lives. Because the process involves the distribution of societal roles and resources, the stakes in it are high in terms of the national investment, the interests and value of the professions that comprise the mental health work force, and the opportunities available for profit including social and professional status as well as monetary reward.

My purpose here is to emphasize the obvious--minority access to the "politics" of mental health personnel and minority participation in it are essential if we are to achieve progress toward assuring the availability, accessibility, and quality of services to minority communities. In order to discuss minority access and participation in the political process, my remarks will be arranged in five major sections: 1) mental health as a national industry; 2) the major partners in mental health personnel development and training; 3) the late arrival of minorities in the personnel field; 4) the impact of lowered expectations; and 5) some selected points to consider in the "politics" of mental health personnel.

The Development of the National Mental Health Industry

The mental health personnel field has undergone vast changes in the last fifteen years. These changes have occurred under the impetus of the expansion of the mental health service delivery system and its increasing interdependence on other parts of the human service delivery effort. We have seen major changes and expansion in the types of services offered, in the number and types of places where services are offered, in the categories of personnel, in how personnel are organized and deployed in providing services, in the nature of the problems for which people seek help, and in their expectations for help and solutions.

These changes have come about for many reasons. Surely a major reason has been the coalescence of government and the professions in engineering programs for community-based care and in supporting these initiatives under various mechanisms, for instance the Community Mental Health Centers Act, health care financing schemes such as Medicare and Medicaid, and supportive service programs such as Title XX. Another reason has been changing public attitudes about what constitutes mental health problems, how and where they should be treated, and by whom.

Growth in the personnel field is evident in the core mental health professions--psychiatry, clinical psychology, social work, and psychiatric/mental health nursing. As the President's Commission on Mental Health noted, the supply of these professionals has more than doubled in the last twenty-five years thanks to a major investment of Federal funds. Personnel growth can also be seen throughout other human service occupations that interface with mental health including social services, corrections, general health, child welfare, and vocational rehabilitation. This growth is further evident in the development of diverse midlevel and paraprofessional categories. The latter comprise almost half the patient care staff in mental health facilities.

This array of specialized personnel with wide ranging and complementary skills has been generated in large measure by our greater sophistication in perceiving and appreciating two factors:

1. The causes of mental disorders are more complex and subtle than was once suspected. They encompass biological, psychological, interper-

sonal, environmental, and social factors--all of which must be studied, understood, interpreted, and respected.

2. Treatment and prevention of these disorders require a national cadre of workers with knowledge, skills, and experience commensurate with the scope and complexity of the problems presented.

As a result of expanded service delivery and financing and the increase in personnel, mental health has become a major national industry employing millions of workers and spending billions of dollars. According to the President's Commission, the direct cost of mental health services rose from about $1.7 billion a year in the late 1950s to about $17 billion in 1976 (when it was about 12 percent of all health costs). Significantly, over 50 percent of these expenditures were for services provided in nursing homes and public mental hospitals.

As specialization in the field has accelerated, the mental health industry has become even more regulated from within by a host of distinct professions and occupations, each with its own specialty, its own entry and practice requirements, and its own organized association which monitors its performance and advocates for its interests before legislators, officials, and the general public. Nevertheless, the long-established core mental health disciplines, though highly competitive among themselves, remain dominant in the industry while newer occupations which include many paraprofessional and alternative service providers must vie for autonomy and recognition.

In addition to this internal regulation, the mental health industry has long been regulated by Federal and state governments because of the large sums spent for personnel training and for services reimbursed under public programs. At times this relationship between government regulators and the mental health industry has veered toward habitual "understanding," support, and reinforcement of or tradeoffs on mutual interests when a more critical scrutiny has been needed to weigh the public good against a host of special interests. In some respects a more critical scrutiny is likely due to growing national concern about the impact of licensure and certification policies on the delivery and costs of services.

Yet, despite the growth and consolidation of the mental health industry, it is well documented that minorities have not substantially benefited from these developments. As the President's Commission dramatized, minorities and special segments of the population--including women, children, youth, the elderly, migrant families, and rural populations--are underserved by existing systems. When available, services tend to be underutilized because they conflict with or ignore cultural and linguistic heritages and values as well as existing social and community supports. Special needs have not been sufficiently understood or seriously addressed by most personnel involved in the planning and delivery of mental health services. In order to alter this neglect, it is necessary to identify and impact on the major partners that exercise power in the "politics" of mental health personnel.

Major Partners in Mental Health Personnel
Development and Training

For the sake of brevity and simplicity, I have divided the major partners into four groups: governmental structures, universities and allied training institutions, credentialing bodies, and special interest groups.

If we consider the "politics" of mental health personnel as a process, we can call these partners the significant actors in this process. They represent multiple organized public and private interests which exert power through advocacy, the shaping of public opinion, lobbying, and legislative and regulatory decision-making. Although each of these significant actors may not achieve all of their objectives in the "politics" of mental health personnel, they all express commitment to a common goal, namely sufficient personnel trained to provide quality services. Obviously in this process the issues are frequently decided not merely on objective assessment but rather on the relative political strengths of the actors. Let us now look briefly at each of these participants.

GOVERNMENTAL STRUCTURES

Governmental structures include legislatures and bureaucracies. At the national level, it is the Congress that authorizes, funds, and conducts oversight on mental health training in public priority areas. These functions are exercised in both the House and Senate by various committees-- health committees, appropriations committees, and budget committees. Congress first opened the door to public support of mental health personnel development and training in 1946 when the National Mental Health Act was passed. For many years emphasis was placed on using Federal dollars to increase the supply of professionals in the core mental health disciplines. Now the emphasis has shifted toward devising incentives to better distribute health-related personnel across geographic and specialty areas.

In the Federal bureaucracy that administers Congressional mandates, the lead role in mental health falls to the Alcohol, Drug Abuse and Mental Health Administration and its three institutes. However, many other agencies and departments have a role to play and money to spend on mental health. They include other Department of Health and Human Services units such as the National Institutes of Health and the Office of Human Development Services. They also include the Veterans Administration, the Departments of Labor and Defense, and the Law Enforcement Assistance Administration in the Justice Department. All of these agencies, whose combined budgets run far in excess of billions of dollars, spend funds for mental health including aspects of personnel training and development.

At the state level, legislatures play a key role in authorizing and appropriating funds for mental health, including training, and in providing for licensure in the mental health professions. It is worth recalling that in the last ten years or so, the states spent more than three dollars for every Federal and local dollar spent on community mental health.

At the state bureaucratic level, each state and territory has at least one governmental unit, be it a department or division, that has charge of provision and/or regulation of mental health services. Many states have separate agencies for drug abuse and alcoholism services. These state units are pivotal in that they administer and distribute the major portion of mental health funds, set standards for care, develop service and personnel priorities, collect program data, monitor affirmative action, carry out mental health statutes and regulations, and control systems of communications.

The last level of governmental structures includes counties, cities, and towns. These are closest to the people served and often exert functional control over the service delivery system and the workers in it. They seldom have the funding power that the states possess.

UNIVERSITIES AND ALLIED TRAINING INSTITUTIONS

These institutions develop and disseminate new knowledge through basic and applied research. Through their graduates and their continuing education programs, they help set the tone for the service delivery system and influence both governmental structures and the mental health professions. They are, in turn, held responsive to governmental and professional concerns through accreditation programs which confer both status and funding opportunities.

CREDENTIALING BODIES

The term "credentialing" is used here in a generic sense. It refers to the process of licensure by a unit or agency of government and to the process of certification by a nongovernmental agency or association. Credentialing bodies exert influence on the mental health personnel system by regulating levels of entry and practice in the professions. Their role is also critical to various reimbursement schemes for financing services and is likely to be strengthened under any national health insurance program.

SPECIAL INTEREST GROUPS

These organized groups represent the interests of the professions, functions within the professions (such as service delivery, research, and training), or specific populations. They have accrued and maintain power because, through their members, they can shape public opinion, muster votes, and contribute to candidates for public office through special political action committees. These groups have a marked influence on the other significant actors in the "politics" of mental health personnel, and they are regularly consulted in the planning, development, implementation, and evaluation of personnel initiatives. Often this consultation is done under contract with public funds.

In brief, these are the major actors in the "politics" of mental health personnel which must be impacted.

The Late Arrival of Minorities in the Personnel Field

With regard to the "politics" of mental health personnel, perhaps its most striking aspect is how it has gone on without, apart from, and oblivious to the millions of minorities that have been in this country for so long. In fact, minority access to this political process has come about and been sustained in large part because of social changes originating outside of the mental health field, changes that have profoundly altered public opinion, minority expectations, and minority behavior. These changes include:

1. The civil rights movement which produced equal opportunity and affirmative action programs.

2. The consumer movement which through its emphasis on individual rights, including the right to treatment and the right of consumer participation in the service planning and delivery process, helped highlight the scope and severity of needs unmet by existing personnel development and training--in particular the needs for cultural and linguistic sensitivities and for specialized approaches in working with special populations such as children, youth, the elderly, and migrants and rural residents.

Minorities have come late to the process called the "politics" of mental health personnel. They have arrived at a time when the major concerns of the significant actors in the process lie elsewhere. In short, they have come on board, ready for new initiatives, at a time when nearly everyone else is talking about lowering expectations in the face of constrained budgets.

Minorities can point with justifiable pride to signs of their increasing involvement in the mental health field. Although their presence is small in terms of overall numbers and how far and wide they are distributed, they are beginning to make some impact. But their immediate impact, and more importantly their long range impact, are highly constrained by a complex set of critical needs mostly arising from their continuing underrepresentation in the mental health work force at all levels--policy making, practice, and training. This is a handicapping situation that is unlikely to improve significantly over the next decade. Even now the outlook is that minorities will be hard-pressed to hold on to present gains in the face of limited, if not declining, Federal support. Let us review some of the critical issues in this situation affecting all minorities.

INCREASING THE SUPPLY

The underrepresentation of minorities in the mental health professions is recognized as a major national problem. As the President's Commission noted, fewer than two percent of all psychiatrists in this country are Black, the percentage of Hispanic psychiatrists is even lower, and there are only 13 who are Native Americans. A recent survey by the American Psychological Association estimated that of all doctoral-level health service providers in psychology, 0.9 percent are Black, 0.7 percent are Asian, 0.4

percent are Hispanic, and 0.1 percent are Native American. In the fields of social work and psychiatric nursing, data reveal a somewhat better situation with minorities accounting for an estimated 15 percent of the members of the National Association of Social Workers and seven percent of the nurses belonging to the American Nursing Association's Division of Psychiatric and Mental Health Nursing. Among candidates preparing for practice, minorities continue to be underrepresented although some gains have been registered, mostly in social work and psychiatric nursing.

The future is even more problematic; hope for improvement rests on longitudinal efforts to stimulate and support an increase in the pool of qualified and motivated minority candidates for the mental health professions, especially those requiring long training. These efforts to recruit and motivate should begin in junior and senior high school, if not earlier, and continue through the postdoctoral level. Moreover they should attract minority candidates not only to service delivery positions but also to teaching, research, and administrative posts. Clearly such efforts will require the redirection of existing training funds and the targeted allocation of funds.

In response to the problem of minority underrepresentation, the President's Commission recommended that a major objective of Federal personnel policy should be to increase the number of minority mental health professionals. An implementation task force responsible for developing proposals to carry out the Commission's recommendations has put forth various suggestions that are mostly in line with the Commission's emphasis on the need to develop a national minority mental health cadre. The task now is to mobilize the political will to act decisively on these recommendations and proposals, even in austere times.

We should also note that minority underrepresentation in the mental health disciplines is further aggravated by the limited recognition and support of other vehicles for entry. More and more, minority students are enrolling in applied associate and bachelor's level college-based programs for mental health training. These programs should serve as steps in a career ladder leading to further training, education, and advancement in the professions for workers who are so motivated.

IMPROVING MENTAL HEALTH CURRICULA AND TRAINING

With regard to mental health curricula, it is vital that we remedy deficiencies by developing and incorporating minority content into the training of all mental health personnel. The goal here is to better equip them to serve minority consumers and to respond to minority concerns in more understanding and sensitive ways. Traditionally, mental health training programs have prepared most workers to provide those services that are either underutilized or not available to minorities and special populations. By and large that is still happening today.

IMPROVING THE SKILLS OF EXISTING PERSONNEL

The retraining of existing personnel is needed to enable them to serve minorities and special populations as well as to work more effectively with those providing nontraditional services such as indigenous therapies and "indirect" services (e.g., consultation and education, prevention, and improved linkages among health, mental health, and human service systems). In this regard, strong leadership in providing opportunities and support for this continuing education effort should be exercised by various entities-- state agencies for mental health, drug and alcohol abuse, and related human services; universities and allied training institutions; and the professions themselves.

EXAMINING CREDENTIALING PRACTICES

We must focus more attention on institutional barriers that affect the degree of minority access to the mental health professions and their services. These barriers at the state and professional levels include the credentialing process, that is, state licensure and in-professional certification policies.

The economic and political clout of professional organizations representing mental health personnel has enabled many to largely determine the requirements for entry into these professions at the state level. By and large, state licensure boards are dominated by members of the professions being licensed. Many state legislatures delegate responsibility for licensing personnel to professional groups that have a direct interest (i.e., a monetary interest) in restraining the number and type of individuals permitted to enter and practice in their professions.

There are three issues that should be touched upon here:

1. In many cases the original purpose of licensure has been transformed. From the original goal of protecting the public, it has gradually moved toward insuring minimal competence, then toward establishing higher and higher levels of practice. Is this sound public policy? The question should be debated. Some suggest that licensure should be limited in scope and directly designed to protect the public from harm while the matter of competence should be left to voluntary professional associations. This decision should properly be made by the public through its legislative representatives. Unfortunately, legislatures tend to be responsive almost solely to professional interest groups on this issue.

2. State licensing practices rely heavily on academic credentials. The notion that these credentials represent a minimal level of competence is being increasingly challenged by educational experts. Some cite evidence that credentials are not causally related or even correlated with work performance. If credentials are not reasonable indicators of nonacademic performance, then other indicators of minimal levels of professional performance such as testing must be considered to protect the public. But the state of the art of test reliability is not

well advanced and cultural bias against minorities in test construction must be eliminated.

3. The majority of minority mental health personnel can be classified in allied health or paraprofessional positions. State licensing mechanisms and professional certification policies can act to stifle innovation, thereby inhibiting the development of new types of personnel or the efficient utilization of existing types. The practical result is the limitation of the professional status of allied health and paraprofessional workers.

ASSESSING MINORITY MENTAL HEALTH PERSONNEL NEEDS

It is essential that we press hard for a comprehensive nationwide assessment of minority mental health personnel needs. This assessment should be made by cultural, racial, and/or ethnic group; profession; and geographic area. It should take into account the specific and differential needs of various minority populations including diverse cultural and linguistic subgroups within some of these populations (e.g., among Asians, Hispanics, and Native Americans).

MAKING GOOD USE OF SCARCE RESOURCES

Finally, as long as we continue to grapple with all of these complex issues, it will be necessary to develop and foster innovative, ingenious alternatives to insure that scarce minority personnel resources are effectively and equitably distributed and utilized. This will require heightened sensitivity and a willingness to match personal and professional goals with the urgent unmet needs of minority communities, both immediate and long-term.

All of these complex and interrelated issues consitute a basic minority agenda for action in the "politics" of mental health personnel development. But who in the process is listening? Who is prepared to work for this?

The Impact of Lowered Expectations

Minorities have been encouraged by the emphasis given to their needs in the report of the President's Commission on Mental Health. To a large degree the spirit and intent of the Commission are reflected in task force follow-up proposals. But implementation has yet to occur. The Congress and the Federal officials designated to take follow-up steps have yet to act.

But now the political debate has become increasingly overshadowed by austere, "belt-tightening" forecasts. Emphasis has shifted from increasing the supply of mental health professionals to concern over the distribution of the existing supply. The only exception is psychiatry; in this case, a strong lobbying effort has been mounted to garner more funds for psychiatry as a shortage area in the field of mental health.

Federal support for mental health training began to decline in 1969. In that year, the Nixon Administration started a phase-out policy, first with psychiatry, then psychology, then social work, then nursing, and finally with training of all types. In response, Congress reinstated a portion of the cuts but never enough to offset rising costs, the impact of inflation, and even steeper cutbacks in successive years. For example, National Institute of Mental Health support for clinical and research training dropped from $120 million in 1969 to $85.1 million in 1976. In recent years, mental health training support has gone up slightly, but for fiscal year 1980 the budget calls for a reduction in clinical training support throughout the Alcohol, Drug Abuse and Mental Health Administration and a continuation of the previous fiscal year's funding level for research training--in effect, a decline given inflation.

Clearly, reductions and hold-the-line funding do not hold much promise for vigorous efforts to improve training in accord with minority concerns and related priorities recommended by the President's Commission. How much will be allocated to minority training concerns is yet to be determined and should be monitored closely, for it is the flow of money that measures agreement between an agency's announced priorities and its actual program operations.

The outlook for increases in Federal training support are not promising. The growing national concern over inflation and deficit spending has undoubtedly affected the willingness of Congress to approve additional dollars for domestic programs including health care. This national trend is equally pervasive at the state level, with "Proposition 13" in California being the most notable example. Given the overall austere mood and climate on fiscal matters, it will be necessary for minorities to work even more skillfully in the political process to insure that their concerns are addressed regardless of the size of budgets.

Selected Points to Consider in the "Politics"
of Mental Health Personnel

The following are a few of the many aspects that minorities should consider when working in the "politics" of mental health personnel.

Mental health interest groups have developed strong national constituencies and have played a leading role in influencing how both state and Federal governments have supported mental health programs and personnel. Interest groups have been successful in helping to mold national legislative initiatives, shaping state legislation which defines who can practice in a given profession, and influencing the execution of legislative and regulatory directives at the local level.

There are several factors that make this interest group-government relationship work:

1. Using a variety of techniques, such as grassroots lobbying and political action committees, interest groups have traditionally supported candidates for state and Federal offices that directly affect the outcome of legislation impacting on their professions. Perhaps the clearest example of this is organized medicine. Organized medicine has played a crucial role in shaping health service, health financing, and health training legislation and has contributed more total dollars to both state and Congressional candidates than any other single occupational group in the country.

2. Close working relationships have developed over the years between members of various state and Congressional health subcommittees and members of the health-related professions which supported their election. In these working relationships, both formal and informal views on the issues are regularly exchanged.

3. Another technique is to influence the implementation process once legislation is passed. Many professional groups have been able to place their members in key positions in state and Federal agencies which administer health-related programs. This is not to say that such individuals are "puppets" of their professions but rather that the training, experience, and background of these individuals probably insures that "understanding" attitudes about the interests of their professions will prevail in many instances.

The principal benefits from the above factors are information and timing; that is, interest groups keep regularly informed of political trends and developments. This, in turn, enables them to act at critical moments to insure that their positions are considered. Perhaps one of the most important gains that minorities can make is to share in the flow of information that is regularly provided to various interest organizations, often far in advance of actual decision-making processes.

Public attitudes, including media interest, also have a vital impact on the political process. Minorities must give greater attention to the ways they communicate their message and advocate for their interests.

Public hearings on legislation and regulations are also vital forums. They are critical because they enable legislators and officials, who may not always have the relevant expertise in a given subject area, to hear and judge various views on a given issue. In some instances, these hearings may be pro forma gatherings; but nonetheless they afford minorities the opportunity to be seen and heard until some action is taken or as a particular program is being monitored and evaluated.

The following lessons to be drawn from this discussion are, in essence, elementary, but they are basic:

1. Minorities must plan and exercise a greater commitment to positively affect the political process at all levels.

2. Much more unity and solidarity must be evidenced among minority groups in working together to help shape national and state mental health policies in personnel development.

3. Minorities must concentrate their efforts on the support of candidates and appointees who merit office because of their demonstrated understanding and sensitivity to minority mental health personnel and service needs.

4. Minorities must work together to keep state and national legislators and their staffs well-informed of their situation. Minorities should suggest new initiatives, needed reforms and improvements in existing programs, and compliance monitoring of these same programs.

5. Minorities must concentrate more on shaping public opinion and media outlook on their special concerns in the mental health field including the need for personnel.

6. Minorities must secure increased representation on the policy boards of professional organizations in mental health along with more appointments to state and Federal offices with mental health program responsibilities. Moreover, minorities must work with these representatives by giving them support and by insuring their accountability to the interests of minority communities.

PART FIVE

RESEARCH

This concluding section deals with the status of mental health research on minority groups. In a wide-ranging article, Stanley Sue discusses previous research themes and trends and suggests new research directions. He goes on to examine the issues of the value of research, who should conduct research, the methods and concepts to be used, and the relationship between researchers and minority group communities. Sue includes sixteen specific recommendations in his presentation and concludes with a plea for ". . . more research, greater systematic efforts, use of proper conceptual and methodological tools, involvement of qualified and sensitive researchers, increased collaboration between researchers and the community, the enhancement of mental health, and more research funds."

ETHNIC MINORITY RESEARCH: TRENDS AND DIRECTIONS

STANLEY SUE[1]

In order to present a state-of-the-art paper on ethnic minority research, two problems immediately come to mind. First, the four major ethnic minority groups--Asian Americans, Blacks, Hispanics, and Native Americans--have similar as well as different mental health research needs and experiences. In order to speak of ethnic minority research, it is to some extent necessary to draw out general trends applicable to all groups and at the same time to refer to each group's separate concerns. Second, ethnic minority research has generated a great deal of controversy and rhetoric because research is not simply a scientific task but rather a process involving scientific methodology, values, needs, philosophical perspectives, politics, and funding. My presentation reflects the roles of a researcher, ethnic minority individual, and consumer of research and represents my **own** perspectives.

I want to cover several questions and issues:

1. What are the research themes and trends that have evolved with respect to minority groups?

2. What themes or areas in mental health, drug, and alcohol research should we focus upon?

3. What is the value of research for minority groups?

4. Who should conduct research on what populations?

5. What methods should we use in research?

6. What is the relationship between researchers, various communities, and consumers?

7. How can we obtain funds for ethnic research?

Obviously, in such a brief presentation, I can only touch upon these issues and concerns, and the recommendations that will be offered are simply meant to be a means of provoking thought.

---

[1] A revised version of this paper will appear in E.E. Jones, and S.J. Korchin (eds.). **Minority Mental Health.** New York: Praeger, in press.

Themes and Trends

It is impossible to appreciate the current status of ethnic research without reference to past research themes. Three general themes can be identified: 1) the inferiority model, 2) the deficit model, and 3) the bicultural or multicultural model. In the foreward to the book **Racism and Psychiatry** by Thomas and Sillen (1972), Kenneth Clark, past President of the American Psychological Association, indicates that social scientists often reflect the trends of society. He states that: "Probably the most disturbing insight obtained from the relentless clarity with which this book documents the case of racism in American psychiatry is the ironic fact that the students, research workers, and professionals in the behavioral sciences--like members of the clergy and educators--are no more immune by virtue of their values and training to the disease and superstition of American racism than is the average man" (Thomas and Sillen, 1972: xii). Indeed, Thomas and Sillen document the historical theme perpetuated by research that Blacks are psychologically and intellectually inferior to whites. Society was largely held unaccountable for the plight of ethnics since the victims themselves were to blame. I do not want to dwell on this point except to say that early research was intended to show the inferiority of certain minority group individuals.

More recently we have moved and continue to move in a direction that attributes the plight of ethnic minority groups to society and social conditions. There were attempts to study societal racism and its effects on ethnic minorities. The victim was blamed less, for it was believed that society was the culprit. Gordon Allport (1954) in his classic book **The Nature of Prejudice** indicated that prejudice and discrimination could not solely be attributed to abnormal personalities or "rednecks." Rather, social psychological processes in society were responsible, a theme reiterated by James Jones (1972) and Thomas Pettigrew (1973). The assumption was that prejudice and discrimination created stress for minority groups. Consequently, many minority group individuals were deficient, underprivileged, pathological, or deviant. Kramer, Rose, and Willis (1973: 355) went so far as to say that "Racist practices undoubtedly are key factors--perhaps the most important ones--in producing mental disorders in Blacks and other underprivileged groups. . . ." Many studies documented the social, economic, and mental health conditions of minority groups. Blacks were presumed to have high rates of mental disorders, a poor family structure, lower intelligence, and high rates of drug addiction; Native Americans were prone to alcoholism and suicide; Hispanics were described as having tendencies toward drunkenness, criminal behavior, and undependability (c.f., Fischer, 1969; Jones, 1972; Kitano, 1974; Padilla and Ruiz, 1973). Interestingly, Asian Americans were believed to have few problems since they were supposedly free from prejudice and discrimination (Sue, Sue, and Sue, 1975). Most ethnic minorities were assumed to have serious problems involving self-identity and self-esteem because of culture conflict.

The deficit model is helpful in focusing on society rather than the individual ethnic minority in explaining the status of minority groups. The implication is that analysis of institutional factors is necessary. We also know that racism does affect the physical, social, economic, and psychological well-being of minority groups. Finally, because of discrimination and unresponsiveness to minority groups, we know that mental heath treatment and service delivery systems are inadequate. The deficit model, therefore, stimulated research into societal factors, the effects of racism, and the adequacy of treatment services.

The deficit model, while valuable in certain respects, also raised grave concerns.

1. The emphasis on deficits neglected strengths, competencies, and skills found in ethnic families, communities, and cultures (Jones, 1972; Thomas and Sillen, 1972).

2. There was a tendency to focus upon treatment or remediation of "deficiencies," rather than upon the institutional roots for the deficiencies, as means of resolving problems.

3. The deficit model implied that certain ethnic group behaviors were psychopathological if they deviated from mainstream norms (Padilla and Ruiz, 1973) so that a strict assimilation model was deemed appropriate.

4. Conceptual and methodological challenges were made concerning the adequacy of research findings. For example, in the areas of ethnic identity and self-esteem (Banks, 1976; Brand, Padilla, and Ruiz, 1974), family structure (Jones, 1972), and rates of psychopathology (Fischer, 1968), many investigators felt that previous research strategies were inadequate. Similarly, the view that Asian Americans are free from, or immune to, the effects of prejudice and discrimination is inaccurate (Sue et al., 1975).

These criticisms stimulated what I call the rise in bicultural or multicultural research. There is a growing emphasis on the interaction between ethnic culture, mainstream American values, and racism, not only as causing conflicts and stress but also as providing seeds for growth and development of competencies. Behaviors cannot be simply judged as being appropriate or inappropriate without reference to the context in which such behaviors occur (Grier and Cobbs, 1968).

In summary, research on ethnic minority groups has moved from an inferiority model to a deficit model and now to a bicultural model. Obviously, these are trends rather than distinct, nonoverlapping stages. It should also be noted that we are still at elementary stages in terms of knowing the mental health status of ethnic minority groups, the causes of mental health needs, and solutions. For those who want more specific information on mental health research on ethnic minorities, it should be mentioned that the following annotated bibliographies sponsored by the Center for Minority Group Mental Health Programs of the National Institute of Mental Health (NIMH) are available: Asian Americans (Morishima et al., 1979), Native Americans (Kelso and Attneave, 1981), Spanish speaking/Spanish surnamed (Padilla et al., 1978), and Blacks (Gary, forthcoming).

Directions for Research

Let me now turn to directions that we should take in ethnic minority research and, in doing so, propose a model by which we can systematize research efforts. I am tempted to say that we need more research in almost all areas involving minority groups: essential demographic data, needs assessment, culture, education, ethnic identity, mental health, community functioning, discrimination, the costs of racism not only upon minority groups but upon all Americans, family structure, psychopathology, sex roles, mental health delivery systems, and ethnic resources to name a few. Where, among these and other areas, should we begin in our research priorities? I would like to introduce a four-stage cycle of research and to indicate important areas upon which to focus, as indicated in Figure 1. The four stages are: 1) status of ethnic minorities, 2) causes of psychological well-being or disturbance, 3) solutions to mental health problems, and 4) implementation of solutions. These four areas are intimately related. If we do not know the status and situation of minority groups, then it is fruitless to look for causal factors. If we do not know the causes for mental health status, then it is exceedingly difficult to plan for solutions. Finally, knowing solutions to problems is of no value unless we can implement programs and policies which in turn affect the status and well-being of ethnics. Let me briefly discuss the four stages.

Figure 1

RESEARCH DIRECTIONS

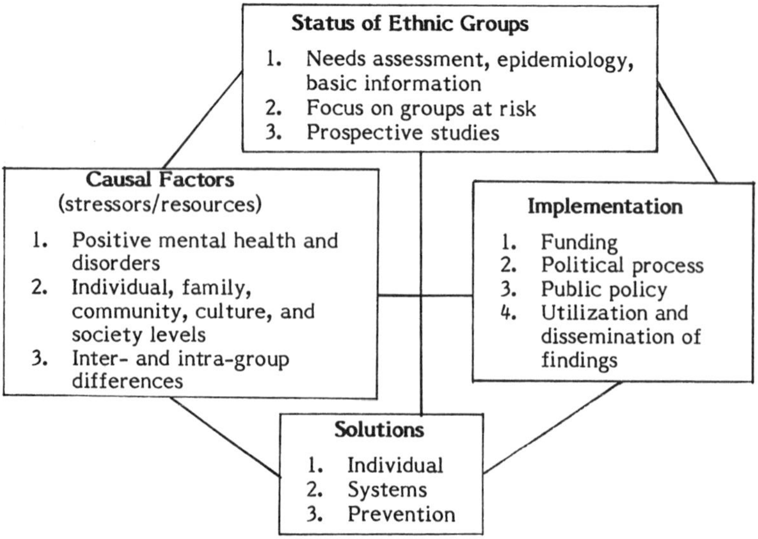

Status of Ethnic Groups
1. Needs assessment, epidemiology, basic information
2. Focus on groups at risk
3. Prospective studies

Causal Factors
(stressors/resources)
1. Positive mental health and disorders
2. Individual, family, community, culture, and society levels
3. Inter- and intra-group differences

Implementation
1. Funding
2. Political process
3. Public policy
4. Utilization and dissemination of findings

Solutions
1. Individual
2. Systems
3. Prevention

First, in the status of ethnic minorities we need an increase in the quantity and quality of research studies. Because of methodological, conceptual, and practical problems in ethnic research (to be discussed later), we are still at elementary levels in terms of having systematic and accurate information on various ethnic minority groups. That is why many researchers are attempting to conduct needs assessments of ethnic groups. That is why researchers are constantly frustrated. We lack basic and essential information. For example, we still do not know how many Asians there are in the United States. Estimates vary between official sources and community leaders. The same situation exists for Mexican Americans. There is still a great deal of controversy over the rates and extent of mental disorders, drug abuse, and alcoholism among ethnic group individuals. My first recommendation is that we begin to systematically, purposefully, and nationally collect basic demographic data and epidemiological information on various ethnic groups and subgroups. My second recommendation is that groups at risk receive a high priority in our research efforts. Immigrants, the poor, the elderly, the powerless, and other high risk groups should receive special attention. My third recommendation is that needs assessments be planned so that we can project for the future. Changes are rapidly occurring so that what is true today is not true tomorrow. For example, Padilla (1977) indicates that Hispanics are the fastest growing minority group and that by the year 2000 they will be the largest. In the state of California, ethnic groups will, in the near future, outnumber white Americans. The Asian population in the United States will double from 1970 to 1980 (Owan, 1975). Native Americans are increasingly becoming an urban group (Trimble, 1976). Based upon demographic statistics, risk categories, and future projections, Morton Kramer (1975), past Director of the Division of Biometry and Epidemiology of NIMH, has predicted that by 1985, there will be a substantial increase of Blacks and other nonwhites admitted to mental health facilities and of Blacks and other nonwhites diagnosed as schizophrenics. That is, the percentage increase will be greater among nonwhites than whites because the former would be more heavily represented in the high risk groups. All of these projections indicate the necessity to address our efforts not only for today but also for tomorrow.

Second, more research should be devoted to causal factors in mental health and mental disturbance. I want to make a distinction between health and disturbance. Health is not simply the absence of disturbance. Individuals may not be "mentally ill" but rather have low positive mental . health (e.g., low self-esteem, anger, feelings of powerlessness, etc.) in the same way that one can be free of disease but have poor physical health. I do not want to carry this analogy too far since medical model concepts are too limiting. My point (and fourth recommendation) is that our attention on causal factors be expanded to include positive mental health as well as what has traditionally been considered disturbed behavior (i.e., psychiatric disorders including drug and alcohol abuse). Development of self-esteem, feelings of personal control, mastery, achievement, self-identity, happiness, etc., would all fall under the rubric of positive mental health. Then too, when one examines causal factors, there is a tendency to dwell on stressors. Culture conflict, culture shock, stereotypes, discrimination, poverty, etc., are stressors that are believed to influence mental health. As mentioned previously, a focus on stressors helps to perpetuate a deficit model orientation. But mental health and mental disorders are also affected by resources that the society provides. The fifth recommendation is that resources and their means of preventing or intervening on behalf of mental health be studied. Note that specific areas of study can be conceived as having potential as stressors or resources. Thus my sixth recommendation is that the individual, family, community, culture, and society be studied as stressors **and** resources. Finally, ethnic minority groups show a great deal of differences. Even among the major groups, there are major differences in factors such as social class, immigrant status, urban-rural residence, integrated-segregated neighborhoods, etc. The seventh recommendation is that we begin to focus more specifically on inter- and intra-group variations and on ethnic conceptions of behavior and disorders.

Third, the search for solutions is crucial. We know that the mental health needs of minority groups are very serious. There is evidence that minority group clients are not preferred by therapists; that even when these clients are in psychotherapy, rapport and good working relationships between client and therapist are difficult to achieve; and that the mental health delivery system is unresponsive. For example, in one study (Sue, 1977), it was found that approximatly half of all Asian American, Black, Chicano, and Native American clients failed to return for treatment after one session in community mental health centers, compared to a much lower failure-to-return rate for whites. I have three recommendations dealing with solutions at the levels of: 1) individuals, 2) systems, and 3) time of intervention. With respect to the individual level, we need more research into the factors that facilitate positive outcomes in treatment (recommendation eight). It has been frequently stated that treatment needs to be culturally responsive, that similarity in race between therapist and client is important, that therapists must be open, flexible, and free of stereotypes, and so on. Nevertheless, questions remain and must be researched. For example, what specific therapist attributes are necessary for effective treatment with minority group clients? How can we better train students and paraprofessionals to work with minority clients? The question of therapist attributes is one that faces the entire mental health field. For ethnic minorities, the question has posed a much larger problem since we have lacked resources to examine the issue and not much attention has been placed on ethnicity by the mental health field. At a level higher than the individual one, we need to focus on systems and community processes (recommendation nine). Research into systems can be divided into ethnic and mainstream solutions. Ethnic solutions are those cultural-community means of resolving emotional disturbances. Medicine men, curanderas, third-party intermediaries, herbalists, and even ethnic churches often play a vital role in treatment. Their impact and value in ethnic communities have been assumed. Greater research must be conducted to investigate their effectiveness so that these resources can be better utilized and that the effective ingredients can be trained in others. Mainstream solutions are those that are in widespread use today. Community mental health centers, hospitals, clinics, and other facilities form the major part of our mental health system. What kinds of changes should occur in our system to better respond to minority group needs? In enhancing the mental health of minority groups, the development and assessment of our system should proceed in three directions. First, evaluation should be made of existing services and programs to meet the needs of ethnic groups. For example, many community mental health centers have hired ethnic specialists, utilized nonprofessionals, and engaged in outreach services or client advocacy programs. Have these been effective? Second, independent (free from existing programs) but parallel (i.e., similar to existing services) programs have been established for ethnic groups. That is, many services or agencies have been created to serve minority groups. An important research issue is to determine their effectiveness and to find out what aspects are particularly responsive so that others can initiate or modify programs to better meet the needs of minority groups. Third, new non-parallel services should be developed and evaluated. New therapies, agencies, or institutions aimed at ethnic groups are important.

Solutions at the individual and systems levels are obviously needed. Time of intervention is also an important factor to consider in our efforts. Recommendation ten is that primary prevention programs in mental health, drug abuse, and alcoholism be given high priority. The reduction of the incidence of disorders through elimination of causal factors or through improved resources must be investigated. Charles Willie (1978), a member of the President's Commission on Mental Health, acknowledges the key role of prevention. He states that "In the past, effective treatment for various disorders including mental disorders have been made available first to the affluent and members of the majority. Prevention, however, benefits both the majority and the minority, the affluent as well as the disadvantaged. Minorities therefore, may help the majority as well as their own members by insisting that preventive efforts pertaining to mental disorders not be delayed."

I am not naive in recommending research on primary prevention. I realize that: 1) priority is often given to urgent and acute problems needing treatment, 2) fruits of prevention programs take years to demonstrate, 3) past prevention efforts (such as in early education programs, headstart, etc.) have frequently lacked sound methodology, and 4) some researchers have doubted whether we know enough to begin massive primary prevention programs. However, if we are to truly respond to ethnic minority groups, reduction in the incidence, not merely in the prevalence of disorders must occur. Research proposals on prevention should be encouraged and supported.

Thus far, the importance of research in determining the status of minority groups, the causal factors in psychological well-being, and the possible solutions have been discussed. The fourth and final step (recommendation eleven) in research is to implement strategies and solutions. Funds are needed for mental health research in general and minority group mental health in particular. In addition, there must be means of implementing the possible solutions suggested by research findings. Here the task is to increase funding, to have influence in the political process, to affect public programs and policies, and to make others aware of needs and problems. I have no simple answers as to how this immense task can be achieved. My point is that implementation is a logical and necessary step in enhancing psychological well-being.

Value of Research

Research has been attacked as having no applied value, as being too abstract and esoteric, and as perpetuating stereotypic, biased, or even inaccurate views of minority groups. Because of the urgent and pressing needs of minority groups, recommendation twelve is that priority be given to research that has the potential for significantly contributing to the betterment and well-being of minority groups in the short or long term. The issue here is not basic verus applied research. Basic research often has applied value and applied research has often failed to produce meaningful findings and practical implications. Research proposals for funding should be explicit in delineating their impact and significance. Very few, if any, instances can be found where a single piece of research has resulted in social change, social action, public policies, etc. Rather, the systematic, rigorous, and multidimensional approach to attacking a problem or issue has probably been of greatest benefit. Seen in this light, research can serve to document needs to the public and to policy makers, to point to the underlying roots of problems, and to suggest possible means of intervention. Research can have tremendous value if properly targeted at problems systematically conducted, and initiated with proper research strategies and tools.

Researchers and Those Researched

Since early ethnic research was for the most part conducted by white researchers and since minority groups often see research findings as being biased and inaccurate, the essential question of who should conduct research on what populations must be addressed. Some feel that only members of a particular group should conduct research on that group. Ethnicity of the researchers would be a necessary (but not sufficient) condition. Others believe that regardless of race or ethnicity, qualifications and ethnic sensitivity are sufficient factors for ethnic research. However, the issue is further complicated by the possibility that factors such as qualifications and sensitivity may be related to ethnicity. For example, Brazziel (1973: 41) states that "Today's white researchers are perhaps counterproductive in Black communities, not because they are white, but because they are poorly trained." Brazziel goes on to argue that white researchers: 1) have less credibility than Black researchers in Black communities, and 2) are affected by their own training and have inadequacies in perceiving racism. Seen in this light, ethnicity of researchers and ethnic background are important factors to consider.

It is unwise and impractical to limit ethnic research to researchers who
have ethnic similarity to the group being studied. First, there is still a
manpower shortage of ethnic researchers. Second, various white researchers (or ethnic researchers who study ethnic groups different from their
own) have made valuable contributions. Third, race relations, racism,
mental health, etc., must be issues and problems addressed by all Americans. Fourth, it is simply impossible to limit research on ethnic groups
according to the race of the researcher. Qualifications, sensitivity, and
credibility should dictate who does research on what populations. However,
since these characteristics may be related to ethnicity and since ethnic
perspectives have been lacking in ethnic research, recommendation thir-
teen is that well-qualified researchers with proposals of merit should
conduct ethnic research; nevertheless, since researchers of the same ethnicity as a studied minority group often have special insights, credibility, and
sensitivity and are just now beginning to have an impact on ethnic research,
these investigators should have increased support and encouragement. The
implication is that ethnic researchers for one reason or another have only
recently had an impact on research. Another implication is that researchers who differ ethnically from the group being studied must develop sensitivity, insight, and credibility with that group, and must seek assistance and
advice from group members.

Methodology and Conceptual Issues

One persistent problem in minority group research is the use of proper
conceptual and methodological tools. This problem in ethnic research
includes: 1) use of culturally biased measures, 2) inadequte consideration
of ethnic response sets, 3) faulty interpretations of minority group behaviors, 4) lack of norms in evaluating ethnic responses, and 5) effects of
experimenter's race or ethnicity upon subjects. Many researchers have
pointed to conceptual and methodological research issues in areas such as
intelligence (Jorgensen, 1973; Williams, 1974), personality and ethnic
identity (Banks, 1976; Brand, Padilla, and Ruiz, 1974; Nobles, 1974), mental
health (Sue, Sue, and Sue, 1975; Thomas and Sillen, 1972), and family structure (Gordon, 1973; Trimble, 1976). These investigators have been critical
of many research findings on minority groups. Strict adherence to traditional concepts and methodological tools has made it difficult to explore
the use of more innovative concepts and methodologies that might be
applied more appropriately to minority groups. I believe that many ethnic
researchers are frustrated by the proliferation of studies that have
methodological and conceptual inadequacies. They are also frustrated by:
1) requirements upon which research granting agencies often insist that
only traditional and well-researched instruments be used; 2) editorial
policies of journals that have similar requirements; and 3) the lack of more
adequate concepts and methodologies to study ethnic groups. In trying to
avoid the pitfalls of previous research, investigators have had to start
"from scratch." The fourteenth recommendation is that support be given to
the creation or development of innovative and more adequate concepts and

instruments in ethnic research rather than to the continued use of traditional strategies that fail to accurately convey minority group experiences. The issue is not so much over whether research should be correlational, experimental, single-subject, field, laboratory, or participant-observer; rather, it is over the issues of culturally biased measures, response sets, etc. mentioned previously.

Community Relations

Within the last decade, many minority group individuals have grown increasingly suspicious of the motives of the researcher and of the outcome of research (Sue and Sue, 1972). Ethnic communities often feel that research is irrelevant at best and inaccurate at worst. They feel exploited as subjects of research and distrustful of researchers. Indeed, funding for research (ethnic and nonethnic) has come under greater scrutiny by the public and by decision-makers. Some of the problems are due to public misunderstandings of the research endeavor. But probably to a greater extent, difficulties have arisen because communities have not been called upon as collaborators in research. Research--especially that dealing with social issues, societal problems, and ethnic minority groups--requires broad participation. Gordon (1973: 94) advises that ". . . parties share in guiding the total research endeavor, including decisions about research conceptualization, design methodology, and the dissemination of the utilization of data. We must recognize that such data are used to influence public policy; they generate political consequences which must be to the benefit of the community involved." Recommendation fifteen is that researchers and ethnic communities collaborate and share in research endeavors.

Funding for Research

It is very clear that funding has a profound impact on the direction, nature, quality, quantity, etc. of research. What is also clear is that while a compelling case can be made for the necessity of substantial funds for research in general, ethnic research must receive high priority. Issues of minority group mental health, drug and alcohol use, and racism are urgent ones that have been inadequately addressed. All funding agencies in the mental health arena must systematically and substantially support ethnic minority research (recommendation sixteen). The problems and issues concerning minority group mental health are not limited simply to ethnic minority groups. Aside from the moral or human rights issue, racism continues to affect not only minority groups but also all Americans. Issues concerning integration, busing, poverty, and well-being affect us all. Funding for mental health research should reflect the magnitude of the issue or problem. It is through research that needs, problems, issues, and solutions can be presented to the public, decision-makers, scientific and professional communities, research granting agencies, etc.

Conclusions

In such a brief presentation, it is difficult to examine the issues of minority group research in much depth. The sixteen recommendations are not intended to be specific or definitive. For example, I have not specified whether research on, say, ethnic families is more important than research on cultural values. In view of the need for research in all areas (e.g., needs assessment and epidemiology, stressors and resources, solutions, and implementation), my plea is for **more** research, greater **systematic** efforts, use of **proper** conceptual and methodological tools, involvement of **qualified** and sensitive researchers, increased **collaboration** between researchers and the community, the **enhancement** of mental health, and more research **funds.** Access to policy-makers and funding sources should be facilitated. Furthermore, if we are to truly respond to research needs of ethnic minorities, the current trend to include more minority group persons on research review groups, in administrative positions, and as decision-makers must be expanded. These suggestions and recommendations are not new for the most part. But they bear repeating in light of the unmet needs and issues regarding minority group mental health.

References

Allport, G. **The Nature of Prejudice.** Reading, MA: Addison Wesley, 1954.

Banks, W. "White Preference in Blacks: A Paradigm in Search of a Phenomenon," **Psychological Bulletin** 83 (1976), 1179-1186.

Brand, E., Padilla, A., and Ruiz, R. "Ethnic Identification and Preference: A Review," **Psychological Bulletin** 81 (1974), 860-890.

Brazziel, W. "White Research in Black Communities: When Solutions Become a Part of the Problem," **Journal of Social Issues** 29 (1973), 41-44.

Fischer, J. "Negroes, Whites and Rates of Mental Illness: Reconsideration of a Myth," **Psychiatry** 32 (1969), 428-446.

Gary, L. **Bibliography of Black Mental Health.** Washington, DC: Howard University, forthcoming.

Gordon, T. "Notes on White and Black Psychology," **Journal of Social Issues** 29 (1973), 87-96.

Grier, W., and Cobbs, P. **Black Rage.** New York: Basic Books, 1968.

Jones, J. **Prejudice and Racism.** Reading, MA: Addison Wesley, 1972.

Jorgensen, C. "IQ Tests and Thier Educational Supporters," **Journal of Social Issues.** 29 (1973), 33-40.

Kelso, D. and Attneave, C. **Bibliography of North American Indian Mental Health.** Westport, CT: Greenwood Press, 1981.

Kitano, H. **Race Relations.** Englewood Cliffs, NJ: Prentice Hall, 1974.

Kramer, M. "Psychiatric Services and the Changing Institutional Scene." Paper presented at the President's Biomedical Research Panel, National Institutes of Health, 1975.

Kramer, M., Rosen, B., and Willis, E. "Definitions and Distributions of Mental Disorders in a Racist Society," in C. Willie, B. Kramer, and B. Brown (eds.), **Racism and Mental Health.** Pittsburgh: University of Pittsburgh Press, 1973.

Morishima, James, et al. **Handbook of Asian American/Pacific Islander Mental Health.** Vol. 1. Washington, DC: U.S. Government Printing Office, 1979.

Nobles, W. "Psychological Research and the Black Self-Concept: A Critical Review," **Journal of Social Issues** 29 (1973), 11-32.

Owan, T. "Asian Americans: A Case of Benighted Neglect." Paper presented at the National Conference of Social Welfare, 1975.

Padilla, A. "Foreward," in E. Olmedo and S. Lopez (eds.), **Hispanic Mental Health Professionals.** Los Angeles: Spanish Speaking Mental Health Research Center, 1977.

Padilla, A., and Ruiz, R. **Latino Mental Health: A Review of the Literature.** Washington, DC: U.S. Government Printing Office, 1973.

Padilla, A., et al. **Hispanic Mental Health Bibliography II.** Los Angeles: Spanish Speaking Mental Health Research Center, 1977.

Sue, S. "Community Mental Health Services to Minority Groups: Some Optimism, Some Pessimism," **American Psychologist** 32 (1977), 616-624.

Sue, D., and Sue, S. "Ethnic Minorities: Resistance to Being Researched," **Professional Psychology** 3 (1972), 11-17.

Sue, S., Sue, D.W., and Sue, D. "Asian Americans as a Minority Group," **American Psychologist** 30 (1975), 906-910.

Thomas, A., and Sillen, S. **Racism and Psychiatry.** Secaucus, NJ: Citadel Press, 1972.

Trimble, J. "Value Differences Among American Indians: Concerns for the Concerned Counselor," in P. Pedersen et al. (eds.), **Counseling Across Cultures.** Honolulu: University Press of Hawaii, 1976.

Williams, R. "Scientific Racism and IQ--The Silent Mugging of the Black Community," **Psychology Today** 7 (1974), 32, 34, 37, 38, 41, 101.

Willie, C. "Stress Producing Social Circumstances that Trouble the Emotions and Thoughts: A Minority Report," in S. Sue and T. Moore (eds.), **Community Mental Health in a Pluralistic Society.** New York: Human Sciences Press, 1978.

ABOUT THE CONTRIBUTORS

Walter R. Allen
Assistant Professor of Sociology
University of Michigan

June Jackson Christmas
Commissioner of Mental Health, Mental Retardation,
and Alcoholism Services
City of New York

William H. Denham
Director, Division of Manpower and Training Programs
National Institute of Mental Health

Russell Endo
Associate Professor of Sociology
University of Colorado

Louis A. Ferman
Director, Institute for Labor and Industrial Relations
University of Michigan

Madison Foster
Professor of Social Work
University of Michigan

Sumiko Hennessy
Director, Program and Therapy Services
Ridge Regional Center
Colorado Department of Institutions

Armando Morales
Professor of Psychiatry
University of California-Los Angeles

Faye Untalan Munoz
Executive Officer,
Talan and Associates

Delores L. Parron
Project Director, Institute of Medicine
National Academy of Sciences

Robert A. Ryan
Director, White Cloud Center
University of Oregon Health Sciences Center

Rodolfo B. Sanchez
Executive Director
National Coalition of Hispanic Mental Health
and Human Services Organizations

Barbara Bryant Solomon
Professor of Social Work
University of Southern California

Marta Sotomayor
Acting Director, Office of Special Populations
Alcohol, Drug Abuse and Mental Health Administration

Sandra Stukes
Researcher
Abt Associates

Stanley Sue
Professor of Psychology
University of California-Los Angeles

Joseph E. Trimble
Professor of Psychology
Western Washington University

Barbara W. K. Yee
Minority Research Associate
Scripps Foundation Gerontology Center
Miami University-Ohio